To Melissa

Original HOK design for Camden Yards, August 1, 1986

To Michael;
    A story about Baltimore on
your fortieth birthday. With
much affection and all good
wishes,
        Don, Bev, Laura and Sarah Waters
                6/12/93

PETER RICHMOND

BALLPARK

CAMDEN YARDS AND THE BUILDING OF AN AMERICAN DREAM

◆

SIMON & SCHUSTER
NEW YORK LONDON TORONTO SYDNEY TOKYO SINGAPORE

SIMON & SCHUSTER
Simon & Schuster Building
Rockefeller Center
1230 Avenue of the Americas
New York, New York 10020

Designed by Pei Loi Koay
Manufactured in the United States of America

1   3   5   7   9   10   8   6   4   2

Library of Congress Cataloging-in-Publication Data

Richmond, Peter.
Ballpark : Camden Yards and the building of an American dream /
Peter Richmond.
p.   cm.
Includes index.
1. Oriole Park at Camden Yards (Baltimore, Md.)   2. Baltimore
Orioles (Baseball team)   I. Title.
GV416.B353R53   1993
796.357′06′87526—dc20   93-14855
                                                            CIP

ISBN: 0-671-74851-3

Front and back endpapers: HOK/Sneary Architectural
Illustration, Illustrator: Dick Sneary

Photo Credits
AP/Wide World Photos, 2, 4, 9, 11, 13, 14; Carl Clark, 8; Courtesy of
HOK, 6, 7; HOK/Sneary Architectural Illustration, Illustrators; Dick
Sneary/Verne Christensen, 3; Tadder/Baltimore, 1, 10; Richard
Tomlinson, 12; UPI/Bettmann Archives, 5.

CONTENTS

◆

BALLPARK

◆

OPENING DAY

◆

THERE IS A CERTAIN SCENT, so strong it's like a taste, thick and rich and promising, of grass being washed by the day's first sun after a long night's dew. Warm to the face, it begins to rise from the infield of Camden Yards in the early morning of Monday, April 6, as the first rays come in over the warehouse and paint the field, from left field to right, as slowly but insistently as the sweep of the minute hand on the center-field clock until, soon after nine, the entire field is bathed in emerald and poised, at last, to be christened by baseball.

In the early hours, the sun's march goes unnoticed. In its first few hours, Camden Yards is an accessory, a stage set, a story line to be stalked in the cool of the shrinking shadow. None of the newsfolk swarming the sidelines stops to see the game that drew them here.

Not Willard Scott, telling Joe Garagiola how much he's earned for his latest endorsement as the two of them trade sound bites down the right-field line—"I couldn't get in!" Garagiola barks, "The bastards wouldn't let me in! They didn't know who I was!"—as the weatherman's Jell-O-bowl laughter careens around the empty seats.

Not Charles Gibson, who squints sincerely into the camera lights and promptly places the park "south of Baltimore"—although it's smack in the middle of the city—then intones, "They don't talk about the Baltimore Orioles here anymore. They talk about 'The Orioles,'" although, at that very moment, staring him in the face, a video screen the size of the Graf Zeppelin in center field is alight with a fifty-foot team logo that includes the word *Baltimore* for the first time in several years.

Not the local news-show types, interviewing the network news-show types. Not the cameramen tripping over each others' cables. Not the program assistants, all checking their watches every few minutes as if, in a stadium built to last a century, for a game that has no clock, a minute could possibly matter.

Not the truck drivers edging their rigs down the service ramp to a chorus of hissing air brakes. Not the man wearing a SWAT jacket walking up and down the aisles in the right-field box seats. Not Lonnie Harris of Metropolitan Maintenance, sweeping an aisle on the first-base side: "Last time I worked was a year ago at the Art College on Mount Royal," he says. "I been actively searching three or four days a week for ten months. There's just nothing out there."

Not Orioles vice president Janet Marie Smith, a sternly pretty woman in her thirties. When Joe Garagiola introduces her to a live national audience, and observes that it must have been hard to get an old-time effect in a new park, Smith says, "It was very easy, Joe. We tried to quantify what the old parks had," as if it was a matter of mathematics, of lines and angles and ingredients; no mention of baseball there, either.

What the place needs is a baseball player, and so, at a few minutes after nine, down the right-field line, a big man shaped like a bowling pin standing on its head turns his back to home plate and regards the warehouse. Big things, both of them—always bigger than everyone else—they size each other up.

"I'd like to get me a shot at that warehouse," Boog Powell says. "Right field, down the line—that was my power."

After years of lazy exile in the Florida Keys working a marina that wouldn't pay off, Boog Powell has returned to the city that loves him. He is about to embark on his first official day as proprietor of Boog's Place, a rib stand in the street-fair plaza that separates the warehouse from the field.

"Look at those power alleys," Boog says quietly, in a baseball player's voice he hasn't had reason to use for more than a decade now. "Three sixty-four. That was my power.

"Man," he says, "I wish I was twenty years younger."

*   *   *

At nine-thirty, down in the basement concourse, the dusty smell of new concrete duels with the choke of diesel smoke. Deep beneath the first-base box seats, in cold lockers the size of large rooms, hundreds of kegs of beer are stacked like ordnance. On the loading dock sit several cardboard cartons labelled LEAFY VEGETABLE, a generic growth genetically designed to embellish the smartly choreographed trays of fruit and shrimp destined for the luxury boxes.

Down the hallway, through a double door—past the Jacuzzi room, past the weight room—Johnny Oates's office is graced by a single memento, a framed poem written by his wife Gloria.

Orioles' manager Johnny Oates walked over at about eight-thirty from his room at the Hyatt on the Inner Harbor, conspicuous in his distinctively compact carriage. He is not short, but he feels well packed in, as if gravity is a little stronger where Johnny Oates stands. Maybe it's that way with all catchers.

"There was a little nip in the air," he says. "It's one of two days—you can tell it in the smell of the flags, the way the flags are starched. It's either Opening Day or the World Series."

That Oates's mind is on the game, and not his new ballpark, is not a surprise. Johnny Oates grew up in a house that stood on piled brick legs on a hillside in western North Carolina and featured neither electricity nor running water; a wooden crate planted in a spring-fed stream out back served as an icebox. He learned to hit rocks with a stick in that backyard—a humble proving ground, but good enough to get Johnny Oates to the major leagues, so it's no surprise that he is unimpressed by network puffery and glistening green steel.

He is, however, nervous. The past several years have not been kind to Orioles managers. After Earl Weaver's unfortunate reprise, and Cal Ripken, Sr.'s impossible tenure, and Frank Robinson's erratic reign, Johnny Oates had been asked, since mid-season of 1991, to return one of baseball's most exalted franchises to some semblance of joy. The team had misfired its way into fifth place, and there was little real reason to expect it to climb much higher. A journeyman who has played for teams of all shapes and sizes, Oates knows that a ballpark can only provide the scenery; a baseball team could play on the stage of Radio City Music Hall and still finish dead last.

He was going to start a pitcher who had spent more time on the disabled list than on the mound in the last four years—moreover, someone who was an old, old friend. Rick Sutcliffe had been given the call over a couple of young pitchers widely considered to be the team's future aces, prompting one Orioles official to privately question the manager's strategy the day before.

And still, on this day Johnny Oates cannot contain his smile, and on Oates's face a smile is a singular thing; a ruddy-faced man, he always looks as if he's just walked off the soybean field.

"You know what's funny?" Oates says. "I was thinking about the first game I ever saw. I can close my eyes right now and feel that day. It was a gray, overcast day. It wasn't hot, but it could have rained at any time—you could feel it in the air. But the Good Lord was not going to let my doubleheader get rained out, 'cause I might not ever see another one."

In a chair in the corner, Oates's teenage son watches his father, who is dressed in a major-league uniform managing a major-league team at the focal point of the entire sports world on the morning of baseball's biggest day, and tries to keep the pride out of his eyes, but fails.

"I like the excitement of it all," the father says. "I think it's going to help us. You want to get caught up in the excitement and have it push us. This attention is going to last all year—the first half, anyway, with each new team coming in, with media that haven't seen it before. That's what I'm happy about. The excitement. That's what it's about.

"Because there's nothing worse than fifty-four hundred people in an empty park in September booing you because they paid for their season tickets and figure they have the right to."

Across the hall, the locker room is huge, disproportionately so. It feels as if all the players have gathered in the meeting room of a large chain hotel. Like the rest of the ballpark, Cal Ripken, Jr.'s locker contains no disarray. Like the rest of Camden Yards, it is poised and empty, waiting to be filled with memories and sensations.

Cal has been allowed to choose his locker. It sits at the end of a row so that there is no locker to his right, and to his left is an empty locker. This is a privilege of merit, and a fact of practicality: The world now regularly marches to Cal Ripken's doorstep, all of it wanting something. As a result he tends to wear the distinct expression of one holding something back. Writers who deal with Ripken on a daily basis know him to be a man given to measured, even responses on matters of baseball, not likely to expand in great detail, nor to paint any particularly vivid picture when he's recreating a play. He speaks in grays. Most often his words are accompanied by a look of not quite being there, as if he's biting back a part of his self—a reasonable posture for an athlete who means more to his city than any other in the land; if he gave more fully of himself, it might devour him entirely.

The look especially figures to be present on this morning, as Cal Ripken begins a season that could mean a great deal to his bank account; the lowest-paid star in the game, Ripken will be a free agent at this season's end, and coming off a grand MVP season in 1992, he is poised to sign for more money than any athlete has ever made. Negotiations are at a standstill. But on this morning Cal Ripken is uncharacteristically animated, even anxious to talk—just not about baseball. About something closer to home.

"Rachel took a dive out of the crib last night," he says. "But she's okay."

On this morning, Ripken's eyes are as blue as Steve McQueen's in *Bullitt,* almost unworldly; it is in the unusually bright tint of those eyes, in a face that is otherwise mostly at rest, that you find the only hint of something entirely different from most of his peers; his singular sense of purpose.

"Last month she cut her nose," he says. "She was bouncing on her bed. We have this shelf over the head of the bed, and she was so glad to be home after spring training that she bounced on it. I could see it coming; instead of bouncing onto the pillow, she bounced past it. I tried to get there in time, but she hit it."

Here Ripken pauses with a half-smile. Ripken's reputation as a fielder is that he makes the play on everything he can reach.

"I knew the cut was deep. I called to my wife in the next room—'Kelly, we got an accident'—and as I said it, the blood just gushed out."

"Cal!" calls a disembodied voice. "You got two minutes!"

Ripken pops up from the seat, jogs out of the locker room, and takes a left down the hall, then a right down another hall, past the players' lounge with its brown leather couches, and a television the size of a drive-in movie screen. The television shows a soap opera.

Past the batting tunnels. Down the dugout steps. Onto the field, where he squints at the green, and blinks at the warehouse, and even though the rest of the team is stretching in the outfield, he pauses to scrawl an autograph on a baseball dangling from a child's hand.

At 10:55, several hundred men and women wearing black jackets and octagonal orange caps—the kind old-time cab drivers used to wear—have filled a section of lower boxes behind the Orioles dugout. The Orioles ushers have always looked archaic; today, from above, they look like an acre of marigolds. Most of them hold lunch boxes or brown paper bags on their laps.

On top of the dugout a small man with a mustache and the demeanor of an aggressive small dog paces back and forth.

"It's a national event," Roy Sommerhof, chief of stadium operations, sings to his army of ushers. "This is on television in Japan. We want to put on our best face, right?"

"RIGHT!" comes the answer, in unison.

"Correct?"

"CORRECT!"

"Right?"

"RIGHT!"

"Let's go!"

Larry Lucchino comes hurtling down the steps in flannels and blazer and overcoat, none of which quite fit, his hair too long, his mustache a little sinister for a minority owner and team president. He is late for his speech. He was supposed to address the orange-and-black troops. He grabs a few random hands, smooths his hair in back.

"We want the ushers to be warm and friendly," he explains. "Disneyworld stuff. Sounds stupid, doesn't it? But it's important."

Lucchino scans the stadium, which has just opened its doors and is slowly filling, fleshing out; the dark green of the steel and the seats now starts to give way to the colors of baseball fandom. Lucchino is seeing, but his mind is elsewhere. Like Johnny Oates, he is concerned with more pressing matters, baseball matters. He owns 9 percent of a team whose book value is ready to soar off the page, and he's overseen and driven and shaped the building of the stadium, carrying out everything his late mentor, Edward Bennett Williams, had dreamed of, and everything his current owner, the enigmatic Eli Jacobs, leverage-buyout king, has demanded—but the baseball team over which he presides is in a state of disarray. More than anything, Larry Lucchino wants to be a baseball man, a part of the action.

Lucchino has hired not one but three general managers beneath him, to the general befuddlement of the rest of baseball and the skepticism and derision of a daily press that widely dislikes him for his often patronizing and haughty manner.

On top of which, while back in New York Jacobs has fielded offers to sell the team—for $200 million—here in Baltimore Lucchino and his hand-picked lieutenant, Janet Marie Smith, are already widely disliked for having demanded so many design concessions for a stadium they paid virtually nothing for. Eli Jacobs stands to clear tens of millions, yet Lucchino and Smith had the gall to ask the state to pay for everything from ornamental brickwork to two additional electrical outlets in the press box, and to charge five-dollar admission to watch the team work out the day before. As a result, the real fans had a sense that the team, like Oz, was hiding behind the grand emerald curtain of Camden Yards, hoping to obscure the fact that a once great and powerful organization had allowed itself to fray so severely that it had become a perennial underachiever, all of its considerable luster worn to the nub.

"Opening Day," Larry Lucchino says, regarding the park, "is like a new start for a lot of people."

At eleven, the pregame workout begins to let some of the wind out of the high-ceremonial feel of the day. With the first ground ball hit out of the batting cage by Billy Ripken, the pageantry is punctured and the game takes over. The box seats are already shimmering with happy conversation—the workday suspended, the work brain let loose with the first taste of hops—conversation heightened on this day by distinctly industrial baffles. Yelps of anticipation bounce off a soaring wall of brick, and high in the upper deck, the rustle of scorecards echo down off a metal sunscreen, along with the scrape of shoe soles on a mezzanine concourse framed in girders of steel. All of these welcome sounds of spring and life and hope are carried on a quiet breeze coming in through the open arches.

A man in orange files into a box seat and holds up an orange sign. It reads, THEY MADE IT AND WE CAME.

At 11:35, out beyond the right-field wall, in the pedestrian concourse at the base of the warehouse, up above the Tall Wall that will feature the out-of-town scores, the first baseball falls out of the sky.

The concourse is meant to evoke the first decade of the twentieth century; the original light stanchions next to the warehouse's loading docks have been preserved, and the brick has been scrubbed to its original rusty crimson. Barbecue smoke drifts out of Boog's Place. Early imbibers drift in and out of Bambino's.

Back in the park, unseen by the strollers, Chito Martinez has stepped into the batting cage and hit a ball to right-center field. It rises, and rises farther, out of the park and into the picnic plaza atop the wall. It hits the concrete and takes one huge bounce, over the turn-of-the-century wrought-iron fence, and lands smack in the middle of dozens of people who immediately freeze, as if confused, and then all at the same time realize that this ball has been kissed seconds before by an Oriole's bat, back in the park.

A dozen people lunge for it; a little boy comes up with it. Then the crowd returns to its milling, except for a few boys, who linger in the hopes that if they wait another ball might descend out of the sky.

If they wait long enough, it will.

At noon, behind the batting cage, Fay Vincent sits in his golf cart, his cane at rest across his knees, casts a long, panoramic glance at the park, and speaks of Comiskey and Fenway and Ebbets—in particular, the Abe Starks sign in Ebbets Field.

"A new stadium," Vincent says, "makes the whole country sit up and take notice."

Fay Vincent, a rounded and delightfully assymetrically morphed man, was, in his too-short tenure, blessed with calm when called for and passion when it was needed. Ultimately, he had too much common sense for the game's owners to allow him to endure. He was at Camden Yards only because his good friend Bart Giamatti, the guardian of all that was good about the game, died in the summer of 1989, having vanquished Pete Rose to great relief in some quarters and dismay in others. Vincent inherited the game, and ruled with Giamatti's gentle philosophy, having found a fittingly dim-witted villain of his own in Yankee-owner George Steinbrenner, whom Vincent toyed with at regular intervals.

Like Giamatti, Vincent loves the game of baseball and on this day would rather be nowhere else, and thus parries dozens of mindless questions from the press. At one point, a radio reporter sidles up in pants that are much too short, sticks a microphone in Vincent's face, and says, "I have one question for you: your thoughts on the new ballpark."

Vincent pauses, smiling; perhaps he realizes that it wasn't a question. Then he says, "The children would say, 'awesome.' "

Around us, several expressionless men wearing natty blazers are popping up like weeds, each with a small pin on his lapel identifying him as a Secret Service agent. A helicopter is ripping a hole in the cloudless sky with an urgent, tight, perfectly repetitive flight pattern, like a bear stalking the same twelve feet of a zoo cage he's lived in for years. In front of the Indians dugout a woman wearing a trench coat has a press pass identifying her as a writer for a Cleveland newspaper that doesn't exist.

Just inside the Orioles dugout a Secret Service man holds the leash of a German shepherd the size of a Volkswagen. The dog is named Rex. Rex is enjoying himself; he is chewing a baseball.

All of this means that the president of the United States will soon be arriving to give the park its federal blessing. In this one all-important arena, the haughty capital city has lost out for good to its long-derided poor sister. Did Edward Bennett Williams fully realize he was condemning his power-slicked city when he signed the lease for Camden Yards?

Fay Vincent does. "Washington," says Vincent, "has conceded."

To Vincent's left, one by one, the Cleveland Indians are filtering out of their clubhouse, down the runway, and into the new dugout. They look out at the crowd much like farmers testing the wind before dawn. Behind them, on the gray rubber runway, they have left the first wet brown splotches of tobacco juice, like modern-day Hansels and Gretels marking the way back to the clubhouse.

From the vantage point of Vincent's cart behind home plate the park is a mural of overwhelming green—of the steel and the walls and the field. The Orioles uniforms against the dark green seem particularly white.

"I miss him," Fay Vincent says, quietly. He does not have to mention a name.

On the eighth floor of the warehouse, in the Camden Club, are youngish men in office suits and a few well-dressed women who have paid a thousand dollars for the privilege to tread upon carpeting emblazoned with the pattern of the Baltimore Baseball Club, circa 1895. Their eyes linger over the purple satin couches, plush, decorated in High Privilege. Entering the formal dining room for luncheon, they pause to admire the grand piano before perusing a menu that features a twelve-dollar hamburger. In the upper level of the club, wooden tables next to the small windows in the lounge have filled early. Set low to the floor—these windows were never intended to provide a view in the days when the warehouse was a warehouse—they require the men sipping imported beer to bend a little low, but the mild contortion is well worth the effort, for the view below is something until now completely unavailable in America: Nine floors beneath them an entire baseball park unfolds, as if scaled down like a model. The players are small, but the effect is perfect: baseball viewed from above, over a beer. The monthly dues are forty-five dollars, the minimum monthly food expenditure is thirty-dollars—this last requirement met easily, what with a bottle of Heineken going for $4.50.

Down in the stadium, on the restricted club level outside the luxury suites, tuxedoed servants stand at attention next to mobile dessert carts, ready to ferry them from suite to suite. Each contains a variety of cakes and confections, and a bottle of Courvoisier.

Still further down, on the field where the featured workers will perform their labors for the amusement of the assembled, Roland Hemond, the Orioles ruling general manager, stands in the sun, smiles, and says, "I can completely and thoroughly enjoy the good things that come about in the game of baseball."

Hemond is the rarest of baseball general managers, a man who has never allowed the buffeting of the business to move him off his wide-eyed love of the game. Another poor Orioles season—another undistinguished show by his catcher Chris Hoiles and pitchers Mike Mussina and Ben McDonald and left fielder Brady Anderson—will most certainly cost Hemond his job. But he wears no tension on Opening Day.

"I was with the Boston Braves when they drew two hundred eight-one thousand in 1952," Hemond says. "And I've always thought since then it's not a bad thing to break in with some adversity, so that each passing day gives you immense pleasure.

"I'm having a ball. Thoroughly. Some things are right. They're right."

Hemond ducks into the Orioles dugout, strides up the runway and walks into Oates's office. "The Lord has the sun shining," he says. "He is an Orioles fan."

Oates rises, smiles, and sticks out his hand. Hemond shakes it and leaves. Neither has spoken.

"I hope I can get a picture with the president," Johnny Oates says. "I had my picture taken in a receiving line with the queen last year, you know. Actually, I happened to be behind Frank when they took a picture of Frank shaking her hand."

"It was in *Royalty* magazine," says his son.

"If I don't, I'll understand," Johnny Oates says. "I know what it's like. If he's busy, I'll understand. But if there's someone around with a camera, I wouldn't mind."

At two o'clock, the president of the United States walks through the locker room, embraced by a phalanx of Secret Service people. Various Orioles shake his hand and several of them wear a small smile they seldom unveil—the naïve and excited grin that even the four-million-dollar men give when they're faced with someone who, they have to admit, is more important than they.

Rick Sutcliffe looks up from his locker at Bush, but doesn't see him. Bush passes his locker without saying hello. Sutcliffe doesn't notice. He is huge, red bearded, and woolly, and on game days he does not shake hands or socialize with anyone before he pitches, although judging from his looks, he might stop and chat with Rex.

An hour later, the opening ceremonies are about to begin. The fans are on their feet; the crowd seems to fill more space than the building, and the portions of the park that are still visible are all green. Despite the presence of forty-five thousand people, it could be a lovely minor-league bandbox.

At 3:08 George Bush comes out of the Orioles dugout wearing a blue sweater and a wary, uncomfortable, lopsided grin. At his side is a teenage grandson—one of "the brown ones," as he calls them. His grandson hums a fastball to catcher Hoiles. Bush then bounces a ball in front of him, and leaves the field to mixed applause and boos, escorted by Eli Jacobs.

Then, at 3:19—prompted by the slightest tensing of the players on the field, all of them dropping into alert, as if some unseen elastic has drawn them all a little tighter together—the park begins to hush. Friends suspend workday gossip, vendors stop their pitch.

In right field, Joe Orsulak stops spitting the first sunflower-seed shells of the season into the tall right-field grass and pounds his glove, once. Shortstop Cal Ripken stops sweeping the dirt with his right foot in lazy arcs, unfolds the glove that he'd held to his chest like a wing, turns its pocket toward the batter, and leans forward. There is no expression on his face.

On the mound, Rick Sutcliffe turns, looks at his team, turns back, and looks in at his catcher. He begins his windup. As he raises the ball over his head, his wrist poised to snap the ball past Cleveland's Kenny Lofton, the crowd noise has quieted to nothing.

Sutcliffe's arm comes forward and releases the ball, and—it's probably an illusion—from the upper deck, from the top row in left field, you swear you can make out the seams.

ONCE AN ORIOLE...

◆

" 'SO-FT CRABS,' " Boog Powell was singing, quietly, into the Florida dusk. " 'SOOOOOft crabs.' That's what you'd hear every Saturday morning in the alley behind my house: 'SOOOOOOOOft crabs.' I'd buy dozens of 'em. There'd be a lot of gourmet dinners at one A.M. with those crabs."

A breeze off the pink horizon ruffled the thatched roof of the poolside bar at Harley's Sandcastle Inn on Lido Beach, Florida, during a break in the Baltimore Orioles' 1992 Fantasy Camp. At the end of the bar Brooks Robinson was sipping a pastel-colored drink through a straw. On another stool, Elrod Hendricks was doing the same.

Boog was standing. The top of his head came within an inch or two of the underside of the thatch. He was drinking a beer from a can. It looked like a thimble in his hand.

In a few minutes the three of them would pile into a small motel room and sign autographs for 106 fantasy campers who'd each paid thirty-four hundred dollars for the privilege of dressing up in orange-and-black polyester pajamas for a week, many of who would, on this night, regale the three ballplayers with reminiscences about the players' careers—moments and occurrences that, as is often the case when it comes to childhood memories, and baseball memories, and memories in general, hadn't happened at all.

So Boog and Brooks and Elrod were bracing themselves with thick drinks of colors that don't, as a rule, occur in nature, and with memories of Memorial Stadium.

"The night I cut my hand open, it wasn't crabs," Boog said. "It was Chincoteagues. It was the night before the first game of the '71 playoffs. I'm shucking some beautiful Chincoteagues with a big old knife. My buddy comes over with two dozen more. So I get down to the last oyster, and I put the knife right through my thumb."

Elrod did not seem to be listening. Brooks was down at the end of the bar talking to a fan. There was no doubt that both had heard the tale before.

"Now, right away I know it's nasty," Powell said. "But the last thing I want to do is go to the hospital. My next door neighbor is a doctor. A pediatrician. He's renting [former Oriole Curt] Blefary's house. So I go over and I say, 'Can you sew me up?' Well, he breaks the needle right off in my hand. He didn't have a needle long enough to stitch me. Now he breaks another one off. Seriously. See, he's a pediatrician! He's not used to sewing up hands like mine. Anyway, he finally sews me up.

"The next day, I get a glove for the hand. I don't want anyone to know. My first at bat is against Catfish. He runs a fastball inside. I pop it up. I *never* popped one up off Catfish."

As he told the story, the veins stood out in Boog Powell's neck. The time to get to Catfish, of course, was early. You never wanted to waste a fat first-inning fastball against Catfish.

"The next time up," Boog said, "he takes me inside and I take him into the right-field bleachers."

Boog took a hit of the beer. For effect.

"So I go back to the bench. I put on my glove. It starts to fill up with blood. It feels like sweat, but it's not. It's dripping out of the glove. Ralph Salvon, our trainer, looks at it. I say, 'Just stop it from bleeding. Sew it up. Whatever you have to do.' The cut is gaping wide open. A half-inch deep and an inch wide. Ralph tapes it up real good. I get another glove. My next at bat I hit a two-run home run."

Boog took another hit of his beer.

"That was kind of a neat day."

Boog Powell played a dozen years embraced by the horseshoe of Memorial Stadium, protecting first base, plowing particularly Boog-like home runs into the right-field seats. For all of the Brooksian expertise, for all of Frank Robinson's majestic feats, no one was more of an Oriole than Boog. It would stand to reason that Boog would be carrying some vivid memories of the stadium.

"I remember me and Blefary buying ammo belts for the Colts games," he said. "Fifty-caliber ammo belts. See, you couldn't take bottles into Memorial. So we bought these ammo belts at an army-navy surplus store and filled them with airline bottles. We'd wear them under big, loose jackets and walk right in."

Here Powell made the pantomime gesture of a man hoisting a small bottle to his lips.

But what about Memorial Stadium's playing surface? Any quirks? The dirt? The grass? The angle of the sun on pickoffs?

"Well, there was the rats in the tarp," Boog said.

"The rats," Elrod Hendricks said, nodding. It was the first time he'd spoken in several minutes. "The rats," he said again, his eyes not leaving whatever it was he was looking at in the middle distance behind the bar. "The rats were huge."

Hendricks was not smiling as he spoke. He was staring at his drink, which was the color of red dye No. 2. Now Hendricks was wearing the expression of a man in a mediocre stage adaptation of an Edgar Allan Poe story.

"There was one night in the bullpen Tippy [Martinez] was leaning against the fence looking in at the game," Hendricks said, "and this rat just walked across his feet. He turned to me and said, 'Was that a cat?' I said, 'No, that was a rat.'

"Huge rats," Elrod said.

"The rats," Boog said, "were big enough to stand flatfooted and screw a turkey."

"What did you say?" said Brooks Robinson. Brooks had been chatting with the fan at the end of the bar, but ballplayers' ears are trained to pay attention to certain words, and Boog had used one of them.

"I said the rats were big enough to stand flatfooted and screw a turkey," Boog said.

"That's what I thought you said," Brooks said.

"See, they'd live in the tarp," Boog said, "and when the fans started coming in and spilling popcorn, the rats would come out. Before the game. I never saw them during a game. Before the game. But you know what? When it rained and they rolled out the tarp there'd never be any rats in it."

"They were in the drain," Elrod Hendricks intoned. "They'd go down the drain. That's why there were so many stray cats out in the bullpen. They'd keep the rat population down. The ground crew would feed them."

Elrod took a sip of his drink, and put it down.

"Huge rats," he said, and Boog Powell nodded.

From the start Memorial Stadium seemed endowed with something special. The first game was played there a day after fire claimed Oriole Park, the wooden-bandbox home of the International League Orioles down on Greenmount and 29th in 1944. A football stadium, then known as Municipal Stadium, it was found to be quite serviceable for both sports. Ten years later, Baltimore's new major-league baseball team—in uniform—disembarked downtown at Camden Station from the overnight train from Detroit, fresh from a two-game season-opening split, and rode up Charles Street in open convertibles as the city lined the street to wave its delirious greetings. The Orioles then stepped onto the field at 33rd Street, now named Memorial Stadium.

"Uppermost in everyone's mind," Ernie Harwell remembered, "was the weather. It was supposed to rain." Ernie Harwell rode that train too. He was the Orioles' announcer for the inaugural year.

Within a few years he had moved on to become the storied voice of the Tigers. But on this Baltimore morning, he was setting up the booth at Memorial for what everyone believed would be his last broadcast for the Tigers on the last day of Memorial's baseball life, a few hours before the final game of the final weekend of 1991. As thousands of fans milled outside on 33rd Street, snapping pictures of the soaring brick façade with its distinctive post-Deco lettering, Harwell went about his business, preparing for one more broadcast. His "retirement" had been declared by Tigers owner Tom Monaghan, a pizza baron, collector of antique cars, and funder of right-wing Central American missionary efforts. Harwell was not pleased about it;

neither were the citizens of Detroit. They would respond by staying away from Tiger Stadium in droves, a circumstance that combined with the downturn of his business to force Monaghan to sell the club to rival pizza baron Mike Illitch, who wasted no time in restoring Harwell to his rightful position behind the microphone.

But on this day in 1991, those events were in the future; as far as anyone knew, Harwell's career was about to end on the last day of a ballpark he had helped to inaugurate.

"No one wanted it to rain on Baltimore's parade," Ernie Harwell remembered of that first day in 1954. "It didn't. They beat the Tigers, two to one. Went on to lose a hundred of a hundred fifty-four games."

It's one of the stranger things about America that a nation still in its relative infancy feels compelled to abandon so many of its physical treasures, to discard the buildings that bear the stamp of its small evolution. This one was thirty-seven years old—newer than most of us. When Cal Ripken was born, Memorial was six.

It was no trophy. It had the look and feel of a minor-league park masquerading for the majors; the brick and yellowed concrete on the outside masked an inner skin of unpainted cinder block. But the park quickly blossomed with the beauty endowed by a legend it nurtured. And yes, up in the top rows of the lower deck you'd almost immediately lose sight of a pop fly or a fly ball. But tucked up there in the dark, nestled in a wooden seat, you filled a baseball space: The cooking-oil scents rose from the stands down below (the food was cooked at the booths, and not in distant kitchens, in modern fashion, to be trucked in and wrapped in foil), and framed by the overhang of the upper deck and the distinctive double concrete columns, the game seemed like a huge mural, an American diorama.

In its lobby—and how many ballparks have lobbies?—in a small glassed-in case sat a brass urn containing a teaspoon of dirt from every foreign cemetery on earth where an American serviceman or -woman is buried: Old-time stuff, useful for nothing; there's no marketing value in an urn, yet it reminded those who saw it that "Memorial" was more than just a name.

It doesn't speak well of the modern march of progress that Memorial's most appealing features were those that spelled its doom, beginning with its scale, which was small, and its profile, which was low. The park lay tucked so deeply into the hills between Ednor Gardens and Lake Montebello that the place didn't even reveal itself to anyone approaching by foot—the approved method of approach, since parking was a knotty snarl—until he or she was three blocks away.

It was the right size for the Orioles' brand of baseball, which meant that it was fairly innocuous as it went about its work, and thus made such a small physical imprint on the city and its landscape that it was unlikely to rally efforts to preserve it. Had Memorial been more obtrusive—had it been an overwhelming structure, even grotesquely so—it might have stamped itself more emphatically on the city's psyche and skyline. But the park was small in all ways—"a place you weren't going to get lost in," Earl Weaver recalled one day—and it could never have prompted a civic shout of rage at the threat of its being vacated, not the way Tiger Stadium has in the wake of its owners' efforts to persuade that city to provide a new park.

Memorial was one of the few parks not hooked into the artificial life-support system of the interstates—which, of course, killed its chances of surviving. Wiser heads in a perfect world might have noted that the traffic and the congestion were a warning—that the game was getting too far out of hand, too big for society to support it. But our society, like any child—we are, as civilizations go, in early adolescence at best—rarely scales back its pleasures; instead, it demands greater and greater accommodations to its desires, even at the risk of growing so huge that the pleasures they provided are compromised if not lost altogether. The revenue in Memorial was a stream, and the modern game requires a rushing river.

Except for Wrigley Field, it was the last neighborhood park. Neat and modest red-brick and clapboard homes spilled away from it on all sides—"All the older streets of Baltimore show thrift and industry," journalist H. L. Mencken wrote in his diaries—and on a walk up Charles Street from downtown for a Sunday-afternoon game you'd find Baltimoreans on their knees, tending their gardens—explosions of azalea, brushstrokes of tulip and daffodil—and hear the buzzing of real bees, bees feeding on pollen, not on the sweetscum detritus of mankind they find in the trash cans outside of Yankee and Shea stadiums.

"I used to drive down Charles Street from the north in the first week of April," Ken Singleton said one day, sitting on the Expos' bench in their spring-training park in West Palm Beach, "and the buds would be coming out, and you'd say to yourself, 'This is what I'm going to see next month—even maybe after the next road trip.'"

Ken Singleton is now an announcer for the Montreal Expos. But as an Oriole in 1981, he compiled a remarkable streak: he hit safely in ten straight at bats. And still, when asked for memories, he spoke not of games but of driving to Memorial Stadium.

"Charles Street was a street that dictated baseball," he said. "It'd start with the early leaves, and then full bloom, and then in the fall, as the season was ending, the leaves were falling. And every year you wished it would go on forever."

Inside the park it was nearly as green: The spruces and cedars and cypress behind the scoreboard grew tall in later years, home for the sparrows that flittered from branch to branch at dusk each night; the grassy slope beyond center field was not grass that had been brought in to look as if it belonged, but had been growing there for years when they built the place, a feature of terrain that reminded you there was life here before there was a stadium. It was a remarkably verdant place, and it didn't have to try to bond with baseball; it did so naturally.

"This was an aesthetically beautiful stadium—I loved it here," John Lowenstein was saying before a Brewers game one August night—the time of the year when Memorial Stadium was wholly alive. Midsummer nights always carry a baseball-park feel—it's the time of the year when the game is *supposed* to be watched, one short season when baseball is the land's only sport—and it was never as good as it was at Memorial, a small park in a Southern town with a mid-Atlantic climate, a green-laden summer smell, up on the hill, where the humidity never oppressed, and the wind was always deeply fragrant.

From Lowenstein's perch you could see the wall in left that would kick a line drive back as quick as a billiard ball, a carom that allowed

Rickey Henderson to throw out three Orioles trying to stretch singles into doubles in a single game. You could see Frank Robinson's flag—HERE was all it read—where he hit the only ball ever to leave the park, in 1966; other, bigger parks shout out their landmarks. In Yankee Stadium the memorials in center field are trumpeted constantly, and there are now so many they're losing significance. In Fenway Park, the numbers of retired players are painted on the façade of the deck in right. They are part of the picture. But in Memorial, Frank's flag was largely hidden, and even once you found it, all it said was HERE. Not Frank, not his number, not any explanation. Just HERE.

Lowenstein nodded at the short foul pole in the left field where he himself curled a home run to the opposite field, to win a playoff game against the Angels in 1979.

"For me, preserving the memories is the most important thing in my life," he said. "They're an inventory of your life that you carry in your hip pocket the rest of your life."

Outside the park, trees and bushes fronted the homes on 37th Street. From Rexford and 37th you could peek in and see a slice of the field, including the mound and home plate; from five hundred feet away you could see the ball break away over the outside corner of the plate. These sound like features from ballparks of another era, but they were the norm at Memorial.

The neighborhoods lapped up on three sides so that it always felt as if the Orioles were playing on the lawn of the biggest house on the block on a midsummer's night, after all the families have eaten supper and all the kids and dads are out throwing a few more balls around before it gets dark. Memorial's link to the gardens and the grass and the small wage-earner's streets was no small thing.

"The parking lot used to be grass," Jim Henneman said. "There were trees in it. We used to sit under the trees and play cards. When my family moved there—it was two weeks after Pearl Harbor, and I was in first grade—I had the choice of going to Blessed Sacrament, which was close by, or another school that was farther away. To get to the other one you had to walk across those fields. I said, 'I want to go there.' I wanted to walk through the fields. I grew up playing in that grass parking lot."

Jim Henneman attended two thousand of the three thousand baseball games played there, including the very first, the day after the fire at Oriole Park, and the first major-league game in 1954, and, of course, the last.

"In 1944, it was four hundred fifty feet to dead center, four forty-seven to the power alleys. Down the right-field line led to an archway onto the street. Eddie Robinson hit one once that would have gone all the way out—six hundred feet or so—just rolling through the archway onto the street, if it hadn't hit the water fountain. The last games they played in that configuration was a doubleheader in '49."

Jim Henneman's dad was a milkman in the neighborhood. Jim sold programs for the 1944 Army-Navy game when it was Municipal Stadium. He ushered. He cooked in the press-box lounge. He was a clubhouse boy for the Triple-A Orioles in 1950 and 1951. His brother Bobby played on the first team ever managed by Chuck Tanner, at Quad Cities. Jim pitched in college, but when he made it to Memorial it was to cover the team for the *Baltimore Sun*. Jim and the old stadium fit very well: nothing flashy, quite dependable.

Henneman grew old with the park, and it grew old with him. You may have seen him down on the field at the last several Opening Days, or the last game, and taken note: Jim was wearing a tuxedo.

"I remember walking down there the morning after the fire [in 1944]," he told me. "I remember seeing big, black charred pieces. And you know what? I remember that ashes from the fire actually drifted—this is the truth, I saw them—ashes drifted on the wind and were carried from Oriole Park to Municipal."

It was a good place to play the game—fair, forgiving. It was a pitcher's park—and thus a cradle of defense, from Brooks and Aparicio to Belanger and Blair to Ripken and Murray—and in its brief life nurtured a remarkable six Cy Young Awards. Before the trees grew up, Earl Weaver would start Jim Palmer on every Sunday at home so that his overhand fastball would come straight out of the white façades of the homes on 37th.

It was a ballplayer's park too; as odd as it sounds, Orioles fans seldom if ever booed their teams. They seldom if ever booed the other teams, either. In many respects, it is an easy town to get along with; there seem to be fewer shrieking nerves than there ought to be.

"In the last few years, players on other teams used to ask me when we were leaving," Cal Ripken was saying, down in the Orioles locker room before a game against Toronto in early September of that last season, "not because they wanted to play in the new one, but because they like playing in this one. If you're a baseball fan of any character, it's a great stadium."

This is not an isolated opinion. Memorial engendered a quiet affection around the league. Not true of some of the older arenas: "I can't win in this place," Sparky Anderson told me one night in Tiger Stadium, although his record indicated otherwise. And a pitcher named Jeff Russell said, "I've played in Little League parks better than this one," although, when the books are closed on the game's history, there's a fair chance that Tiger Stadium's name will appear in a larger typeface than Jeff Russell's.

"My earliest memory was a World Series game in '66," Ripken said. "I remember seeing Frank Robinson hit a home run. A line drive in the left-field bleachers. Walking in the first time, the field seemed so perfect. Everything seemed so . . . ideal."

On this day Ripken was sitting in a prototype chair that the Orioles were considering for the new locker room at Camden Yards. Cal was the only Oriole with the new chair.

"I remember shagging flies when I was a teenager. I worked out here for the first time when I was fourteen or fifteen. I remember once when my dad was pitching BP [batting practice]. He told me to go out to shortstop. He said, 'Make sure you stand on the edge of the grass, and not chew up the field for Belanger.' I stayed back as far as I could, to not leave any footprints whatsoever.

"It was easier to dream then, having been on the field," Cal Ripken said. "Before that it didn't seem realistic."

"I remember the first game I saw there," Mark Belanger said one day in his office on the twenty-sixth floor of a mirrored office building on the Upper East Side of Manhattan, the home of the Major League

Baseball Players Association. He lit another cigarette and stared out the window. He was seeing Memorial Stadium.

"The scouts—Joe Cusack and Frank McGowan—they flew me down and took me to a game. I sat in the mezzanine on the first-base side and saw Aparicio go into the hole to make a play. My scout says, 'You'll be making plays like that.'" Belanger laughed at this, because, of course, he did make plays like that. For a decade.

Belanger grew up in Lanesborough, Massachusetts. His dad's people were from French Canada, his mom's from Italy. His dad worked maintenance at the U.S. Gypsum plant outside of Pittsfield. His mom worked in the G. E. plant. He has commuted to New York from his home in Baltimore for a decade now, and expresses hope that his own children will raise their families there, too.

Belanger still looks like a French existentialist film star—a dark-complected, handsome man with an expression that can be frighteningly intimidating across the bargaining table, but soft as worn leather when he talks about baseball. He spent most of his career in Baltimore, and had a woefully weak bat most every season, but it's a measure of the town—its size, yes, as well as its generous scope—that he carried a near-heroic stature.

"Memorial was pretty damned good," he said. "The upper deck blocked out the sky and helped me concentrate. Other players would come from places like Cleveland and say, 'How can you have such a great field?' Our groundskeeper, Pat Santarone, worked on the turf so well because we were supposed to be a pitching and defense club.

"I enjoyed going to the park because I knew it was going to be manicured properly. Which kept up my confidence. Which I have no doubt made me a better fielder."

There was nothing cosmetically stunning about the place. The warning track of gray gravel could take out a chunk of your skin if you dove onto it. The home dugout was so small that the man in the hole—on deck to be on deck—would have to stand in front of the bat rack to practice his swing. Jon Miller, the announcer, frequently found his view blocked by the visiting television crew.

"I'm the only home-team announcer in baseball with an obstructed view," Miller noted once. "You think I'm going to miss that bullshit?"

"Oh, it was never a good baseball stadium," Jim Henneman said, and he should know. "If the White Sox or Rangers had played there it'd just be another stadium. It was what happened on the field that made Memorial Stadium special."

For fifteen years, they were the American League's dynasty; from 1966 to 1983, they won three world championships ('66, '70, '83), six pennants ('69, '71, '79) and eight division titles ('73, '74), but the dominance riled no one. The A's and the Reds inspired vitriol. The Orioles inspired respect. Maybe it was because there was no longer any Jimmy Cannons chronicling the game, but even if there had been, it's hard to imagine someone writing, "Rooting for the Orioles is like rooting for U.S. Steel." Like everything else in Baltimore, they did what they did with very little self-puffery. While the Reds were dominating the National League as the Big Red Machine, no one was giving the Orioles any nicknames.

It was a good baseball town, of course. Baltimore had had teams in three different leagues in 1884, and in the 1890s a remarkable National League team won three pennants in a row with a style that was known as "Inside Baseball"—trying for every edge you could find. "The Orioles, who operated in the 1890s, were one of the fiercest teams in baseball history," noted the *New York Herald Tribune* the day after the Browns' sale to Baltimore had been approved in 1953, "as can be proved merely by listing a few of their heroes—John McGraw, Wilbert Robinson, Kid Gleason, and Wee Willie Keeler—great men all. They terrorized opponents and umpires alike, and they left an undying imprint on baseball through the creation of 'the old Orioles spirit' by which is meant a determination to play to the hilt regardless of personal injury or illness."

Orioles spirit also embraced such strategies as the players sharpening their spikes on the bench in plain view of the opponent, and hooking a finger into the belt of an opposing man trying to tag up on third, and hiding a few extra balls in the high grass in the outfield for quicker throws into the infield on opponents' hits.

Later years brought a spirit of a less sinister nature, but spirit nonetheless—apparent to anyone who has known the team since the sixties. Outside of the city, they've been known as a good club with a great deal of talent and little affect to attach to the numbers. In town, they have helped a small city through a great deal of racial and economic troubles. They have always addressed their obligations in town.

Every winning team, of course, carries a legend of one kind or another, and most ball players are savvy enough to pay lip service to traditions that may have never existed at all. With the Orioles, though, the spirit is now a tangible thing; it never strays far from any conversation with anyone who has played the game in this uniform. Even when they trade the uniform for another.

This happened in a hotel room in Philadelphia in the middle of the 1991 season: Dennis Martinez of the Montreal Expos answered his telephone and said, "This is Dennis Martinez." Then his face lapsed into a smile.

"Thank you," he said. "Yes. Yes. How are you? Yes. Thank you. Thanks. Good-bye."

"That was a woman who calls me to wish me a happy birthday every year," Martinez told me. "No matter where I am. Her husband was the postman who delivered mail to Memorial. She never forgets. She calls every year."

Dennis Martinez, who hadn't worn an Orioles uniform in six years, smiled and shook his head at the same time.

In the winter of 1967–1977, sixteen Orioles and their families lived in Baltimore in the off-season. That was a routine number, sometimes higher, sometimes lower. It seems inconceivable today.

"Once an Oriole, always an Oriole," Don Baylor said. "No matter what team you go to it's never like what the Orioles have. It wasn't 'maybe you could win.' You *knew* you could win. That was how they ingrained you. Rookie to majors."

Baylor was sitting in the visitors' clubhouse of Memorial Stadium, wearing a Milwaukee Brewers uniform. It could have been a Yankees uniform, or a Cardinals uniform, or a Red Sox uniform, or an Oakland uniform, or an Angels uniform; he's worn them all. He will tell you, though, that there is only one uniform to which he feels an allegiance. And you'll believe him. Baylor is not a man given to frivolous thought for the sake of hearing his own voice.

We were sitting on a couch that you might expect to see in a college student's room; it had the desperate, overworn look of a vagabond. Behind us was the grating rumble of a clothes dryer dating to the Taft administration. Next to it, a coat hanger had been bent into a small basketball hoop and fastened to the wall with dirty adhesive tape.

The Orioles' visiting locker room, once the Colts' locker room, always felt like someone's basement. Two years ago, Yankee Mel Hall—piqued over some Mel Hall-ish injustice, real or imagined—slammed the old wooden door of the manager's office as he walked out, taking it off its hinges. One wall of the manager's office featured a blackboard on which no one had written in decades.

"The Orioles always recruited the kind of players who could coexist with others," Baylor said. "The team actually liked each other. Etchebarren, Boog, McNally, Belanger—everyone sitting around, drinking a Bo, long after everyone showered. They'd still be in there shooting the shit. . . . When they traded me to Oakland in the spring of '76, Earl had a cry and I had a cry. The last trip through the clubhouse, it's like being kicked out of the family. I can still see their faces. Palmer, Etchebarren, Belanger, Shopay. Lee May, Singleton. It was hard.

"The year we were ten out with thirty-two to play, we all went to Brooks's house for a meeting. The entire team. The Orioles always knew how to advance runners. The Oriole always knew how to play the game. So we decided to start doing it all the time. We decided, 'Don't look for the sign, just get him over. And when he comes back, everybody better be on the top step to shake his hand.' We met until two-thirty in the morning; we won ten in a row. The Sox lost ten."

I asked Boog Powell about team meetings.

"I remember a party in '66 trying to throw Drabowsky into the pool," he said. "But I hit my head on a pillar. We went to the hospital and Mo tried to put me on his Blue Cross. They wouldn't take it. I woke up with guacamole and sour cream in my hair. I'll never forget that one. It was hosted by this one-armed undertaker. That's the truth.

"That was the night Frank almost drowned. Etchebarren saved him, I think. He jumped in. Someone looked over and said, 'There's Frank at the bottom of the pool.'"

*   *   *

It was a good town to lose in, something that can be said of few baseball cities. On the final day of the 1982 season, on what was supposed to be his final day in an Orioles uniform, Earl Weaver's team could have won the division, and lost it instead. The capacity crowd stayed in the stadium to applaud him for forty-five minutes.

In 1988, the Orioles lost twenty-three of their first twenty-four games—including an 0-21 start—and came home to a capacity crowd.

"Oh and twenty-four, well, then you could have seen it for the curiosity factor," Jon Miller recalled. "But one and twenty-three? All that is is an incredibly bad record. People react to something like that by not showing up. Instead, the town said, 'This is the Orioles, this is Baltimore, this is something special.'

"The first pitch of the game—Jay Tibbs was pitching—was a strike, and the crowd went nuts. Then the batter pops up for the first out, and the crowd goes nuts. It was one of the most exciting games I've ever broadcast, and that's the truth."

"Mark Belanger in Baltimore was as big as Mickey Mantle was nationally," Belanger told me without fear of sounding boastful; it *was* the truth. Belanger, perhaps more than anyone, epitomized the quiet grace with which the team and the city engaged during the Orioles' best years. It was a relationship that did not translate out of the city limits because of the absence of both team media and national media attention. But anyone who was there, anyone who watched the Orioles of the seventies, could sense something going on.

"The difference between home and here," Mike Flanagan said, on an August night in 1991 over in the home dressing room, "was that at home in New Hampshire I was a star, but here I was an Oriole. Here I wanted to be one of the community."

This was Mike Flanagan's season, this last season, in a way that could only happen to a Baltimore Oriole, in a way that surprises no one who has lived in the town.

Mike Flanagan spent thirteen years with the Orioles—and won their last Cy Young, in 1979—before he was traded to Toronto in 1987. He started for three years, and was released at the end of 1990. In the spring of 1991, at the age of thirty-nine, he was invited to the

Orioles' camp. So was Jim Palmer, already a Hall of Famer, a star for whom the limelight never seemed quite bright enough in Baltimore. Palmer's heavily publicized contract attempt fizzled after just one spring outing. But Flanagan, the Oriole, made the team. On the last Opening Day in Memorial, when he was introduced with the rest of the team, Mike Flanagan received the longest ovation. And through the season, remarkably, he proved to be not only adequate but exceptional coming out of the bullpen. As the season neared its end, the New York papers had the Mets seeking a trade.

Flanagan often said that he'd hoped to pitch the last pitch in Memorial Stadium. As the season wore on, though, he mentioned it less and less; even though the team would finish a dreary sixth, Flanagan knew better than to emphasize a personal desire over the fortunes of the team.

"A lot of us had chances to go the free-agent route through the years," Flanagan said. "But we didn't because we knew we had a good thing here. Until I left, though, I didn't really know what it meant to play here."

"Now players don't like each other," Don Baylor said, and his face grew hard. "Oh, they say they do. They don't.

"I never do old-timers' games. I just won't. But when the Orioles asked me to come for the final weekend, I said, 'Just tell me where and when.' "

For the final weekend at Memorial Stadium the Orioles promise surprises.

On Friday night they lose to the Tigers in fourteen innings.

On Saturday afternoon they assign players to stand at every ticket entrance, to greet and thank the fans, and to hand out calendars featuring the new park.

Boog is assigned a gate down the first-base line, with Luis Mercedes, who, not long ago, threw a batting helmet at an opponent in Rochester and broke some of the man's teeth. The Orioles are a little worried about Luis's temperament. They figure they should instill a little of the old Orioles in him. They pair him with the right man.

"Boog!" says a big blonde, bestowing a big hug.

"I remember you—section eight," Boog says.

"Boog!" says a man. "You retired ten years too soon."

"Tell me about it," Boog says.

"I wish you could still play," says another man. "You made me very happy, many times. You playing today?"

"Yeah," Boog says. "Temporary comeback."

Then he shakes his head.

"Temporary insanity is more like it."

A crowd has assembled, and they all laugh. To the side, Luis Mercedes watches with the expression of a man watching a play being performed in a language he doesn't understand.

The Orioles place Earl out in right field, for the general admission seats. The crowd at the gate grows so large so quickly that the entrance is soon clotted. People do double takes. Triple takes.

"That's Earl Weaver," says one man to his son. "That's Earl. That's the one. That's the man."

"Earl Weaver with me!" says Fannie Sauer from Hollandtown.

"It's a privilege, sir," says a man.

"Thank you," Earl says, again and again—for once, taken aback, even embarrassed, as the crowd pushes in; at a loss for words to express his real emotion, he frantically hands out the calendars.

The Orioles were Baltimore's team, they were Frank Robinson's team, they were Boog Powell's team, they were Eddie Murray's team, they were Mark Belanger's team; but above all else they were Earl Weaver's team. His domination of its style and tone over a long period of time, his ability to stamp it with his overriding imprint, these belonged to an earlier era; what John McGraw was to his Giants, what Casey Stengel was to his Yankees, Earl was to his Orioles.

His five one-hundred-win seasons tie him with Joe McCarthy for second place, behind Connie Mack. A ball field was his stage. He liked his beer, he liked his bluster, he liked his stomp. It was theater, it was caricature, and it worked. His teams hated him and loved him, all at the same time, and they would have followed him anywhere.

"One game I pitched I led off an inning by getting the first batter to hit a ground ball to Cal, and it took a bad hop," Flanagan recalled. "The next guy hits an easy fly to Singleton in right, but he loses it in the sun. Now there's two on. Earl comes out, says, 'Don't let them hit it on the ground and don't let them hit in in the air,' turns around and walks back. I get a line-drive double play. As I walk into the dugout, Earl says, 'Am I a fuckin' genius, or what?' "

And then, there was one night in Memorial Stadium, 1979; random on the face of things, but the perfect summation of the *Earl of Baltimore:* The Orioles have won a close game in a season in which they seem unable to do otherwise. Most of the players are showered and dressed. In Earl Weaver's dark, tiled office, he stands naked, which he often did. A cigarette is clutched between the fingers of his left hand, extracted from the pack that he carries inside his shirt in the special pocket sewn to the inside of the lapel. With his right hand he sprinkles salt into a can of National Bohemian beer.

It is the perfect office for Earl Weaver, painted in a dim beige, like a cell devoted to the interrogation of political prisoners in a Central-American oligarchy. The cinderblock walls make for abrupt and emphatic acoustics. The floor is cement. The radiator hisses in a corner. (Memorial was never meant for luxury—a fact borne out fully when, in the middle of the 1990 season, manager Frank Robinson had the office redone in High Men's Club, with real wood panelling, blue leather wingbacked chairs, and faux-antique end tables. He took to talking about the three televisions he'd have sunken into his walls when they moved to Camden Yards. He was relieved of his duties a few weeks into the following season.)

On this night Earl has a bounce to him, an ungainly elfin gait, as he circles the desk, takes hits of the beer, and rewinds the game in his head. Eventually, only two writers remain. Tom Boswell of *The Washington Post* asks Earl for the name of the game's most valuable player.

Earl thinks for a long time. Pulls on the beer, pulls on the cigarette. Blinks at Boswell.

"I was," he says.

Now, on Memorial's last weekend, Earl shakes a boy's hand, and hands out calendars, and smiles.

"They don't seem to care if you lose in this town," Earl says. "That was important. They didn't seem to care if you lost.

"How my teams appreciated that," he says, in a most un-Earl-like syntax.

But then, he seems most un-Earl-like on this day. It's something in his expression. It was always marked by wrinkles that evoked nothing more than a relief map of the Mississippi River delta, always pulling down. Now, his face has relaxed. Now, there is nothing left to be angry about.

Sunday dawns cloudily. The main concern is the weather. At game time, a layer of blue clouds hovers to the east.

The Colts' band plays the national anthem. The lead cornet misses a few notes.

In the top row of the upper deck down the left-field line, autumn rides a wind coming in from Lake Montebello, shining steely. To the east of the park, in someone's back yard, a half-dozen men play touch football. From above, the trees are tinged with yellow at the edge of all of their leaves.

Bob Milacki's third pitch bounces five feet in front of the plate. Milt Cuyler beats out a bleeding, hopping infield single. Lou Whitaker grounds a ball right through Glenn Davis's legs. Lloyd Moseby singles to right on a hit and run. Cecil Fielder pops one foul, and catcher Melvin drops it. Mickey Tettleton singles up the middle. Tony Phillips drops a single into left. Dave Bergman singles into center. It is 4–0. The Orioles are obviously going to lose the game, emphatically. It is just as obvious that the day's purpose is not to be found on a scoreboard.

In the bottom of the eighth, Baltimore is losing by eight runs. The crowd next to the bullpen starts to chant Mike Flanagan's name. In the top of the ninth, it has spread throughout the park, breaking out like pockets of wildfire, then growing into a plea raining down from all reaches:

"We want Flanagan!"

Greg Olson opens the ninth on the mound for the Orioles. The first batter grounds the ball to Davis at first. He bobbles it, then frantically flips it to Olson, and the pitcher steps on first, beating the runner by a half-step. As he crosses the bag, Olson thrusts a fist into the air.

Oates walks to the mound and Olson flips him the ball with a smile. The manager motions for Flanagan, who walks in slowly, not giving in to the temptation to doff his hat to acknowledge the standing ovation.

You fancy him soaking all of it in, the sound of fifty thousand people.

Flanagan goes to 0–2 on Dave Bergman, then throws three straight balls. Then he throws a screwball and Bergman swings and misses. Bergman flips his bat in disgust.

When Travis Fryman comes to the plate, the crowd is on its feet to stay. Flanagan alternates balls with strikes until the count is 2–2. Flanagan's fifth pitch misses just outside. The entire stadium is shaking. Up in the top row, a man from Lutherville notes that the upper deck hasn't shaken like this since an Eddie Murray at bat in the 1979 Series.

Flanagan goes into his windup. It's a distinctive motion, a slow one, almost balletic, in which all of his limbs stretch out and then come together. It's so slow that you can feel the heft of the ball in the palm of his left hand. It seems impossible that he could get anyone out with it.

Then Fryman swings and misses, and in the immediate moment that follows, in the sudden freeze-frame where Fryman is out and Flanagan knows that he's done it, Memorial Stadium is elevated with a sensation that fills you up to your fingertips. It's a moment entirely free of thought.

But for all the dictates of drama and poetry, baseball has its rules, the Orioles must bat, and so Tigers pitcher Frank Tanana will throw the actual last pitch in the park. When he does, it is to Cal Ripken, who grounds it into a double play, and the crowd is almost relieved. It turns out that Ripken is giving way to history, graciously stepping aside.

No one knows what is to follow, and when Frank Robinson steps out of the dugout, in uniform, rounds the bases nonchalantly, and steps on home plate; when a white limousine drives in from the outfield, seeming incongruous and jarringly inappropriate, and several men in white tuxedos dig up the plate to drive it down to Camden Yards; when James Earl Jones's voice starts to weave its stentorian tones out of the center-field scoreboard speakers, a sound bite lifted from the movie *Field of Dreams*, inauthentic, almost heretical—reality having to turn to fiction to celebrate itself, less than the stadium deserves—everyone assumes that the festivity is complete.

But then Brooks Robinson steps onto the top step of the home dugout, pauses for a moment, hefts himself to the field, and jogs to third base.

And now everyone knows.

Then Frank Robinson jogs to right, turns, stops, takes the place he always took, and listens to the ovation. And Boog lopes to first, and then Jim Palmer to the mound. Rick Dempsey to the plate. One by one they take their positions, each man waiting long enough for the man before him to reap his own ovation.

The sound in the stands is an unusual mixture of cheers and gasps and applause; there is no precedent, so no one knows how to react, although many people in the upper row of the upper deck are crying unashamedly.

Dave Johnson and Bobby Grich and Rich Dauer go to second. Lee May, Pat Kelly, Elrod Hendricks. Dave McNally, Pat Dobson, Mike Cuellar. Doug DeCinces. Russ Snyder. Mike Flanagan, Dennis Martinez, Scott McGregor.

For ten minutes they keep coming, and when it becomes apparent that it wasn't just the star Orioles who had returned, but everyone who had worn an Orioles uniform, life really does start to imitate art: Each successive name—Glenn Gulliver, Dave Skaggs, dozens of them— adds an extra chill to the moment.

By now the ovation has settled to a steady roar, like a waterfall, just as insistent; it is thanks for nothing less than thirty-seven years of baseball.

Finally, Cal Ripken comes out alone. And then Earl.

And for that single moment, there isn't anyone in Memorial Stadium who wasn't finally grateful for the ballpark's youth; because of it, the men who played in it—almost all of them—could return to bid it good-bye, all of them alive. Other parks speak of their ghosts. Memorial needed none. It had never happened before that a stadium could be visited by virtually all of its former players.

Beyond the rim of the stadium, the setting sun cast a tinge of purplish pink on the undersides of the clouds over Lake Montebello. It hadn't rained after all.

Down on the field, the players formed an enormous circle around the infield and joined hands. And then, without signal, they went away, down through the dugouts.

Then the field was empty.

GOOD-BYE, OLD FRIEND, said the scoreboard, and for a moment it was unclear whether the Orioles were saying good-bye to the park or the other way around.

"When I started to warm up it really hit me," Mike Flanagan said. He was locked in a sea of reporters, all of them frantically scribbling at notebooks. It was so quiet in the locker room that you could hear the collective scratch of the pens on the paper, an effect that was heightened by the other Orioles, most of whom were taking care not to make noise in their own lockers so that Mike Flanagan's words could be accurately heard and correctly transcribed.

"I asked Elrod to warm me up. He'd warmed me up for three or four hundred starts. He said, 'I'd be honored to.' I've walked in from that bullpen three, four hundred times. This was the last one. I didn't want to rush it.

"To me, it was still like pitching in the seventh game of the World Series. I had the honor of being the last guy to throw."

At the beginning, writers had been asking specific questions, and Flanagan had answered them in measured tones—no, he couldn't even remember if Fryman swung or was caught looking; yes, he heard them calling his name; no, he was not surprised it worked out so well: "Most of the season has felt like it was out of my hands."

And then, into a silence, Flanagan began to talk.

"I felt like I wasn't doing it for me," he said. "I felt like I was doing it for all the guys I played with. I felt like I had the weight of all the generations before me.

"I *tried* to make it for me. I tried to make it 'Do it for yourself.' But I've never been able to do that. I've always done it for the guys before me," he said, as if trying to convince someone otherwise, although no one doubted a word of it.

Tears were beginning to well in Mike Flanagan's eyes. Not a single writer was looking up from his notebook to see it. The water caught in his lower eyelids and reflected the overhead lights of the Orioles locker room.

"It was always the game. It was never the stats. It was all in the winning. It was the Orioles concept. You have to say, 'These were the best days of your life.' And they were.

"I spent the best day of my life," Mike Flanagan said, "with the best friends I ever had."

As the last stragglers padded their way down the grassy divider on 33rd Street, lit only by the blue-white of streetlights filtering between maple branches, it was easy to be carried away by the simple and stunning clarity of one baseball team's emotions. In a game in which so much emotion has learned to fake itself, in a sport whose championship celebrations must be bloated for the cameras and choreographed for the sponsors, in an age when reporters have forgotten how to look and are compelled to ask for descriptions of emotions that are often best left unuttered, it was a remarkable afternoon.

There was, though, outside of Memorial Stadium, a sliver of fear to accompany the joy riding the cool night air: that a chapter of history had been closed, and had taken—deservedly—all of the names and all of the moments with it, so that Camden Yards would be starting anew, amid all of the pomp and glory, without the Robinsons, Eddie Murray, Powell, Weaver, even Ripken; none could loan themselves or the accumulation of their feats to the new park. Nor would the new park be bold enough to presume to borrow them. Memorial Stadium had closed and taken the Orioles—the real Orioles—with it. The ballpark had lived its life during a time in which such lives were possible—during an era in our society when a single small baseball team from the neighborhood could fill a small, odd little mongrel of a ballpark, and together they could elevate their entire time and place. The fear was that it could not possibly happen again.

Then came the march of a couple's footsteps down the sidewalk off 33rd Street, a loud and crisp autumn sound, and they were laughing, and they turned left on St. Paul Street, and together they began to head downtown, away from Baltimore's baseball, toward its baseball dream.

HIZZONER AND THE LION

◆

BALTIMORE DIDN'T NEED a new baseball stadium, but it was more than grateful for the deliverance of a national showpiece. Mired in the cultural crevace between the imperious capital city to the south and the mainline strutting of William Penn's cobbled town to the north, the brick-built village with its quilt of marble-stepped row-housed streets tucked into a crook of mid-Atlantic coastline has been nursing, for quite a while now, an inferiority complex the size of H. L. Mencken's ego. This complex was not without some justification.

"The last thing that happened of any importance in Baltimore," says journalist and novelist Frank Deford, Baltimore born and raised, "was the writing of 'The Star-Spangled Banner.'"

Deford's childhood experience was not a particularly normal one; raised in the northwest corner of the city, the son of an executive of Pemco Porcelain and Enamels, his background was more rarified than most. This did nothing to lessen the shame, as Deford went on to Princeton and out into the world, of repeatedly having to explain to his more worldly acquaintances just exactly where it was that Baltimore lay on the map.

"We were a second-class place," Deford admits. "We were looked down on. We had a tremendous inferiority complex. We never had a major-league baseball team—the sixth largest city in the country when I was growing up, and we didn't have a major-league team! You wanted to absolutely *scream*!

"We clung to things that no longer distinguished the city: Mencken. The Duchess of Windsor. The old Orioles. The War of 1812. We were clinging to the past because there was nothing to distinguish the city in the present. We'd always been passed over. You know in the Bible when one of the apostles first hears of Jesus Christ, and is told he's from Nazareth? 'What good,' he says, 'could come out of Nazareth?' I remember thinking, 'That's what they think about Baltimore.' "

Throughout its history, whatever natural treasures the town did cultivate were methodically seized by marauders from all directions. Babe Ruth became the symbol of the New York Yankees. Edgar Allan Poe was appropriated by everyone; New York, Richmond, and Philadelphia now have Poe museums. And while no one would claim the town's one true towering figure, after the publication of Mencken's diaries who would particularly want to? They revealed him to be a racist of the first order, and quite insufferably full of himself.

It was Baltimore that built the first monument to George Washington—but the District of Columbia went on to build itself a far more priapically impressive version. The District won the Hirshhorn art collection by building a museum to house it all, paid for by federal funding. The *Sun*, once a newspaper with European bureaus to rival the best, took a backseat to the post-Watergate *Washington Post.*

The Baltimore & Ohio, the nation's first railroad, was so insecure that it designed a logo with the Capitol dome in it, Baltimore itself lacking any landmark distinctive enough to emblazon the cars; oysters, after all, are not all that distinctive in profile. (Of late, pollution in the Chesapeake has dropped the oyster harvest so low that the state has considered importing a strain of Japanese super-oysters.)

By the sixties, the only thing about Baltimore for which Washington would deign to drive up the turnpike was The Block, its neon-scarred neighborhood of vicely temptations. Washington had Jefferson and Lincoln. Baltimore had Blaze Starr and, on a slightly lesser level on burlesque's phylogenetic scale, Irma the Rose—best known, as you might imagine, for her imaginative use of a floral prop.

The sports ledger was no less dismaying. The Bullets fled to ignominious anonymity in a ghostly vacant arena down on the Beltway. The Colts may have been championed as the jewel in the city's sports crown in the late fifties and sixties, but the truth is that none of the city's own financiers had been willing to preside over this natural resource; the glory Colts were owned by a Philadelphia man, Carroll Rosenbloom, who ended up swapping them, of all things, to a Chicago sheet-metal baron, Robert Irsay. And after the team's fortunes sank so low that John Elway told the team not even to bother drafting him, and after the state built them a state-of-the-art practice complex, the Colts left town in the middle of the night, during a snowstorm, to a city known as Indiana-no-place, where, for all practical purposes, the team disappeared. Maryland's faithful were left without a team. (Venturing down to RFK Stadium was quite out of the question. As Baltimore novelist Tom Clancy put it, "I'd rather sell my children to gypsies than be a Redskin fan.")

These days, in downtown Baltimore, the department stores at Lexington and Howard, once the greatest shopping hub in the Northeast, have long closed their doors, and their windows stand as empty and unblinking as the eyes of the dead—while the fastest-growing section of the state is Maryland's Alsace-Lorraine, Prince Georges and Montgomery counties, suburbs of the District. The renovation of the harbor was a step in the right direction, of course, but who wants to see their city reduced to a theme park?

Certainly not its proudest booster and staunchest advocate, Baltimore mayor-turned-Maryland-governor William Donald Schaefer.

In the sixties, when the town was in desperate need of a moral lift, it elected Schaefer, president of the city council, to be its mayor. After he'd returned from the war to start a law practice, friends remember, Schaefer would walk down to the harbor with them as early as 1945 and remark, "You know, this could be another San Francisco."

He was the last of the one-man, one-agenda urban American politicians, unencumbered by academia's political science theories, full of passion for nothing but his town—the man former governor Marvin Mandel once called "the most nonpolitical politician I've ever met in my life," a billing Schaefer lived up to when, as one of America's highest-profile Democratic mayors, he skipped the 1984 Democratic National Convention for a trip to the San Diego Zoo.

He'd never had time or patience for the Beltway strut. But when

Baltimore's fortunes were at stake, he was as tenacious as Robert Moses building his bridges across the rivers of New York City. No one could dispute Schaefer's devotion to his town. "William Donald Schaefer never would have said we were second class," Frank Deford says. "He just embraced the city. 'Follow me. I love you, and I'm proud of you.'"

He was in a private law practice after two unsuccessful runs at the House of Delegates in 1950 and 1954, when he was tabbed by Irvin Kovens, a furniture dealer, and Phillip H. Goodman, a former state legislator, to run for city council in 1955. Kovens had a knack for fund-raising, and Goodman would eventually be elected mayor. Together they headed a West Baltimore Democratic cadre, and with their backing Schaefer was elected to the city council and was elevated to that body's presidency ten years later. The Baltimore city council, it was once said, had about as much power as the Soviet Proletariat—until Schaefer used his position as a sort of deputy mayorship.

Despite his powerful backers, Schaefer was beholden to no one. In 1966, when Goodman and Kovens backed Thomas Finan for governor, Schaefer supported his rival, Carlton Sickles—and was the leading city politician to do so. And most recently, he astounded his entire party by endorsing George Bush for the presidency. His style was not to give or grant favors, or to do favors for others; rather, he found the best person for the job, and worked with him or her. "If you want to get things done," he once said, "you can do it two ways: order people around, or ask them to work." He preferred the latter, since he was always willing to pull his share of the load.

At the same time, Schaefer was not disposed to work with those whose views didn't gibe with his own, and was quite unafraid to use the office as a pulpit. Woe to the visitor to City Council President Schaefer's office seeking compromise or reason on a matter of politics qua patriotism. "In '68 there was a resolution in the city council against the Vietnam War," recalls native son Jimmy Rouse, the proprietor of Baltimore's fabled Louie's Bookstore and Café. "I was protesting the Vietnam War outside of City Hall. We wanted to meet with Schaefer, then president of the city council. Well, he sat us down and proceeded to give us this incredibly fiery lecture about how great the United States was and how wrong we were, and he built up this crescendo—the more fired up he got, the more he was a man out of control—and then he dismissed us! He was so condescending he wouldn't listen to a word we said."

Schaefer never married. "He was married to the city," says Rouse. He spent eighteen years on the council, making friends and building coalitions, but none of it was modeled on the old-style Democratic machine with its taint of vote getting by forceful persuasion, of block captains herding reluctant enlistees, of contracts doled out as favors, and wheels being greased by the green. Schaefer wasted little time on deal making, concentrating instead on getting things done, and finding the people to help him do it, whether it was picking up litter around Roland Park or pushing for the inner harbor's rebirth. As a truly beloved mayor, Schaefer was a builder and a promoter and a marketer—always with a finger held out to test the political winds. When his proposal to extend the interstate through Fells Point—and rend several city neighborhoods—was defeated, he did an immediate turnaround and became the advocate for rebuilding the city; his subsequent buy-a-house-for-a-dollar became a model for cities across the nation, and soon the national press was touting him as the champion of gentrification.

In 1972, with his election, the skyline began to rise around him. But Schaefer never rose with it. He stayed rooted to his streets. He'd knock on the doors of homes in neighborhoods that had allowed trash to accumulate in vacant lots, and threatened to move into empty buildings and harangue the neighbors unless they cleaned it up. In public he retained a nearly comically homey public image—he once jumped into the harbor wearing an old-style bathing suit and a rubber duck to promote a new harbor venture—and was often at odds with reporters who would question any of his decidedly eccentric means. If the *Sun* published a letter critical of his policies, the letter writer could expect a personal visit from the mayor. If the *Sun* ran too much bad news on the front page, the executive editor could expect a missive from the top.

"It's one of the outstanding moments of my life to be able to stand and chat with the press," he once told *Regardie's* magazine, during one of his many tenures as mayor. "It's one of the things I look forward to each day: 'If I can only get downtown, then I'll be able to see the magnificent press there.' Then I start to puke."

It isn't only in the media that he finds his perceived enemies. At a dinner for the NFL trainers in 1990, a festive occasion graced by the still-faithful Colts band, Schaefer was the only one in a crowd of three thousand who seemed to divine a few boos in the middle of the ringing applause following his speech.

"I heard it!" he said. "I heard you in the back! I heard the boos." He then launched into a defense of his policies. It was vintage Schaefer: setting himself up as an underdog, all the better to come back swinging from the heels, with popular opinion behind him.

The fight for Camden Yards proved to be a classic Baltimore battle, with classic Schaefer ingredients: He was able to set himself up as the humble underdog battling the intellectual giant from the capital, gathering the town behind him, and fighting for his most memorable public works achievement. As it took William Donald Schaefer to reinvigorate the city, it took Schaefer to keep its prime jewel of a team within the city limits. That's all it took, and that was everything.

In the early seventies, the fledgling mayor, prompted by Rosen-bloom and Jerold Hoffberger, whose family owned the Orioles, had seized on the idea of a ballpark next to historic Camden Station, the downtown railroad terminal. The two owners had floated the idea of a dual-purpose stadium on the site as early as 1967, but it was given little credence—the same fate suffered by subsequent stabs at getting the city and state to help them build a new home. In November 1972, for instance, Hoffberger publicly asked, "What does the team mean to the city?" and had to backtrack quickly: "This was no 'Build-me-a-stadium-or-I'll-leave-and-the-city-will-fall-apart' threat." But Orioles executive Frank Cashen said at the time there'd be no long-term lease without a new stadium: "We are not going to be able to do anything in terms of a long-term lease unless a stadium is built downtown." In 1972, when Irsay was rumored to be considering a move to Tampa, William Boucher, the head of the Greater Baltimore Committee, had written to Governor Marvin Mandel to suggest resurrecting the stadium proposal. But it was not a good climate for public expenditures; the city was losing its tax base, and fast. Standard Oil, Crosse and Blackwell, Revere Brass and Copper, and American Smelting were all leaving, prompting a letter writer to the *Sun* to observe, "The city is full of ruined houses, the jails are overcrowded, the dome is falling off City Hall, there are potholes in the streets, crippled children can't get to school, taxes are going up and services are going down—but we're going to have a sports complex."

In the face of such sentiment, in 1973 the Senate Finance Committee voted to abolish a body being funded to look into a downtown sports complex: "People in my county just don't want to go into downtown Baltimore," said one Carroll County senator. James Kraft, chairman of the Stadium Task Force, admitting that racial considerations are "an issue. There is a contingent that fears the blacks." In 1974, Brooks Robinson suggested a new stadium. But governor Mandel said he wouldn't support the effort, and it died.

Nonetheless, when Schaefer was elected mayor in 1972, he immediately saw the sense of the Camden Yards site: The railroads were clearly on the way out, and one hundred acres of downtown land were going to depreciate quickly. At the same time, the location for a park was perfect: a rail hub is, by definition, located at a city's most accessible location.

And when William Donald Schaefer got his mind wrapped around an idea—an idea that would mean building something new in Baltimore—he tended to hold on to the notion, clamp his teeth onto it, and never let it go.

When the time finally came to sell the stadium to the state's legislators once and for all, or let it sink, Schaefer seized the day.

In the words of Edward Bennett Williams's financial advisor, Bob Flanagan, the man who spent a decade crunching the numbers between the town, the team, the state, and the ballpark, "If you're looking for a hero on Camden Yards, it's Hizzoner. He never let up."

"He was," Frank Deford believes, "simply magnificent."

The ballpark was his greatest challenge. But first he had to wrangle with his most worthy foe.

*   *   *

It is a sunblasted March morning in 1985 in Miami Stadium, a tin-roofed palace from baseball's past. Orioles owner Edward Bennett Williams is passing the time in one of his favorite fashions— oratorically. Pressed for a prediction about the upcoming season during a slow, aimless amble down the right-field line after a morning in court, he doffs his suit jacket and eases into a parable that reflects two of his many passions, politics and baseball.

"There's a way to be a genius as a prophet," he says. "All you have to do is combine the Henry Kissinger Principle of Prophecy with the Henry [Zeke] Bonura Theory of Chance."

It's a typically intriguing Williams introduction, followed by a pause long enough to allow a companion to fish for a notebook and pen.

"The Henry Kissinger Principle of Prophecy says that you always prophesy doom. That way if it comes to pass you are hailed as a prophet. And if it doesn't, you're given credit for having forestalled it."

We are out near the right-field wall. It is emblazoned by a hand-painted advertisement, in Spanish, for the Blood of Christ Church. We have paused for Williams to rest. Up close, he does not have the look common to most franchise owners, the big-business boys—the flat, gray, disinterested stare of the robber baron who has no use for you if you have use for him.

For one thing, his hair is too long to be intimidating: unruly, graying, flicking over his collar like a mane in back, the coif of a man who abides by no one else's rules. His manner is polite and comfortable and seems to indicate, startlingly, that unlike so many of his peers he trusts whomever he meets, until he has reason to feel otherwise.

On the other hand, there is no way around the sensation of being in the presence of living history, although, if the aura that surrounds him seems a tangible thing in the heat-heavy humid air, it is also remarkably easy to penetrate.

"Now," he says, "you mix this with the Zeke Bonura Theory of Chance. Zeke was a journeyman first baseman in the thirties and forties with a terrible glove. But baseball has this absurd rule that says if you don't touch the ball, you can't make an error. Well, Henry never touched the ball. He was the worst first baseman you've ever seen. But he always won the fielding title because he never touched the ball.

"So: If you prophecy like Zeke Bonura played first base, and use the Henry Kissinger Principle of Prophecy, you'll top the Delphic Oracle, Teiresias, Cassandra, Nostradamus and all the rest."

It is, of course, nothing more than a neat evasion. At this point the doom has already come to pass: a fifth-place finish in 1984 after the championship season of 1983. And less than a week before this morning he had undergone his fifth operation for cancer in eight years.

Suddenly, Williams stretches out his left hand and rests it, gently, on the right shoulder of his companion for support; ions leap—it is a stunning sensation. He is weak, but hardly fragile; there is a stem of steel to his grip.

He always attacked the disease the way he attacked everything in life: head-on. At the first sign of any recurrence, he underwent the knife. With his baseball team, though, it was Williams who wielded the machete.

In his own mind, on this day he is sharpening the blade.

"I never should have stayed with the same roster," he says, with a shake of his head. "There's a saying a baseball: You don't break up a winning combination. But do you remember the portrait of Dorian Gray? It grew old before your eyes. That's what happened to the Orioles last year. Five Orioles died before your eyes. Bumbry, Singleton, Ayala, Palmer, and Underwood."

They are painfully blunt words. But Ed Williams saw things in extremes, the easier to identify the adversary. He'd once described himself as having two speeds: none and full. In 1984, against the advice of his own front office, he had turned himself off, choosing to stay with his fraying veterans to reward them for their years of service. It was a strategy that proved disastrous. It has been said that Ed Williams couldn't wait so much as a week for revenge, and now he'd had to endure months of stewing in last year's failure. He'd let emotion get in the way of logic, and he had paid for it.

He had already started to act to rectify things. He had just hired a former manager, Frank Robinson, to look over the shoulder of his current (but doomed) incumbent, Joe Altobelli. He'd signed three overpriced free agents, all past their prime, who would shatter the clubhouse camaraderie that had long been the team's trademark. And, of course, he was plotting more moves.

"Life is dynamic," Williams says. "It moves all the time. You can't be intractable. You have to shift. You have to move."

Here he stops and lifts his hand, and slowly, ceremonially, pulls his suit jacket back on. Even in his weakness, the jacket is a tight fit. He is a thick, substantial man, and he fills space. The air stirs, as if in deference, around him.

He turns and begins to stride back to the clubhouse to observe his baseball team. In his mind, no doubt, resonate the words of his friend Eleanor Roosevelt, who, when asked by Williams at a 1958 dinner party how she managed to accomplish so much, had answered, "No indecision, no regrets."

The words might have well been Edward Bennett Williams's manifesto—when it came to his baseball team, at any rate: Three months later, Williams lopped off the head of his manager, in squalidly Steinbrennian fashion. Less than three years later he would fire another—eight games into the season. Then he fired his general manager and farm director, and hired himself three general managers.

Off the field, he would pass the baseball reins of his team to a good friend whose main experience with a baseball was negotiating the contracts of the men who hit and threw it.

And, finally, he would convince the state of Maryland to build him a ballpark, simultaneously blessing the game with its finest playing field in half a century and cursing it by playing off a city's fear of losing its final sports franchise, to carve himself an even bigger place in history.

He was loved, revered, and vilified. But on this point, all will agree: Edward Bennett Williams was a big man in a sport populated by so many very small ones. In a fraternity of barons bonded by nothing as much as their love of petty pursuits, he brought to sport a magnificence that transcended the lowly yearnings of the fast-food monarchs and the felonious blowhards. He could exult wildly over his victories and despair with astounding severity over the losses, but he never lingered in the dull gray middle grounds. Nothing he touched in baseball ever felt quite the same.

So while some will say that baseball is more of a game because of what he did, and others will say it's less of one, no one will disagree that his stamp was indelible.

"The Lion of the Law," Nicholas von Hoffman called him in his biography of Roy Cohn. But it was sport that long boiled in the blood of this man who viewed his life as one ongoing contest. Williams's conversation was sprinkled with baseball's metaphors: He'd rather "play than umpire" was his response to questions of Supreme Court ambitions, and his most relaxed and revealing moments were spent in the company of that greenback-ion-charged atmosphere of high-money athletics, from the private suite of a Trump hotel on fight night in Atlantic City to the high-society owners' box at RFK.

"Sports was the thing he liked the most," said Baltimore attorney and sports agent Ron Shapiro, "because it gave him a recognition not even the law could give him. And he loved recognition."

The son of a Welsh department-store floorwalker who earned forty-two dollars a week, as a child Williams would stand on a chair and imitate FDR's radio speeches. He attended daily mass and excelled in high school. "He always ruled with an iron hand and a dominating will," said his high school yearbook. In 1944, after graduating from Holy Cross and Georgetown Law School, he joined a prestigious Washington law firm, then quit five years later to strike out on his own and make a name for himself—which he did, in 1954, when he represented Joseph McCarthy at the Senate censure proceedings following the Army-McCarthy hearings. His law career was on its inexorable way.

But sport was never far away. Williams's first bid to enter the elite company of entrepreneurs who deal in sports flesh came with a failed attempt to buy the 1961 expansion Senators, who shared the surname of his own childhood team, the Hartford Senators of the Eastern League.

"He talked very infectiously," said his protégé and student in sport and law, Larry Lucchino, "about growing up in Hartford and going to the game as a kid and selling red-hots and ice-colds or whatever he called them." That first foray was embellished with typical Williams flair; he enlisted Joe DiMaggio as part of his prospective ownership team.

Five years later, Williams became minority owner and president of the Washington Redskins under Virginia's hunt country sports baron, Jack Kent Cooke. Cooke lived in Los Angeles, leaving Williams to rule the Redskins roost in the owners' box at RFK—still one of the most prestigious addresses in the District. Society writers took envious note of Williams's Sunday visitors, and chronicled their comings and goings as studiously as Fleet Streeters keeping track of the queen's guests at Epsom Downs. "Ed was a brand-name guy," Lucchino says, and this was obvious from the roster of regular guests in the owners' box at RFK: Joe Califano, Ben Bradlee, Art Buchwald, DiMaggio, William Simon. In 1976, when Simon tried to buy the Orioles, Williams represented him in the negotiations. Simon pulled out when Jerold Hoffberger, whose third-generation Baltimore brewing family owned the club, backed off at the last minute to give Baltimore interests a last chance to buy. Simon was furious and vilified Hoffberger in the press. Williams remained mum; he burned no bridges with Jerold Hoffberger.

In 1978, Cooke—quite Williams's match for intellect and cunning, more than Williams's match for self-celebration—sold the Lakers, the Kings, and the Forum to move back to Upperville, Virginia, and take over hands-on management of the Skins. At that point, Williams began to seriously consider buying the baseball team up the turnpike. He sold his 15 percent in the Redskins for $10 million, and stopped doing legal work for Cooke—in fact, stopped talking to Cooke altogether.

"Jack was entrenched with the football team," recalls Bob Flanagan. "He left Ed in the lurch."

By 1979, the Orioles were the most successful franchise on the field in all of baseball; they'd won more games than any other team in the preceding twenty years.

It was not for nothing that Williams left bridges unburnt.

Jerold Hoffberger, the grandson of an emigrant from Kiev who landed in Baltimore and founded the National Brewing Company in

Baltimore's brewery heydey—there were seventy breweries at the industry's peak—had been trying to sell the team for years at the request of his family, which saw the enterprise as a meaningless drain on the family coffers.

"My family would say, 'Don't let the team break our back. Don't lose money. Try to run it as close to the vest as you can,' " Hoffberger recalls, and there's no doubt that the collective family voice had some influence; according to a source at the closing of the sale of the team in 1979, Hoffberger's side of the table spoke for 122 relatives.

At any rate, close-to-the-vest Hoffberger stayed. Orioles salaries were traditionally low. The marketing budget was lower; according to Schaefer, Hoffberger expected the city to do the promoting. Whoever was responsible, they weren't doing much of a job. Of course, the good folks of Baltimore deserve their fair share of blame. When Williams did buy the team, it had won seven division titles in the previous fourteen years—from 1966 to 1979, there was an even chance, in other words, that the team would win its division—but the townspeople had supported the club halfheartedly at best. During the 1969 World Series against New York more than five thousand tickets went unsold for two games at Memorial. In the 1970 World Series, the Orioles won the deciding fifth game before a crowd of 45,531—nine thousand under capacity. In 1971, the third consecutive year of hundred-plus wins, a team that had Cuellar, Dobson, McNally, and Palmer each reaching the twenty-win mark, drew 44,174 and 47,291 for games six and seven.

"We ran a pretty lousy organization," Hoffberger admits now. "We did okay in other ways—building up growing young people and getting them into the baseball world, men like Harry Dalton and Frank Cashen and John Schuerholz, fifteen or twenty guys who have important jobs.

"But even though we ran a lousy organization we only lost money in two of the years I ran the club. There was no evidence you couldn't stay alive even if you were as pisspoor an operator as I was."

By 1974 Hoffberger was willing to meet the right buyer. Bowie Kuhn, one of Hoffberger's least favorite people, wanted him to sell to Washingtonians—"it would have made him a big man with some of the people in Congress," says Hoffberger, who has been angry at

Kuhn ever since the commissioner invited Hoffberger to dinner—
then left early, leaving Hoffberger to pay the check.

According to Mike Veeck, son of the late baseball impresario Bill
Veeck, Hoffberger and his father consummated a deal in 1975. Veeck
was living down on the Eastern Shore, and had long loved the city. He
had known Hoffberger ever since the Baltimore brewer had reached
out to Veeck when Veeck owned the faltering St. Louis Browns,
offering some financial assistance in the form of a sponsorship deal.
Eventually, Hoffberger tried to help Veeck move his Browns east, but
the American League wouldn't allow the Browns to move unless
Veeck sold the team outright.

So when Hoffberger began to cast about for someone to buy the
Orioles in 1974, Veeck's name naturally came to mind. "Hoffberger
and Dad had a deal," says Mike Veeck, who earned his college degree
in Baltimore. "Jerry said to Dad, 'You own the O's.' He made a deal.
He shook hands. He said, 'You can buy my ball club.' That's enough
for my dad. But Jerry Hoffberger screwed him. He really screwed him.
He got pressure from everyone, sure. But Dad never expected Jerry to
cave. Much to Hoffberger's chagrin, Dad never spoke to him again."

"Veeck wanted it back," Hoffberger remembers. "But there was a
tax issue we couldn't resolve. It think he felt until the day he died that
I'd been unfair to him."

Mark Kram, Jr., a sportswriter whose family was close to the Veeck
clan on the Eastern Shore, remembers visiting Bill Veeck soon after
the failed negotiation. He recalls discovering that, whereas in past
visits there had been cases of Hoffberger's National Bohemian beer
on hand, on this occasion a single can remained.

"He told me he refused to buy it anymore," Kram says. "I drank
Bill Veeck's last Bo."

(Epilogue, sixteen years later: "Hoffberger had one of those
services that sent birthday greetings," Mike Veeck said. "On September one this year it sent one to my mother. She said, 'Send a
message to Mr. Hoffberger that Mary Francis Veeck is dead.' ")

In 1979, Hoffberger and Williams made the deal for $11 million,
Williams borrowing much of the money. On August 2, 1979, Williams
and his attorneys sat with Hoffberger in his office at Memorial
Stadium. Four hundred pages of documents sat on the table, the result

of nine months of negotiations. An aide walked in and handed Hoffberger an envelope. It was another bid—from a consortium organized by the bulldog mayor of Baltimore, William Donald Schaefer. Williams's face went white.

"Buying the Orioles was a longtime dream, and he was an all-pro worrier, the prince of pessimism," Lucchino said. "It wasn't Yogi Berra who said, 'It ain't over 'til it's over.' It was Ed, and he told it to Yogi. Ed figured if anything could go wrong, it probably would.

"But Hoffberger, to his credit, said, 'Enough. I've been waiting for years and certainly I'm not going at the eleventh hour to go with these folks after bringing Ed Williams this far.' Ed's vision of the adverse ways life turns was almost a reality. Hoffberger stuck it in his pocket. I don't know if it was more money or not. But Williams's deal was real.

"On the drive back to Washington, he was simply euphoric."

Baltimore, as suggested by Schaefer's last-minute effort, was not. There had never been any love lost between their city and D.C., and now a Beltway baron controlled their baseball team. When Williams and Hoffberger first went public with the agreement in August 1979, "the entire city of Baltimore shuddered," wrote one local columnist.

With good reason. The District was slavering in anticipation. A city that had lost two Senator teams, both to the whims of owners from Minneapolis, finally had one of its own power brokers poised to turn the tables. District baseball fans were well versed in carpetbagger doublespeak. In 1959, Calvin Griffith had pronounced, "The Senators will never move in my lifetime," and moved them two years later. In 1969, Bob Short had intoned, with a little more verbal duplicity, "I didn't buy the Washington Senators to move them"—a statement that, of course, did not preclude moving them, which he did, two years later.

So when Williams started serving up his own public proclamations for the people in Baltimore, few hopes were actually dashed down in the capital.

"For so long as the city [Baltimore] will support this team," Williams told *The Washington Post*, "it will stay here." But he then added, "If someone sees fit to build a magnificent new stadium between here and Washington, that would be great." Williams knew that if he could draw on both markets, the TV and radio audience would make up the fourth-largest market in the nation.

In Baltimore, those words had an ominous feel to them. No one could blame the town for springing to its own defense, which it did, with emphasis. THE ORIOLES BELONG TO US! bleated the headline in the *News-American*, whose columnist, Tom Coakley, leapt in with his characterization of the new owner as "a smooth professional from the high-powered martini set."

"I'd rather have somebody from Arabia buy the club, than someone from Washington," a Baltimore secretary told the *News-American.*

There was no questioning this much: Williams had bought the team with the intention of moving it. Considerations of rupturing a city's fabric aside, it made sense economically. Unlike the real estate, pizza, beer, and fast-food kings in the owners' fraternity, Williams did not have bottomless pockets, and had invested a sizeable amount of his own money in a team that he had every right to expect would continue to draw its twelve thousand a game.

"When he was negotiating for it, when he signed the contract in '79, [moving] was on his mind," says Bob Flanagan. "But by the time he bought it in '79, he wasn't going to do it. He nevertheless thought that the seed that he might be crazy enough to do it wasn't a bad thing to . . . not necessarily plant, but maybe to fondle between his index finger and thumb.

"It was masterfully done. It was always hanging in the air."

Entirely unexpectedly, though, came the first real confirmation of Roland Hemond's notion about God and the Orioles: A remarkable ray of light shone upon the 1979 team, unwavering, all season long. They began to play like the 1927 Yankees. Led by Eddie Murray and Mike Flanagan, the Orioles won twenty-three of twenty-nine games in June. They played an unheard-of .732 for 97 games, going 71–26. Anchored by the beery semaphores of an out-of-work cab driver named Wild Bill Hagy—who took to contorting his less-than-athletic physique into the shapes of the letters O-R-I-O-L-E-S in the upper deck as the crowd chanted along—and scored by the seventh-inning anthem of John Denver's "Thank God I'm a Country Boy," they won 102 games, took the division by an eight-game margin, beat the

Angels in the playoffs in four games, and took a 3–1 lead into the fifth game of the World Series before dropping three straight to the Pirates, the seventh in horrendous fashion, as the Pirate batters polished off Orioles reliever after Orioles reliever.

But the real transformation was off the field: The club drew 1,681,000, averaging a very respectable twenty-one thousand per game, half a million more than anyone had expected. Williams was understandably impressed. And still, the familiar clouds began to gather within a few weeks of the season's end. When the city announced that it would increase seating at Memorial—at a cost of $24 million—at the request of Robert Irsay, the hated Colts owner who once journeyed to the sideline to fire his coach in the middle of a game (Howard Schnellenberger refused to quit), Williams was miffed: "I think, naturally," he said, "it would be ideal to have a baseball-only stadium which would be brand new."

And then in November, Williams told a radio reporter, "I have a dream of a magnificent stadium. Just for baseball, just for the Orioles. Not for football. Just a magnificent baseball stadium . . . parking for fifteen thousand, maybe seats for forty-two thousand. It's kind of like my Walter Mitty dream. I have that dream in my head, and it's not going to go away until I try to execute on it."

There was an added worry: Hoffberger's lease had provided for thirteen games to be played in Washington each year, a clause inserted in 1975 at Hoffberger's insistence. In Williams's hands, that allowance loomed sinister.

"I know he wants desperately to bring this team to Washington," the *Post* reported, quoting an anonymous friend in December, and then this in February: "Privately, EBW has had discussions about building a baseball-only stadium on I-95." Kuhn, the commissioner who'd grown up tending the scoreboard at Griffith Stadium, added his one cent's worth: "I always felt the best solution was to see the Baltimore club take over the entire territory," he said, to the accompaniment of a Washington headline that read, KUHN PREDICTS NEW O'S PARK BETWEEN CITIES.

The grimmest toll of all was struck when American League president Lee MacPhail said publicly that he was unopposed to the idea—

testament to Williams's personality and reputation as much as anything else; for a league president to advocate relocation was heresy.

Things went smoothly enough through the beginning of the 1980 season. The Orioles didn't pull up to .500 until June, but then they took flight. Behind Al Bumbry's line drives and Steve Stone's unlikely twenty-five victories, the Orioles began to crowd the Yankees for first.

Then amid this growing feeling of security, Williams let slip a few more bons mots to the *Post*: "This is a trial year for Baltimore attendance, and the trial is about to begin." Williams was prepared, he said, to exercise "all my options."

Baltimore was stunned—although, in retrospect, it doesn't seem illogical to wonder if Williams knew exactly what he was doing. The Yankees were coming to town two weeks later for a five-game series; perhaps inflamed by the remarks, a quarter-million Baltimoreans pushed past Memorial's turnstiles—a baseball record for a five-game series. As the seeds of doubt kept growing, though, another seed was planted: It was in Williams's box that memorable weekend that Schaefer first spoke to the owner about building a new park at Camden Yards.

"I said I would keep the team in Baltimore as long as the city supported it," Williams said in another interview, "but there seems to be some grave incredulity about this."

And why not? Folks on both sides of the Beltway well knew that Williams was quite capable of promising one thing and delivering another. "George Allen is the last coach I'll ever hire," he once said as the Redskins' president—a year and a half before firing him, and hiring Jack Pardee.

There was very little standing between the man and his appointed city—just a small, balding politician from the near West Side, a simple man of earthen language, possessed of a strictly local vision and unremarkable tastes: a Hector to Williams's Achilles.

Small, perhaps, compared to the soaring, leonine fast talker from down the Beltway. But smart enough to know that there was no shame in a draw. Not on your home turf. On its home turf, a bulldog can fight a lion to a draw.

*   *   *

"Oh, Mr. Williams would have moved the team to Washington," said Governor William Donald Schaefer, his American Gothic visage embellished by a smile of self-satisfaction. "I was absolutely convinced he would. I'm sure he bought the club to move it to Washington. There's no question in my mind."

Schaefer was in a mood for remembrance, and it was easy to flow along with him. On this day, Schaefer was mild, unbarbed, indulging of a visitor in search of the past. The halls of the state house were bone quiet. It was late on a Friday autumn afternoon, and everyone in Annapolis had left work to get a start on the weekend—everyone except Schaefer. He was sitting back in his cluttered quarters and reflecting on his greatest triumph, which was arising out of a web of steel girders back in the city.

He was wearing a garish floral-print tie. A clumsy oil painting of his row-house home sat on a shelf, near a sign that said, IT'S DIFFICULT TO SOAR LIKE AN EAGLE WHEN YOU WORK WITH TURKEYS, not far from a commemorative dinner plate emblazoned with a likeness of FDR. A clock on the fireplace mantel didn't work.

"He used to say, 'I'm not going to move the club,' and then in a very quiet voice, 'unless the fans don't support the club.' I remember one meeting—'I WILL NEVER MOVE THIS CLUB' he said, and then, quietly, 'if I have fan support.' I heard those quiet words. I heard the quiet words."

In April 1982, *Post* columnist Dave Kindred wrote, "A thousand times [Williams] has said he doesn't intend to take his team out of Baltimore; a thousand times William Donald Schaefer has said, he will do almost anything to make EBW happy. 'Marry me, marry me,' the city said to EBW. And the lawyer said he'd do it as soon as he saw the dowry." The next night, at a banquet, Williams took out a bride's veil and slipped it over Schaefer's head. It was all vintage Williams, and vintage Schaefer.

The governor remembered it well.

"He'd just finished telling me, 'I will stay in the city as long as you support the team.' 'Yessir, Mr. Williams,' I said. 'I'll never sign a long-term lease unless I get a new stadium!' 'Yessir, Mr. Williams,' I said.

"Then he gets up at this banquet, and says, 'Here is my

commitment to this city. I just signed a lease with your mayor. Isn't that right, Mayor?'

"I'm saying, 'Yessir, goddamnit, you're right, that's right, Mr. Williams!' Then I heard those little words no one else heard. That time it was [only] three years, that lease—that year, another year and an option year. Of course, he couldn't have built a new park in less than two years anyway.

"Everyone was saying, 'We got him! We got Mr. Williams!' But I heard the quiet words."

Schaefer found himself caught between a city that had no desire to build a new ballpark—the old one, after all, was serving the team quite well—and an owner who would not sign a long-term lease. Williams insisted on a series of one- and two-year leases. The annual and biannual wrangles, as Schaefer tells it, followed a ritual form.

"He used to send Mr. Lucchino, and Mr. Lucchino would be against everything, and bust up everything, and my people would get in here and say, 'We're so close to a deal, we're in fine shape,' and I'd say, 'Has Mr. Williams called?' And they'd say, 'No,' and I'd say, 'You're not even close.' Then I'd get a call from Mr. Williams—up to the roof of the Brookshier Hotel, lunch all set on the table—and he'd sit me down and he says, 'This is the way you treat me? After all I've done for you? I'm on my belly!' It was like he was pleading in front of a jury. He'd walk back and forth, back and forth. 'This is the appreciation I get from you? I'm astounded.'

"I want to laugh. He's just taken me to the cleaners. Everything he wants we've given him, except for maybe one minor thing, and finally we give in on that. He had to go through this, this system. He had to go through these machinations. He'd say, 'Donald, this is what I want to do. I want this, this, this, and this,' and I'd say, 'Yes,' and the negotiating was over."

In 1982, Williams proposed a stunning arrangement—a split of profits, with no liability for the team if it ran in debt, save the operating expenses it cost the city. Schaefer agreed, to the outrage of much of the city, but it proved to be a fortuitous deal.

"He said to me one day, 'I want to be fair. What do you say we enter into a partnership? We split profits. No profits, you have a base rental, that's it.' 'Okay,' I said, 'fine.' The most important thing in my mind was keeping the Orioles in the city of Baltimore. We got a fair contract. We had basic expenses. I really never felt like the city didn't get a break."

But there would still be no long-term lease. Williams would not commit himself to a municipal stadium controlled by an eccentric small-town politician with a long memory for enemies, who might, with the team safe in his city's pocket, never again return a phone call. As things stood, whenever Williams was inconvenienced in even the slightest fashion, Schaefer would jump to rectify it. One day the owner's chauffeur, taking Williams back to his home in Potomac, got lost leaving town, and was stopped by a freight train. After the *Post* carried Williams's account of sitting in his car, counting boxcars, and finally slumping in exasperation with his head in his hands, Schaefer commanded police captain Regis Raffensberger to follow him, unsuspectingly. "Damnit, get him out of town!" Schaefer railed to his captain. "If he can't get out of town, find him a way!"

"I used to like that guy," Schaefer said. "Oh yeah. I used to like negotiating with him. I did. I had great respect for him. He was fair. When he'd take you to the cleaners, he was still fair with you."

Bob Flanagan remembers it slightly differently.

"Oh, Schaefer would always give you this horseshit—'I know I'm not as smart as you, I shouldn't even be carrying your briefcase.' Dumb? He was dumb like a fox.

"But they trusted each other. Unfortunately, that rapport is not there now [between Eli Jacobs and the state]. The trust is not there. The partnership is not there. The love of Williams and Schaefer."

Schaefer's passion for a park at Camden Yards, in truth, was waning in the middle of the first Reagan administration, as federal funds for cities began to shrivel. Renovate Memorial, Schaefer said: forget the new stadium. Schaefer's answer to Irsay's persistent threats to leave town was to formulate legislation that would forbid the team from leaving. But on March 29, 1984, at the height of Schaefer's tenure as mayor, Irsay and the Colts left town, leaving a scar across Hizzoner's record and a wound in the city's heart. There was no love lost between Irsay and the city—Colts attendance had been flagging consistently, and had dipped below an average of thirty thousand in the first half of 1981. But the team's flight represented Baltimore's worst fear about itself: It was a second-rate town again.

And Schaefer took it personally. Chris Delaporte, then the head of the city's parks department, recalls having a breakfast the morning after with Schaefer.

"He was white knuckled," Delaporte recalls. "He couldn't even talk."

But while the rest of the town pulled out its hair and vilified Irsay, Schaefer was acting. He saw, finally, a chance to get Williams his new stadium by appealing to the panicked climate in the city—and with it, an opportunity to finally get Williams's signature on a long-term lease. Behind the scenes, soon after the Colts flight, he mobilized a secret meeting at the Martin Marietta airport north of town between Williams, Governor Hughes, Cleveland Brown owner Art Modell, and Larry Lucchino. It was Schaefer's idea: The state would donate the land, private capital would be raised, and Art Modell, a friend of Williams, would buy an NFL team, put it in Cleveland, and bring his Browns in.

"There's going to be a ballpark with you or without you," Schaefer said to Williams that day. The plan fell by the boards, but it represented the first real signal to Williams that Schaefer was serious about building a stadium.

"The new stadium was never about EBW and that regime making more bucks," Jon Miller says. "It was about William Donald Schaefer realizing that when he died they could have been the St. Pete Orioles."

While keeping the Orioles in Baltimore was always Schaefer's driving passion, with time it was becoming Williams's desire, too. Slowly, unmistakably, he was growing fond of the city and its team. As talk of a new stadium grew, the specter of a move to Washington dimmed. Those around Williams watched the hook of his team take hold, and no one was surprised when the Orioles began to consume his heart and, unlike his ownership peers, Edward Bennett Williams began to live the game.

In Baltimore, the sight of Williams dining in Little Italy on a Friday night grew more and more common, the sight of the black limo inching its way up 33rd Street with the rest of the traffic a regular thing.

"Six or eight times a year he'd entertain a lot of people," said Ned Williams, his son, "but what he really liked was going up on a Wednesday or Thursday night with me or [sons] Tony or Larry, one or two other guys and quietly watching the game on a midweek night. He didn't like a real fancy deal at the game. He preferred a Polish dog and a beer. He really enjoyed getting away from Washington."

Visitors to Williams's box with business to discuss learned quickly to conduct it before the first pitch. Writers in the Memorial Stadium press box grew used to the sight of Williams banging a fist on the ledge in front of him. The studious observer would note, in games the Orioles were winning when Williams was in a good mood, the exchange of small bills between Williams and friends, the result of the constant side bets he'd make with his guests.

"Reagan would come to the opener," said Williams's close friend Jay Emmett, a former member of the Orioles' board, "and Ed would be saying, 'Fucking presidents. He's going to be late, the pitcher's going to warm up and then sit around and get cold.' I'd say, 'You're going to be sitting next to the president of the United States!' He'd say, 'Yeah, but look what he's doing to my pitcher.' "

The most pressing affairs could not budge him. Ron Shapiro remembers a game near the end of the 1984 season when the team was about to embark on a postseason tour of Japan, and out of the blue, John Lowenstein decided that the team was not going to go. The players, he said, wanted to be paid enough to make the trip in light of where salaries had gone. Shapiro and Scott McGregor had to spend the whole game shuttling between the box and the bench, negotiating a settlement. Williams would not leave his box while there was a game going on.

"And when we did," Shapiro said, "I remember I had to take a shower in the Orioles' shower during the game, and I ended up putting on Cal's shirt. I was exhausted. But he did it when it had to be done."

"He was the greatest fan in history," Jon Miller said. "Once in '83 in the final week after they'd clinched it, I brought him on the air. He never went on during the season, but after they'd clinched it I convinced him. Well, they get behind, and they needed two or three runs, and he started pounding the table. In a meaningless game! I've got a stand mike. There are these explosions going out over the air. *Bam! Bam!*"

"Oh, he cared," said Ned Williams. "Maybe too much. He lived and died with every pitch. He agonized. That's why he loved the blowouts. His favorite game was a thirteen to nothing blowout. That was the greatest game imaginable."

"Baltimore adopted him," Schaefer says. "And he adopted Baltimore. He really got to like this town. He'd drive up and people would wave at his limo—'Mr. Williams! Mr. Williams!'—and I think he really enjoyed that."

Within reason, as Lucchino recalls: "One night, I said, 'You always make a left into the special parking area. We should make a right. Experience what Joe Fan experiences.' He looked at me and said, 'I didn't work like a sonofabitch for fifty-nine years so that I could experience bumper-to-bumper parking and stand in line for tickets. Let's take a left and can that idea.'"

Williams's obsession with the game led him to develop a few eccentricities. If he and a son were at Memorial one night, left early, and listened to the game on the drive home—and the Orioles won—the next night, at home, they'd pile into the Lincoln Town Car and drive around the streets of Potomac listening to the game. "That's how he'd bring home victories," Ned said.

"And he had this phone line set up where he could dial the radio broadcast from anywhere," Emmett said. "I remember we're at the wedding of Arnold Schwarzenegger and Maria Shriver. He said, 'I gotta go get the score.' I said, 'Do me a favor. Don't get it. Don't get it.' Because he hated to lose."

Employees found themselves wrapped up in the persona. Ken Nigro, a former sportswriter and a longtime Orioles employee who was widely adjudged to be the most eccentric member of the staff—"He was so far out, he was in," Emmett says—grew especially close to Williams, who would drop into his office and eat his jelly beans. Nigro was in charge of special promotions, supposedly far afield from any policy decisions—except that it was Nigro to whom Williams turned in 1987 when he needed a man to rework his farm system. Nigro had worked for the Yankees, and Williams tapped the connection. Nigro came up with Yankee scout Doug Melvin, now the assistant general manager.

"He'd freaking mesmerize you," Ken Nigro said. "He had this awesome presence. When he came in Big Ed was the only guy in the room."

"He made me a much better broadcaster," said Jon Miller, whom Williams affectionately called Voice; Williams had the Orioles rewire his box so that, instead of getting the Home Team Sports audio from the cable television network, he'd get Miller's radio broadcasts. "And because of his stature and brilliance I wanted to be perceived by him as being very good. Every game, he was my audience. Doing the O's games I didn't work for the O's; I'd look right at him and say something to see if he was listening. And he'd turn around and look at me.

"I'll never forget the night before the final game [of the World Series in 1983], we're in Philadelphia at Bookbinder's, we're leading three to one, and he put his arm around me. He was overwhelmed. He was filled with joy."

For the most part, Williams engendered similar loyalty in his players. He could work the locker room the way he worked a courtroom, and his infrequent but legendary clubhouse motivational monologues left his players in varying states of awe.

"He'd work up to a pitch, back down, raise his voice again," recalled Ken Singleton. "You know how ball players can drift when they're not interested. Well, you know how they can drift when they *are* interested.

"But there wasn't a word out of anyone. He had us all on the edge of our seats."

"He compared baseball and law," Jim Palmer remembers. "Talked about how he didn't like to prepare for two and a half months and walk out a loser. He said, 'I believe you should emotionally, physically, intellectually, and spiritually commit yourself. If you do that, no one can ask anything more of you. You've done everything you can do. That's what I want you to do today.' That wasn't an easy speech to understand. You had to think about the words. You started thinking about their meaning. *Emotionally* meant enjoying what you're doing. *Physically*, well, a lot of guys don't. *Spiritually*, do you trust the people you're playing with, and can they trust you? Can they count on you? I remember that speech as if it were yesterday."

When Palmer starts talking about Williams his voice is as passionate as you'll ever hear it. Palmer has borrowed from Williams's speeches for his own. When Williams was defending Victor Posner in Miami one spring, and was hoarse from his speechifying, it was Palmer who would bring tea with lemon and honey to his hotel room in Key Biscayne.

"He thought that everyone should look at life the way he did," Palmer said. "He thought your attitude was something you could control. Ed thought that everyone . . . should look at winning as a full commitment. He expected it of everyone.

"His oratorical style was so great that I used to root for us to go out on strike so that Ed would talk to us."

Ron Shapiro remembers being mesmerized by another Williams performance, during the team's trip to Japan.

"We went to a restaurant and there was all this Japanese art on the walls. He spent the whole meal telling stories about the people in the paintings. We were amazed. When we were walking out, I said, 'How did you know all that?' He said, 'I didn't.' He'd made it all up."

"When I was going through a divorce, he was always there," said Palmer, the man who fled the press conference announcing his release in 1984 in tears. "He'd say, 'My door is always open,' and then when you got there, when you wanted to the door to open, it would open."

Mark Belanger disagrees. Now, no one was ever more of an Oriole than Mark Belanger. And when Mark Belanger talks, as so many of his adversaries on the owners' side of the table have discovered, it's very hard not to listen.

"I don't want things to be said in a negative fashion, because he's passed away," Belanger said one afternoon as he lit another Marlboro and composed his thoughts, in his office at the union headquarters in Manhattan. He spoke, as always, through a cloud of gray smoke.

"Jerry Hoffberger cared about his players. Cared about his city.

He'd talk to us every spring, and he'd say, 'If there's anything I can do, if you need any help, if there's family problems—whatever, just see me.' And he meant it. EBW said it, too. But I'm not sure he meant it."

As could be expected, as the 1981 strike dragged on Williams tried an end run, and met his match in stubbornness in Belanger, the Orioles' player rep. It was during the strike that Belanger's union leanings became solidified; he's been a philosophical, emotional backbone to the union ever since.

Belanger will not soon forget that year. "I knew EBW better than anyone on the club. I was involved in the 1980–81 negotiations. He was in to make a dollar. Which he was entitled to. But I think in many respects he was unfair to the people of Baltimore.

"I was part of the negotiating team of the era—five or six players, me, Steve Rogers, Rusty Staub. EBW was one of the hard-liners. One day he said, 'Mark, we got to get this straightened out. Come to my office. We'll get it straightened out.' "

(Williams had already earned his reputation as a loose cannon on the owners' side. Of commissioner Kuhn, American League president Lee MacPhail, and National League president Chub Feeney, he'd said, "It appears they would screw up a two-car funeral.")

Belanger: "Marvin [Miller] and Don [Fehr] said to me, 'Why don't you go? So me and Ron Shapiro went down. I'd never been in the office. Monstrous, decorative. I didn't know why then, but I know why now. He was huge. Him and his little hot-shit lawyer Larry Lucchino. We talked about the pool concept for two or three hours. He was trying to get me to commit to giving up the compensation player, the fifteenth or sixteenth player on each club.

"I said, 'Look, I don't have the authority to do that, but I can tell you it's unacceptable to me. It isn't going to happen. And we're going to sit.'

"He stood up and did one of his eloquent speeches. . . . He said, 'You're a great player, but you're overmatched in this field. You really don't have a chance.' I stopped and said, 'Maybe you're right.' Then, as I reached the door, he said, 'I'm a hard-liner now. We're going to sit. Fuck you. I'm going to go back to my guys and tell them, Fuck it. There's going to be no baseball in 1981.'

"This guy didn't give a fuck about baseball. The man just did not care about baseball. No one can play the game without a love of the game. I was a clubhouse lawyer, sure. But I loved the game. I still love the game. It bothers me to have anyone who is an owner or a general manager who goes into this business and doesn't give a shit about the city or the game. I can do this and still love the game. And so can an owner. Remember: He has an obligation to the city and players as much as the players do to the city and the club."

Whether Mark Belanger is on target about Williams's indifference to baseball as an institution will forever be debated; an equally plausible explanation for the man's confrontational stance with Belanger can be found in Williams's addiction to "contest living." A Williams arguing a case without passion was no Williams at all, and in Belanger, the admitted clubhouse lawyer, Williams had found an adversary he could finally see, after months of fighting the nebulous forces of the players' union. His tete-à-tete with Belanger was another courtroom appearance, a challenge of the kind that fueled the man's life. But Belanger made it clear that his opinion of EBW was informed by more than their confrontation.

"As soon as he bought the club he raised the ticket prices," Belanger said, "—substantially. He said, 'The cost of salaries went through the roof. It's unfair to the people of Baltimore. But it has to be done.' It happened to be untrue. I happened to know that the salaries that year increased by sixty thousand dollars. The ticket hikes sent his revenue up two million. That pissed me off. That really pissed me off. He was not being honest. I said, 'This is fuckin' *Mark*, Ed. That's bullshit. This is highway robbery. You know what a dollar means to these people? That's a lot of fuckin' money.'

"When you buy a baseball team, you're buying a part of a city. You're buying people. You're buying a city. You have responsibility."

Ramsey Clark once said of Williams's law work: "Somewhere along the line, money rather than justice seemed to become Ed Williams's passion."

"During the strike in '81," Shapiro said, "Williams couldn't understand the owners or the players. He couldn't understand how people could invite potential disaster on themselves without sitting down and working it out. I'm sure when he invited Mark down he thought he could create logic the way he could create logic in a courtroom. But it didn't work out.

"This man did have a way with words. He was always above you. He could make you feel this tall," Shapiro said, indicating a spot some six inches off the ground. "There were times when he pontificated. Once we went in and he tried to intimidate us. With his grandiose office and his grandiose arguments, he wasn't talking to us. He was lecturing that day."

Shapiro's perspective is unusual; an attorney and player agent in Baltimore, he once represented as many as twenty Orioles in one year. He had ample opportunity to observe Williams at his most arrogant and aggravating—and at his more inspiring.

"He represented the greatest challenges of my career," Shapiro said. "You always want to be up against the star people. What he was always capable of doing was being flexible. He was a tremendously loyal man. When he did a deal, when bidding came up, he always leaned toward the old folks, the client he already had, even when it was partially to his detriment."

On occasion, Shapiro found himself inspired enough to stand up to Williams's raw bluster. Shapiro recalled a government investigation of a drug dealer who lived in the same apartment complex as several Orioles.

"In July 1983, I got a call from the FBI," Shapiro recalls, "to tell me that several players were being watched on the Orioles. Some were my clients. I called [general manager] Hank Peters. I was supposed to be on vacation. Well, we met all day long with the FBI. The players agreed to work with the FBI, the club was going to satisfy its end of the bargain, none of the players was a target of the investigation.

"Now, in walks EBW. 'GODDAMNIT, THIS IT THE DARKEST DAY OF THE FRANCHISE! THIS IS THE BLACKEST DAY IN THE HISTORY OF A GREAT FRANCHISE!'" He was screaming and hollering at me, and one of them wasn't even my client. I said, 'Ed, you sonofabitch,' and slammed the door. I remember a trophy fell off the shelf. I wasn't that mad. It was mostly show. Two minutes later he was out in the hallway inviting me back in. He apologized and came back to earth. More often than not, that's what happened with his bravado.

"He was great about getting negotiations done. When he wasn't a bull in a china shop, Ed was a good interest bargainer. He didn't pretend to be a baseball man, except just often enough to get himself into trouble. The best and the worst thing that ever happened was winning it in '83," says Shapiro. "When that happened, he thought it would happen every year."

And he would never hesitate to rip players, manager, or management behind their backs.

"Once during a seven-game losing streak," Jon Miller said, "I'm sitting in the press room eating a crab cake, and he says, 'Well, Voice, I can't tell you how depressed I am about this.' This mathematician friend at American University had given him a lineup, and he gave it to [manager Joe] Altobelli. Altobelli, of course, won't do it. I'm so astounded he's doing this, talking like this, he was asking my advice. I didn't want to give him my advice. Mine was, let Hank [Peters] and Altobelli get on with it. Teams go through slumps."

Hank Peters didn't want the free agents—Fred Lynn, Lee Lacy, and Don Aase, all signed in 1985, all past their prime when they signed. But Peters, who had replaced Frank Cashen in 1976, was not Williams's man. Peters was an even-tempered man given to nothing spontaneous, a man who engendered loyalty on the part of his players, often in touching fashion—to this day, Dennis Martinez, one of the game's finest pitchers but released by the Orioles in 1986, will say nothing but nice things about "'Mr. Hank."

"EBW and Hank Peters did not get along," said Mark Belanger. "Peters was a baseball man. Here's a man who doesn't know baseball. I'd have listened to my baseball man. He went over Peters's head a lot, and most of the time it turned out to be bad. He lost sight of the fact that this is a pretty close organization. We like each other. Now you spoil what you got. Peters recognized that. EBW didn't *care* about players."

Nor managers. In 1985 Altobelli came to camp for the third season to discover that Williams had hired Frank Robinson—twice a major-league manager already—as a coach. EBW's pride on civil rights matters was well known—he would fire his farm director, Tom Giordano, at the end of the 1986 season when it was publicly written that there were six black players in the entire farm system. It seemed quite conceivable that Williams had in mind that Robinson would sooner or later ascend to the manager's office. At the same time, as if to increase Altobelli's discomfort, he had also already referred to Earl Weaver's absence as a "self-imposed exile." Weaver, of course, had retired after the 1982 reason. Altobelli, then the manager at the Orioles' Rochester farm team, was never Williams's choice to replace Weaver.

"He wanted me to manage the ball club, in '82, when he thought I'd win three hundred," Jim Palmer said. "After Earl left. He called me to Washington and we met at Mo and Jo's. I told him I'd take Ray Miller. But they didn't want any Weaver guys, so they chose Altobelli."

Williams knew that to choose Ray Miller over Cal Ripken, Sr., or vice versa, would slight the loser. On top of which Williams was convinced the team would play for anyone, so determined would they be to prove that they could win without Weaver.

But Altobelli was everything Edward Bennett Williams did not want in a manager. On the field, his moves exasperated the baseball intellectuals. And still, in the 1983 season, every move he made turned to gold. In the playoffs, Altobelli outmanaged the rising star in the White Sox dugout, Tony LaRussa, the very model of a major-league modern manager. No one who was in the winning locker room the day the Orioles won that Series will ever forget Altobelli's huge, goofy, disbelieving smile amid the shower of champagne, after the likes of Benny Ayala and Terry Crowley delivered key pinch hits to make up for Eddie Murray's slump through the first four games.

"If I'd managed," Williams would say a few years later, "if anybody had managed that team, we would have won."

Altobelli had this response: "He also called me 'cement head,' but that doesn't make him right."

Asked if he had indeed called his manager "cement head," Williams said he wasn't sure, "but it was not inconsistent with my thinking on the subject."

The year 1984 was a disaster; in an August 24, 1984, game that will forever be etched in Memorial minds, Altobelli managed himself into a situation where he had outfielders John Lowenstein at second and Gary Roenicke at third, and infielder Lenn Sakata at catcher. Tippy Martinez picked off three Blue Jays in a row, so eager were they to steal. Privately, Williams fumed that Altobelli had found himself with such a comical lineup.

By the beginning of the 1985 season, the writing was on the wall. The pressure weighed heavily—unjustly—on Altobelli. Williams was itching to make a change. After a June sweep at the hands of the Red Sox, Williams told reporters he "wasn't going to sit by idly and let things go on like this."

A few days later, Altobelli came to the park midmorning to find out that his bosses, Peters and Williams, were downtown, meeting with Weaver. At ten-thirty Altobelli was asking staff people, "Am I fired? Does anybody know if I'm fired?" At twelve-thirty Williams hired Weaver. Again.

He had not yet dismissed Altobelli. Altobelli found out at three P.M.

"The Orioles no longer hold the high moral ground," Tony Kornheiser said in *The Washington Post*.

"I thought this was a class organization," Altobelli said a few days later. "I was sadly mistaken."

In fact, Weaver said, he had tried to talk EBW into giving Altobelli a stay of execution. Wait and see if the team slides back.

"I said, 'Give Joe a chance,' " Weaver said. " 'I mean, he won a pennant. Wait until we get a certain number of games out of the race.' And I named a figure, more than they were out at the time."

But Weaver took the offer. It was simple, he explained at the time: A carton of Raleighs cost six dollars when he'd quit in 1982; they were up to nine dollars in 1985. It was costing him $150 just to take the grandkids to Six Flags Over Whatever: "The last time I visited my kids, I went through two grand." Golf was wearing thin: The week before he'd shot a seventy-eight on the course and still ended up losing fifty bucks to Lucky the Champ and Speedy. Then the Orioles kicked in with the perks—flying his wife to the road cities, and covering all of her expenses back in Miami. "They keep going with this stuff, until you say to yourself, 'How the fuck can I say no?' "

But where Earl got to see the courting, persuasive side of Williams,

Altobelli's experience of the ice-cold judgmental side was not unique. "If you weren't in his group," Ron Shapiro said, "he could be not only critical, but sarcastic and demeaning."

As offhandedly as he could discourse about figures on a Japanese restaurant wall, Williams could cut to the quick. One such offhanded comment caused an irreparable break with one of the team's signature stars, Eddie Murray; the discord festered over the years into a poison strong enough to harm the team's fortunes.

It was Williams's mishandling of the most fragile psyche in his employ—and the most potent bat—that best symbolized his inability to govern the Orioles with the same wisdom he brought to the law. The relationship between the domineering attorney and the inscrutable first baseman had not started out so badly. When Williams sat down with Murray and Shapiro to negotiate his contract in 1985, Murray refused to sign for less than $1 million a year, and Williams found a way to get it done by deferring some of the money. Then he asked Murray, "What do you think the [new] stadium should have?" Eddie said natural grass. Williams was delighted; he figured that the state wouldn't fight him on that point if Eddie Murray wanted the grass.

"Right then, he and Eddie were on the same wavelength," recalled Shapiro.

But it was not to last. On August 21, 1986, during a rain delay at Memorial, Williams gave an impromptu press conference in his box touching on a half-dozen players and subjects. When it rolled around to Murray, who had pulled a hamstring and then reinjured it, then hurt his right hand, Williams said, "Murray hasn't given us a good year. You look at his extra-base hits and his fielding, and you see that. He faces a challenge next season because he's at that age where he has to work hard to get ready for a season. Reggie Jackson was doing eleven hundred sit-ups a day to get ready for this season. And he was in the best shape of his life. Getting ready to play baseball has become a twelve-month-a-year job."

"The article read as if he'd called a press conference to rip Murray, which is the way Eddie saw it," Jon Miller said. "I think Eddie felt that EBW was, at the core, dishonest. He felt since EBW defended criminals, he was a guy who said whatever it took to get the guy off.

"The whole city never understood Eddie."

Perhaps Williams, unfamiliar with Baltimore custom before 1979, hadn't realized the significance of Murray's feats: A Southern city that hadn't integrated its schools until the sixties—not until 1954 did they let the black schools play in the Maryland State Athletic Association—a city that had roiled its way through racial tension and riots and curfews that made it a war zone in the sixties, prompting a white middle-class flight in the seventies, had found something great in Eddie Murray.

"It's been said the Orioles didn't attract racial diversity," says former state senator Catherine Riley. "Eddie meant a lot to the city."

Certainly Williams should have recalled the fans in the upper deck in Memorial Stadium in the fourth game of the 1979 Series chanting, "ED-DIE." And certainly Williams should have understood the significance of Murray's performance in the fifth and clinching game of the 1983 Series; how four years earlier, the Orioles had a 3–1 lead over the Pirates, and lost the next three; how in the same situation in 1983 Eddie Murray singlehandedly ensured that there would be no ignominious repeat by clocking two home runs to right-center in Veterans Stadium. No one in that park that afternoon will forget the profound silence that greeted his second shot, as Murray, who seldom celebrated himself, paused for just a moment as he let the bat drop from his hands, while still wearing the Eddie Murray look—if ever there was a look of proud defiance, that was it. Murray's home runs turned the crowd's derisive chants of "MVP! MVP!" to simple acknowledgment of an obvious fact.

The next day, in War Memorial Plaza on Holiday Street, as the city gathered to honor the team beneath an arc of balloons—black and orange balloons, the Orioles colors, the most unchic color scheme imaginable, reminiscent of high school colors, Halloween colors, and perfect for Baltimore—the chant of "ED-DIE! ED-DIE! ED-DIE!" rippled in pockets, a giddy plea, for the crowd well knew that Eddie never liked to talk. Suddenly, out of a fourth-story window in the old municipal building, Eddie Murray's face appeared. A city worker rigged up an extension for the microphone, someone took it across the courtyard, and finally reluctantly, Murray leaned out the window.

"We sure appreciate everything you've done for us," Eddie Murray said, and the crowd hushed. Then he said, "We'll be back here again at this time next year."

Then, spontaneously: "Hey, I kind of like this."

It was the last time the city and Eddie would smile at each other.

By 1985, Murray was fast growing disenchanted with his owner's habit of importing outside players wholesale: "Every guy we get don't know how to play," Murray told Jon Miller. "When you came to the Os you used to know how to play."

"That's what pissed Eddie off more than anything," Ken Singleton said. "That the guys they brought in to maintain the winning tradition didn't care about winning."

By 1986, when Williams criticized him, Murray had already had enough; struggling with various injuries, Eddie watched from the disabled list as his replacement at first base, one Jim Traber, a native Marylander with a penchant for swinging at pitches a few time zones out of the strike zone, put together a home-run-laden July that led the team to within two and a half games of first. Traber was an immediate hit; he began doing local television commercials. Murray felt slighted. And then Williams raked him through the press.

If Williams never understood Murray, he was not necessarily alone. Most Orioles fans were in the dark about the real value of Murray's low-profile leadership, of how he'd assumed the mantle from his clubhouse predecessors, Lee May and Don Baylor. Few Baltimoreans knew that Murray literally did not follow his own statistics day to day, so concerned was he instead with the team's overall fortunes.

Fewer still understood his value to the team off the field. Murray would open his home to the rookies and new arrivals, let them stay until they found a place of their own. He found them cars, introduced them to the right people. And, most importantly, Murray instructed the arrivals in the Orioles way of doing things. Soon after Wayne Gross arrived in a trade from Oakland, the team travelled by bus from Rochester, their AAA town, to Cleveland on a three-hour bus ride. "This is bullshit," Gross said loudly. Suddenly, from the back of the bus, out of the silence, Eddie's stern voice was heard: "Hey, we don't do that here."

But in the clubhouse in the summer of 1986, Eddie began to tell people he was going to make Williams trade him. He began to tell friends he was going to stop making an extra effort. According to Jon Miller, he went in to Hank Peters and said, "Why don't you trade me?" Somehow, the news leaked, and the *Post* printed it. With the public news that Murray had asked to be traded, the city turned, and that was a very big thing in a town whose newspaper's front page daily ran a cartoon of an Oriole on page one, the bird's facial expression indicating whether they'd won or lost. The Orioles were everything, and Eddie was the Orioles, and now, many thought, Eddie was ungrateful.

The upshot of Williams's indiscretion? The team collapsed in spectacular fashion. The Orioles went 14–42 in its last fifty-six games, one of the greatest collapses in major-league history.

Murray and Williams never reconciled. The years of the Williams-Murray discord were the worst the team had seen in a decade; whether there was a cause and effect at work is a matter of conjecture. What is certain is that when Williams took over the team, Eddie Murray was its franchise, on the field and in the clubhouse; nine years later, when Murray was traded, he was its enemy.

Murray wasn't the only Orioles icon whose significance Williams misjudged. In the case of the disastrous reenlistment of Weaver, it was Williams's impatience for a quick fix, colored by his eternal appetite for the high-profile hire, that obscured his better judgment. But there were parallels with his Murray mistake; once again, Williams revealed his ignorance of the Orioles' ethos. Earl Weaver went out on his shield that day after the forty-five minute ovation at season's end in 1982, and Williams should have seen that bringing him back was a fundamental crime against baseball nature—not to mention a tactical blunder too. When Earl left the first time, he was leaving his family. When he returned, it was to ride herd on a handful of stepchildren and strangers.

In the glory days, the team was known for the continuity of its style of play, from rookie league to major league. But upon his return Weaver was stunned to discover that his players did not know the Orioles system. Early on in his unfortunate reprise, a player did not rotate to the correct base on a bunt play.

"What the fuck were you doing?" he said.

"That's the way we do it in Rochester," said the player.

"No it's not," said Earl. But it turned out that it was. The Rochester manager, a career minor-league manager in other organizations, had stopped trying to teach the Orioles way of doing things. The carefully crafted set of baseball fundamentals was being undermined, carelessly, from within. And Earl's heart was not in the monumental task of setting a whole organization straight.

Williams knew he'd made a mistake by changing a man's heart with the lure of money. It came out a month before the season ended that Earl was a lame duck. "Look, it might be a good idea if I go home now," Earl said. "I'll be happy to let you go if you'll give me the money back," said Williams. But the money was why he was there, so Earl stayed on to the bitter end of the 1986 season.

And so there would be no repeat championship; the graceless firing of Altobelli, the desperate turn to Weaver, Williams's inability to divine what it was that made Eddie Murray work—or what Eddie Murray meant to the baseball team—these were the outward signs of decay of what it was that had made the Orioles special. For all his heartfelt passion and acute intelligence, Edward Bennett Williams the baseball owner was too much a slave to his impulsive side, too addicted to the notion of winning it all, all the time; a man of far-reaching wisdom, he nonetheless harbored a blind spot when it came to tact and grace where his athletes were concerned.

But it was that same mania to have exactly what he wanted that would ultimately mean success for his new stadium—especially when he joined forces with a man of similarly impulsive impetuousness, a man with a drive as relentless as his own. William Donald Schaefer, too, was not the most agile of men at tempering his words or opinions, or of steering on the safe side of tact, but his own intense desire to plant his ballpark smack downtown was now in mesh with Williams's wishes.

Face-to-face, they were rivals. Joined together, facing the same constituency—the people of Baltimore and Maryland—they were unbeatable. If their fans had no real desire to see a new park—especially a park that would rise from the lining of their own pockets—this would not be a stumbling block to the two visionaries.

Williams, after all, had overlooked the chemistry of his team in his quest to assemble a champion. And more than once Schaefer had had his way against popular opinion.

Even if the people didn't know what was good for them, Edward Bennett Williams and William Donald Schaefer surely did.

The Orioles' on-field malaise did nothing to blunt the mayor's agenda.

As Williams's baseball team was unravelling, the legislature of the state of Maryland finally took action, creating the Maryland Sports Authority on April 3, 1987, ostensibly to oversee the state's billion-dollar sports industry—most of it thoroughbred-racing money—but in fact with one purpose, and one purpose alone: to build Schaefer and Williams a stadium.

As soon as the Colts left town, Schaefer had put together a mayor's task force to study the city's faltering sports fortunes—specifically, what it would cost to sufficiently renovate Memorial for football to lure the NFL back to town. Like anyone with half a brain thinking of doing sports-stadium work in 1985, Schaefer's people called Hellmuth Obata Kassabaum, the huge sports architecture firm in Kansas City whose designers and engineers had had their hands in dozens of the sports arenas and stadiums that sprouted across the land in the seventies and eighties. HOK's vice president Rick Deflon told the task force that unless they were willing to spend a lot more than they wanted to spend, Memorial would never be better than a second-rate multipurpose facility. It was then that the task force suggested looking at the possibility of a new multipurpose park.

HOK jumped at the chance, and in December it submitted a five-pound tome listing twenty-two possible sites for such a facility, exploring every site in sight from large backyards in West Baltimore to toxic waste dumps down the Patapsco. In the closing section of the report, HOK narrowed the choices to three: Camden Yards, Port Covington to the south, and the renovation of Memorial Stadium. HOK concluded by recommending that the park be built at Camden Yards, and their tome finished with a detailed, full-color rendering of the park they would build. (See the front inside cover.)

It was a combination football-and-baseball park, and, as such, undistinguished and unremarkable. HOK had knocked down the warehouse, and slapped a skirt of asphalt parking lots around the stadium. In defense of HOK, architect Joe Spear recalls, the stadium was generic, and had not been designed to fit into the Camden site; the task force, he says, suggested the drawing of the park be set in the rail yards. On the other hand, the conclusion of the study was clear, in its summary section: Camden Yards was the best choice of all of the twenty-two.

But Governor Harry Hughes preferred a stadium outside of the city. When Schaefer's task force recommended Camden Yards, Hughes had his friend Bernard Manekin conduct his own search. Manekin enlisted the stadium development firm of Howard Needles Tammen Bergendoff—the only other logical place to turn if you wanted a nationally recognized expert who could disagree with HOK.

The lines were clear-cut: on one side, Schaefer (on behalf of the city) and HOK; and on the other, Hughes (representing the state) and HNTB. Hughes's own committee, not surprisingly, recommended a site no one had considered—Lansdowne, just south of the city. When it turned out that the HNTB team had used land surveys from the fifties, underestimating the costs of site acquisition and road building by several tens of millions of dollars, Lansdowne fell out of favor.

Both logic and history stood on the side of Camden Yards. In so many ways the site was perfect—for reasons unique to Baltimore but generic to the game of baseball.

TO THE CAMDEN STATION

◆

NOT LONG AGO—ON A GLACIAL TIMETABLE, anyway—Baltimore
was the driving wheel of the nation's economy. Its port lay one
hundred miles to the west of its rival ports to the north, which meant
that transatlantic shippers who sent their goods through Baltimore
were faced with one hundred miles less terrain to cross. In 1802
Congress appropriated funds for the first National Road, and it
signalled good news for Baltimore: The terminus would be downtown,
heading west, providing the natural route to carry the nation's
supplies. But the ground breaking for the Erie Canal in 1817
threatened to divert the commerce north—until, on a trip to England
in 1826, a Baltimorean named Evan Thomas saw George Stephen-
son's new steam-powered railway in the north of England, and hurried
back with the news.

On the Fourth of July, 1828, Charles Carroll, the last surviving
signer of the Declaration of Independence, turned the first spadeful of
dirt for the nation's first railroad. Operating out of the Pratt Street
station—the building from whence issued Samuel F. B. Morse's first
telegraph message, "What hath God wrought?"—the B&O's early
station stops carried names like Deep Cut, Vinegar Hill, and Licking
Branch, decidedly humble in scope. But when the B&O reached
Washington in August 1935, Andrew Jackson dismissed a cabinet
meeting early to scramble on down to witness the first train from
Baltimore arriving with one thousand passengers.

By 1853, the railroad's Great Central Route was heading for
Cincinnati and St. Louis, and the B&O needed a station to compete

with the stations of its rivals in Baltimore: the President Street terminal built by the Philadelphia, Wilmington, and Baltimore Railroad; and Calvert Station erected by the Baltimore and Susquehanna company. In fact, dozens of railroad palaces had sprung up from Kansas City to Washington, grand places that signified the somberness and weighty import of a cross-country trip, their waiting rooms all marbled and muraled; yet the town that had founded the American railroad had no particular palace of its own.

So the nation's biggest railroad set out to design the nation's biggest station. The architectural firm of Niernsee and Nielson came up with a variation on a style known as railroad Italianate, patterned after the stations in King's Cross and Paddington, the building to be topped with a Normanesque tower 185 feet high.

"What a fascinating place, this fine new Camden Station," ran the account in the *Sun* upon its opening in 1858, "with the long rows of yellow railroad coaches tightly emparked within it; with huge balloon-stacked locomotives cautiously feeling their way into the great and shadowy train shed! Long beams of misty light coming down obliquely from the interstices of the great roof . . . A place of many, many noises. Of ceaseless comings and goings. What a stage for tremendous drama; what a setting for the unending comedy of human life!"

In 1861, the station welcomed Abraham Lincoln's inaugural train, although Lincoln wasn't on it; his security chief, Allan Pinkerton, having heard in Philadelphia that Rebel sympathizers planned to bomb the train in Baltimore, had Lincoln's car detached and joined with a different engine. Four years later, the station was host to Lincoln's casket on its funeral train back home to Illinois.

Camden Station was the site of the first blood spilled in the Civil War: On April 19, 1861, as the Sixth Massachusetts Infantry was being drawn down Pratt Street, mobs lobbed stones at the men, and the soldiers fired back. Four soldiers died, and nine civilians. The violence was worse in 1877, when the railroad asked Governor John Lee Carroll, grandson of Charles Carroll, to restore order in Cumberland, where Baltimore workers had stopped work and closed the Gap to protest a pay cut. The Fifth and Sixth Regiments of the Maryland

National Guard marched to Camden Station to board a troop train west. One hundred twenty guardsmen found a mob of fifteen thousand at the station; stones were hurled, gunshots rang out, and ten lay dying beneath the wail of "Big Sam," the B&O's riot alarm. Fifty-nine of the 120 men made it to the transport train.

In the first half of the twentieth century Camden Station was the terminus for the B&O's Royal Blue and Capital Limited, both with their distinctive blue and gray design, the vision of famed German industrial designer Otto Kuhler. With its train sheds reaching more than half the length of the warehouse, it was a station to rival the grandest Europe had to offer.

And in 1954, the American League's newest franchise, the Baltimore Orioles, pulled into Camden Station after a two-game season-opening trip to Detroit. The team changed into its uniforms on the train, disembarked into the hallowed central waiting room under the ornate chandeliers, each with its carved-glass shade shaped like a frosted buttercup, and rode a parade of gleaming new convertibles up Charles Street to their new park.

At Camden Yards, the game returns, then, to its logical home and its favored means of transportation. The train mirrors baseball's pace—its rhythms of start and stop, rushing and frantic one moment, slowed to a crawl the next. Baseball has always been a train-age game, ever since teams crossed the countryside by rail, the engine's whistle carving somber, tuneful bites out of the American night as the players huddled in the parlor cars over card tables and cases of beer, cultivating friendships and animosities over the course of the twenty-hour St. Louis–to–New York ramble.

On the trains, baseball ritual was as rich as it was on the field. In the Pullman cars, for instance, the star players were assigned to berths in the middle of the car, as far away from the wheels as possible. The lower berths were reserved for the regulars, because the lower hammocks rocked less and the regulars needed their sleep—which led to the show of honor displayed by Kid Elberfeld of the New York Highlanders who, after Jimmy Austin took his starting spot at third base, refused to let Austin climb into his customary upper berth one night, grabbing him by the ankles and pulling him back, insisting that Austin take over his own berth down below now that he was starting.

Train comforts were scarce; Hank Greenberg said that his retirement was hastened by his inability to get a good night's sleep in the swaying hammock. But the small hours on the rails that bound the baseball cities were spent engaged in more interesting recreations than the jet age has been able to cultivate. The Pirates' train trips back east from spring training in California were legendary for the number of women and the length of card games. In Cincinnati they still talk about the Reds' voyage back from Pittsburgh after the last game of the 1949 season; when Walker Cooper and Doc Bohm left the train in West Virginia to get more beer, the train left without them, but a half hour later the train had to stop for a taxicab that was straddling the tracks—from which emerged the two men, each hoisting a case of beer.

In fiction, Bernard Malamud gave us The Whammer—pointing, just before Roy Hobbs's third pitch, to the spot where he boasted that he'd hit the ball: to "where the gleaming rails converged on the horizon—and beyond was invisible." That night, after Hobbs's triumph as he headed East, savoring his feat, "the train whistle wailed, the echo banging far out against the black mountain."

Reality was just as delightful and curious when baseball and railroad conspired, from the part-time scout and full-time conductor who would always stop his train behind the outfield wall in Fulda, Minnesota, to watch George Pipgras each time he pitched a semipro game, to the night Big Ed Delahanty fell to his death off the Niagara Falls suspension bridge after the train had stopped.

Rube Marquard rode five days' worth of freights into Waterloo, Iowa, to pitch his first professional game—cartwheeling into a heap off the moving train in front of the Illinois Central depot for his grand arrival. Marquard beat the last-place team the next day, but when the manager refused to give him a contract, he rode the one A.M. freight back out of town that night.

Of course, all of the romance in the world doesn't do much to fatten the tax rolls, and when the 1954 Orioles headed uptown, they turned their backs on Camden Yards, as did the rest of the nation soon thereafter. Camden's European-classic train sheds had been razed in

1951, and by the sixties the nation's railroads were losing hundreds of millions of dollars a year on passenger travel. Passenger service went exclusively to Amtrak in 1970—in Baltimore, that meant it was located exclusively in the Pennsylvania Station, up Charles Street, with its distinctive maroon-and-gold trim; it was another sign that Baltimore had lost out to its haughty Society-Hilled neighbor to the north. Down at Camden Station, the neon sign that had counselled strolling nighthawks to GO B&O had long been dimmed, and was finally dismantled. The heartbeat of the site of the nation's once-busiest rail hub had been reduced to a murmur—along with, in large part, the heartbeat of the city.

It was only natural that Camden Station's ultimate resurrection would be entrusted, in part, to a man who had fond and distinct memories of the days when downtown was alight and alive.

Herb Belgrad's father owned men's clothes stores back when downtown retail was thriving. These days, if you're a clothier and you're not in the Inner Harbor, you're as good as dead. But one generation back, Herb Belgrad's dad owned Nate and Leon's, and Harold's Men's Wear. However, Belgrad's ambitions lay beyond the clothing business. After earning his B.A. at Johns Hopkins, he went on to get his law degree at the University of Maryland in College Park, and subsequently set up his law practice in Baltimore.

When Harry Hughes left the governor's office in the fall of 1986, his last act was to appoint Baltimore attorney Herb Belgrad to take over the Stadium Authority. It proved to be the most insightful and farsighted move of his administration. Herb Belgrad would shape the park as significantly, if not as obviously, as the owners and the architects. He would control only one ingredient of Camden Yards, but that one was a crucial one.

The checkbook.

The Baltimore attorney wasn't all that interested in aesthetics. He was not willing to have the Orioles dictate to the state, either. He had been chosen to spend the state's money, and Herb Belgrad, a small and wiry man of subtle and sparse humor who evokes nothing so much as a rod of iron, was not going to waste it.

Belgrad was intensely aware of the state's considerable history of favoritism in the awarding of government business, which peaked in the 1970s when Spiro Agnew was alleged to have taken cash kickbacks from Maryland engineers. To Herb Belgrad, good Marylander—and more: the former head of the state's Board of Ethics, not to mention the president of the Maryland Bar—giving the taxpayer value for his dollar was a large part of his mandate. The rest, of course, was making sure Maryland kept its pro team— the Orioles—and attracted more of them. Which meant a football team . . .

Thus the creation of what would prove to be the most architecturally distinctive baseball park in several generations was entrusted by the state to a man who, by his own admission, was never a particular fan of baseball, or, if the furniture in his law-firm office is any indication, of distinctive taste. The chairs and tables in Herb Belgrad's office were not obtained in auction at Sotheby's. They could have been slipped out of a Motel 6 in the middle of the night.

They are, however, functional. Everything about Herb Belgrad is functional. The man functions, and above all, the man functions for Maryland. There is no way to know if, outside of the small and self-secure arena of Baltimore, Herb Belgrad would be as compelling and powerful a figure. It's the nature of the place; it's a curse and a blessing. The city is small enough to allow a few men to have a great deal of influence.

But also, invariably, they are men whose entire universe consists of Baltimore and Maryland, quite defiantly so, and the decisions they make are designed to take care of their own. Fortunately, for Belgrad this meant not friends or cronies but rather the state and city as a whole.

When Hughes tabbed him to head the sports body, Belgrad recalls, he was surprised. "I said to Governor Hughes, 'If you put all my background qualifications and experience together, I wouldn't even show up on the screen.' He said, 'That's exactly what I'm looking for. I'm looking for someone to analyze the facts objectively.' "

Belgrad had first met William Donald Schaefer when Schaefer was on the city council and Belgrad was the assistant city solicitor in charge of housing and labor; Schaefer was interested in legislation for vacant housing, and so was Belgrad. Working together, they devised a law that allowed tenants to hold rent in escrow if the housing was substandard.

He'd first met Harry Hughes in 1978, when the Maryland Legislature finally enacted its first Public Ethics law. Belgrad was the chairman of the bar's ethics committee, and Hughes, who had just been elected, asked Belgrad to form the first ethics commission. Which just goes to show how slippery this thing about ethics can be: Soon after the Colts left town, the papers and airwaves were full of ethical outrage at the notion of one city luring another's football team away. But on one wall of Herb Belgrad's office is a picture of Belgrad wearing a Baltimore Cardinals uniform, a photo taken on the day he thought he'd lured Bill Bidwell's team out of St. Louis.

In 1986, the Democratic gubernatorial primary pitted Maryland Attorney General Stephen Sachs against Schaefer in a clear-cut state-versus-city battle. Schaefer, according to some speculation, was not even terrifically excited about being governor, but decided to run so that Sachs would not gain the office himself. Sachs had spent years criticizing Baltimore's domination of Maryland politics, and had called Schaefer "parochial" for his efforts to secure the stadium for the city.

Two weeks before the primary, Belgrad was asked by Hughes to take over the Stadium Authority; given the difference of opinion between Hughes and Schaefer on stadium issues, Belgrad suspected his tenure might last all of two weeks, for one reason in particular: Schaefer's memory for perceived slights. Belgrad had campaigned for Sachs when the latter had run for attorney general.

On the other hand, when Belgrad was installed as president of the Baltimore City Bar Association in 1981, at a meeting at the Hyatt, Mayor Schaefer showed up unexpectedly and was invited to the podium; he wanted to publicly congratulate his old friend. And when Belgrad was elected president of the state bar in 1985, Schaefer sent a handwritten letter that ran three pages, offering congratulations.

Prior to the primary, Belgrad refused to comment on his own preference publicly. His wife, though, campaigned for Sachs. She even put a Sachs placard on their front lawn. The primary took place on a Tuesday. In his last press conference as mayor, Schaefer was asked if he'd follow the advice of the newly appointed stadium authority. Schaefer was noncommittal and terse: He said he wasn't sure. Belgrad was certain that his appointment would be gutted.

After his victory in the primary, Schaefer called Belgrad and arranged a fifteen-minute meeting that lasted two and a half hours.

"Rather than being elated and jubilant about his victory," Belgrad said, "he seemed angry. 'You've been my friend,' said Schaefer. 'You are my friend. I just couldn't believe you would not support me.' I said to him, 'What you may not appreciate is that today a woman is her own person.' "

"Let's put it behind us," Schaefer said. "I want you to do exactly what you were appointed to do."

Belgrad had no funding. The legislature wouldn't convene until January 1987, and in April it would vote on whether to empower funds for a stadium at all. Belgrad had all of six months to put together a plan for a stadium so compelling that the state would give him the money to build it. The nature of the funding was undecided; the only relative certainties at this point were that the stadium would be multipurpose, and it would likely be located at Camden Yards.

He immediately called some friends—Jerry Sachs, the president of the Cap Centre, and Benjamin Civiletti, former attorney general of the United States and onetime captain of the Johns Hopkins basketball team. They rounded up a team of consultants of their own, including Gene McHale's American Sports Associates, and Peat Marwick out of New York. They visited NFL cities. They visited major-league cities. They spent the fall touring various stadiums. And something began to make an impression on Herb Belgrad: The Jets, the Giants, the Colts, and the Raiders had all shared multipurpose stadiums and had been very unhappy. The Falcons were threatening to leave theirs. The Twins had relinquished all control of design at the Metrodome. Wherever teams shared stadiums, there was an inevitable problem of second-class citizenship.

Belgrad asked his consultants to question the common wisdom: Was a single multipurpose stadium necessarily less expensive than two stadiums?

"The consultants got together with HOK," Belgrad said, "and came back with a very startling analysis: If we built a single multipurpose it'd be forty-one million dollars more than were we to build a single baseball only. Multipurpose had to be designed to be converted with double clubhouses. Had to be built on surface rather than excavation. That would be more costly. The consultants recommended two instead of one."

(Larry Lucchino remembers it a little differently. Lucchino says that it was *he* who thought of suggesting a baseball-only stadium to the authority, and that Williams told him, "They'll think you're crazy, but go ahead and try.")

At any rate, Governor Schaefer conceded it was an interesting concept. Belgrad asked his team to have a full report in by December. His team came back with a quick response: Build two stadiums at Camden Yards.

By now, the debate was heating up in the legislature, in the streets of Baltimore, and the editorial offices of the *Sun*.

"The city is being held hostage," said State Senator Jack Lapides, a Democrat whose district included Memorial Stadium, "because [Williams] wants to make every cent possible."

"The mere fact that he's a millionaire, does that make him a bad person?" countered Senator Thomas Bromwell. "Without a stadium, with no baseball or football, we'll be on a line with cities like Roanoke and Butte. Mayberry is what we'll be."

"I have never asked anyone to build me a stadium," Williams barked, in February of 1987. "I would love to have a new stadium downtown. If someone wants to build one. But I am definitely not holding the city ransom for it." This prompted *Sun* columnist Roger Simon to opine, "If blackmail is a crime, how come rich and powerful people seem to practice it around here without any problem? How can we be told that, unless this state builds EBW a new baseball-only stadium, he'll leave town?"

Williams returned the salvo: "I've become an SOB to a lot of people because everyone assumes I could be an SOB. But I've never been an SOB. I don't know how much time I have left, but I'm not going to start being an SOB now. At no time have I ever threatened I was going anywhere. I don't think there's any fear of me leaving Baltimore. I think the concern is I might die and my estate might sell the franchise."

In February, HOK submitted its first plans for two stadiums. They showed no warehouse. The baseball park was symmetrical. The rendering had four pedestrian ramps stuck to its outside façades. It lay smack in a veldt of asphalt.

During spring training in 1987, in a meeting unknown to the general public, Belgrad and HOK vice president Rick Deflon showed Williams the plans for two stadiums. Build me a baseball-only stadium, Edward Bennett Williams said, and it's a deal. No specific terms had been agreed upon, but it was clear that EBW was ready for a long-term commitment. HOK had not been hired, of course. Not officially. But for Williams, aesthetics were not the primary concern. He was very happy about having the state build a ballpark for his baseball team.

Herb Belgrad had fulfilled his first mandate. Herb had hooked the Orioles. Now all he had to do was get the legislators to give him some money, in the face of widespread public opposition.

Sun columnist Dan Rodricks subsequently formed the Punk Task Force to Name the Thing. He suggested Smokey Robinson Stadium: "It's gonna take a miracle to get the thing built. And a miracle to pay for it."

Schaefer had floated the idea of a ten-cent-per-bottle beer tax to pay the interest on the bond issue—not a popular choice in a city that once boasted seventy breweries. Then, in March, Belgrad confirmed that a financial expert at Morgan Stanley said that two instant lotteries a year would pay for initial borrowing for acquiring the site. He fleshed out the plan: Maryland would borrow $216 million through the sale of three sets of lease-backed revenue bonds that would not hold the taxpayer liable.

On March 4, a joint hearing of two senate committees chaired by Senator Cathy Riley was called. Belgrad and Schaefer knew that the bill would be a tough sell. Together they decided they could swing the legislature with a coup: They'd get Williams himself to speak.

But no one had cleared Williams's schedule. Or told Williams, who, it developed, would be in Boston that morning, Ash Wednesday, for a session of chemotherapy. The day before, Schaefer steeled himself and called: "I said, 'Mr. Williams, you're an essential part of this.' He said, 'All right, if you think I'm needed.' We had lunch at the mansion, in the private dining room."

"We had prepared an outline of questions we thought he'd be asked," Herb Belgrad recalled. "I've never been with someone who could so instantly look at the questions and immediately develop his own answers. I remember I offered at the time that if he gave me a signal, I'd arrange for a signal and they'd cut the hearing, in case he was tiring. That suggestion was contemptuously rejected. 'My health is my private business, and no one else's business,' he said, and I wasn't to mention it to anyone else."

As Williams entered the chambers, Lucchino handed him a copy of the current *Sports Illustrated*—with three Ripkens, manager Cal, Sr., and his two infielder sons Billy and Cal, Jr., on the cover. The same magazine had two years earlier pronounced Memorial Stadium the second-best baseball park in the American League.

The chair of the Senate Finance Committee took note of that cover more than anyone. State Senator Cathy Riley's district included Aberdeen—the rural hometown of the Ripken clan—and now she was presiding over the most crucial meeting the stadium proponents would face. Riley was key to the stadium drive. The strongest opposition had come from outlying representatives and senators: Representatives from Prince Georges and Montgomery counties were Redskins fans, while representatives from the western part of the state, out near Hagerstown, were Pirates fans. Neither group was disposed to aid the Orioles or their city. But Riley, despite hailing from Harford County, had been a maniacal Colts and Orioles fan since childhood—as a girl, her first Orioles game was a doubleheader in 1954 against the Indians; she remembers Al Rosen playing third. Her father, an assembly-line worker at Martin-Marietta, took one day off from work in thirty-nine years, to take his daughter to the all-star game in 1958.

Riley had already shared with fellow legislators some inside information she'd gotten from a friend of an NFL owner, that the city would be number one or two in line for expansion. She'd also been told that if Williams died the family did not intend to keep the team. She thought it had been a mistake not to get Irsay in front of the legislature. And she thought the key was getting Williams.

"Once we got Williams to come in—and the idea was to say, 'Mr. Williams, we want to know, are you going to move this team?'—in front of God and the press, and have him say, 'No,' then we've satisfied just about everybody."

Williams hadn't only come to sell the stadium.

He'd come to sell himself.

Williams knew as well as anyone that, for the gallery of legislators looking down at him, seated behind a bank of a half-dozen microphones, the questions about his own character and integrity were far more pressing than those concerning the details of the stadium complex. The stadium complex was a matter of dollars and cents; one way or the other, the stadium could be finessed.

But the issues surrounding Edward Bennett Williams, the power broker from down the turnpike, were far cloudier. When Williams intoned to his audience, "I'm not an outlander—I'm a Marylander; I've lived in Maryland for thirty-seven years," he knew it wasn't that simple; Williams's residence was Bethesda, nothing more than a suburban satellite locked into orbit around the nation's capital.

And so Williams went straight to the core of the issue—and set out to sell them on his integrity.

"I have never threatened anyone that we need a new stadium or I get out," he said, appearing frail beneath the bath of television lights. But the firmness of his tone made his physical appearance moot.

"I have never said to anyone in any conversation—and I challenge anyone to produce any witness," he said, pausing dramatically to scour the standing-room-only chambers with his gaze, "that I have ever talked to anyone about leaving the city of Baltimore.

"I have no intention to leave the city of Baltimore. I believe that I hold that franchise in trust for the city of Baltimore."

He stopped, his forefinger at his own chest. Then he leaned forward, and lowered his voice.

"And I don't break my word."

He went on to speak of the economic necessity of doubling the number of prime seats he could sell to season-ticket holders—"We cannot get enough first-place seats to generate the revenues that are necessary to break even. We have seventy-five hundred seats that are saleable as season tickets. I believe a new stadium will be necessary if the Baltimore Orioles can stay a viable franchise economically—in other words, if I can break even. That's all I've ever asked. Let me break even, and I'm here for life."

He heard the echo of his words, as well as the echo of his own mortality, and quickly amended them: "I'm here forever."

He spoke of the Orioles' outstanding record on the field during the first six years of his tenure, and spoke of how the NFL had told him it'd come back to Baltimore only in a new football stadium: "The darkest day in sports was when Mr. Irsay backed his trucks up and fled into the night. The NFL owners—insofar as they are capable of guilt—are riddled with guilt. They want to make reparations. They will not do it at Memorial Stadium."

His voice rose and fell, the words insistent and yet lyrical, the emphasis pointed. He rolled with the infrequent punches and played up the self-deprecation. But if one theme emerged from one of the most impassioned and important summations of his career, it was his own character.

"You are not looking at a greedy owner sitting here today," he said. "I have never taken one dollar out of the Baltimore Orioles. I have taken no salary. Sometimes dollars have been spent imprudently, and I plead guilty to that. Sometimes we've signed contracts of which I'm not particularly proud. But every dollar has gone back into that franchise. I'm not rich enough to operate a major-league baseball team in the red."

It was Jack Lapides, of course, who'd opened the questioning. He made his agenda obvious, talking about the correspondence he'd received from his constituency: "I can tell the supporters of the stadium by the content of the stationery. If it's one hundred percent bond, all the fancy-pants want the stadium. That stack is very small. The ones from Rite Aid—the cheap envelopes—the real people do not want the stadium, at Camden Yards. The only ones who want it are the fat cats."

And it was Lapides who drew the only blood of the hearing.

"I'm not sure I know what you mean by 'saleable seats,'" he said. "Is that a euphemism for expensive seats? I don't understand what's wrong with Memorial Stadium. Is this [new stadium] going to fill up with yuppies? Is [the first-class clientele] to not mix with the public?"

"The economics of the game," Williams said, patiently, "have become such that you have to sell fifteen thousand seats on a season basis."

"It might be cheaper," Lapides said, "for the state to buy fifteen thousand season tickets."

The applause from the gallery was loud and sustained. Williams set his face impassively. He let the seconds pass, and when the sound subsided, he'd framed his answer for the high road.

"I didn't come here to ask for a subsidy," he said. "I don't think we should have a subsidy. I'm against subsidies for the private sector . . . I can make this thing go in the private sector if I get the tools."

It was a neat reply. And nothing more than a semantic dodge. For what was a quarter-of-a-billion-dollar gift of a stadium, designed to help a private enterprise meet its payroll, if not a subsidy?

Williams spent the next thirty minutes answering easier forays from the various legislators—questions of lease agreements, and of multipurpose versus single-purpose stadiums. He was, by turns, respectful, deferential, and polite. He never raised his voice. He raised the magazine once or twice.

By the time the last question rolled around—again from Lapides—the tide had begun to turn toward the Orioles owner. In a discussion of parking, Williams cited the massive traffic tie-ups at Memorial. Lapides had an answer: "If you think it's hard to get out of Memorial," he said, "wait 'til you get to Camden Yards—and I hope you never get there."

This time, the applause was mixed with several boos. Lapides had overplayed his hand.

Wan, thin, the long hair wispy over his collar, Williams just smiled—a gracious smile, not an angry one.

"I hope and pray," Edward Bennett Williams said, "that you will see the way to making it economically feasible to build this stadium."

With ash on his forehead and chemical poisons running through his veins, using what Larry Lucchino would later characterize as "the essence of sweet reasonableness," Edward Bennett Williams had charmed the legislative beast.

Riley: "He captured his audience. He was absolutely candid. He didn't try to dodge the questions. There was a new level of respect for him—how he was operating the franchise and his commitment to Baltimore.

"That was the turning point in our legislative success."

Cathy Riley thought she saw something else, too—respect on the other side. In Williams's eyes.

"You knew he didn't want to be there, but—and there's no way I know this—I had the sense that day that he was almost glad he was there. And that in a way, we as a state gained some respect from him. He never would have made that deal without meeting face-to-face with his adversary.

"How we got Bob Irsay God only knows. How sad that was. We were due for a change of luck."

Williams's rhetoric swayed the day. On March 27 the Senate Finance Committee voted for the stadium, 11–0. The Budget and Taxation Committee passed it 9–4. On April 1, the whole senate passed three bills—giving the Maryland Stadium Authority the power to raise funds, approving Camden Yards as the site, and empowering a new instant lottery. Schaefer signed the bills the next day. Three days later, all three bills cleared the house. Not everyone was proud of the achievement.

"The senate of Maryland has taken a fateful step," said Senator Howard Davis. "The tradition of the senate has gone up against the power of greed, and the power of greed won." And this from Senator John Coolahan, D-Baltimore County: "The issue is extortion. We're a bunch of damn wimps. That's what we are. The entire state of Maryland is kneeling down."

"The city was blackmailed into building a new stadium—that's the despicable part," said Jack Lapides. "It is simply unconscionable that cities are forced to succumb to blackmail by pro football and baseball. You should not capitulate to blackmailers. You don't deal with hostage situations. You don't deal with terrorists. I put these teams in the same category."

On Martin Luther King's birthday in January 1992, a wind rakes the crest of the hill at North Milton and Gay like a razor. Inside Lucky's

Liquors a man named Smiley dispenses pints of Wild Irish Rose through a small revolving door in the bullet-proof glass. Several men mill about inside, talking, seeking refuge from the wind outside.

A Christian Brothers Brandy Certificate of Appreciation is on display behind the plastic. On one wall hangs a public-service poster that reads, "A tisket, a tasket, a condom or a casket."

Another wall is covered with advertisements for the Maryland instant lottery games that are paying for Camden Yards, a few months from completion. PLAY FOOTBALL AND YOU COULD GET SACKED says a poster on the wall, which features a drawing of sacks of money. WINNER WONDERLAND. JOKERS WILD.

A man in a worn gray double-knit jacket with a heavy cough pulls a dollar out of his pocket, smiles, and laughs. "I have a dream."

Behind the bullet-proof plastic a woman named Pam Jackson takes his dollar and hands him his ticket. He scratches it. He drops it on the floor. He walks out the door.

"It's a very sad dream we have foisted on the poor," Jack Lapides says now. "It's being financed on the backs of the poor. The very poor, in Baltimore city and Prince Georges county, which is about 25 percent of the state's population, spends about 63 percent of the lottery. It's our third highest source of revenue, the lottery. That's the irony. The whole purpose was to sell a lot of yuppie seats to service the rich and the season-ticket holders. The poor guy who's financing it is going to be in left field."

Jack Lapides is in his thirty-first year in the Maryland State Legislature, his twenty-seventh in the senate. He grew up in Southeast Baltimore, played stickball in Carroll Park. He saw three games at Oriole Park before it burned down. Jack Lapides went to City College, a castle of a high school perched on a hill across 33rd Street from Memorial Stadium. He grew up daydreaming about playing in the bowl across the street. It was Lapides who led the drive for a referendum to derail Schaefer's stadium.

"This is the first time we have ever dedicated a lottery fund," Jack Lapides says. "We have resisted it for schools, the elderly, every other special interest. But we could not resist it for the stadium. When you dedicate lottery money to that purpose it precludes you from dedicating it to areas like low- and middle-income housing. And the money you get from the instant lottery is a finite thing. Four games seems to be a maximum number they can sustain. It's not like the Lotto or the daily numbers, which is an open-ended thing. The instant has only a certain number of players. It was determined we hit the saturation point. As long as the funds are being dedicated to pay off those bonds, we are precluded from using that revenue source."

"It's terrible, using the instant lottery," says Jerold Hoffberger, the old owner. "It's awful. [Using it] ought to be condemned. They won't even be able to afford the buck that it takes to get there on the subway. The underclass that plays the lottery so significantly, they are not the people who buy season tickets to baseball games."

"We ought not be building stadiums until we're building schools," *Baltimore Sun* writer Carl Schoettler said one day. "We ought not to be building stadiums until we're paying teachers sixty thousand dollars a year. But people don't vote for that. Tell them to allocate money to pay teachers, they'll tell you to take a running jump at the inner harbor."

"It's not going to be found money," says Eric Garland, the former editor of *Baltimore Magazine*. "It's existing money. Schaefer gets the money from people who don't have an advocacy. Who's going to argue for people who are addicted to gambling? It's being built on the backs of the poor addicted gamblers."

It was not always so. In the first state lottery, in 1569, to raise money to dig the harbor, the winner received tapestries. Two hundred years later, in 1753, Baltimore held a town lottery to raise 450 pieces of eight to build the first wharf in the harbor. In 1763, 510 pieces of eight paid for firefighting equipment, including leather buckets. A lottery in 1788 paid for the paving of Fell's Point and the straightening of Jones Falls. They became a regular means of raising money to keep the harbor dredged. Even the Washington Monument on Charles Street, the centerpiece of the city, was built in 1809 via a state lottery—$100,000, gathered with a little help from the fund-raising efforts of Ben Franklin.

The lottery's long tradition in Maryland means nothing to the customers at Lucky's.

"I ain't think they needed a new stadium," Pam Jackson says. Pam grew up here. She's wearing faded jeans and a white blouse. She plies the machine the way a pianist would ply a keyboard. Men who buy their tickets inevitably try to navigate the bullet-proof barrier to convince Pam to join them for a drink, or dinner. Pam parries them with good-natured rolls of her eyes.

"What's wrong with the old one? That Memorial Stadium was fine. All these people out here losing jobs. Dying on the street. Hungry. Homeless. People out here don't *have* things. This light rail? Why? So the people in the suburbs can come downtown? Tell 'em to drive!"

Pam stands behind the bullet-proof plastic and dispenses her tickets. WARNING! says a state-issued communiqué taped to her machine. ALTERED SCRATCHOFF. PLEASE CHECK ALL $25 WINNING INSTANT TICKETS. Another read, AGENT ALERT! CHECK INSTANT TICKET CODES CAREFULLY. HIGH LEVEL OF ALTERED TICKETS REPORTED IN BALTIMORE AREA.

In Pam and Smiley's sanctum, it is quiet and peaceful. The floor is a clean pink linoleum. Compared to how she looks through scratched and filthy plastic, Pam and her armies of liquor bottles seem in remarkable clarity. With the barrier between them, she is a comfortable conversationalist with her customers and quite sure of herself.

"See that Porsche in the alley? That's my car," says a well-lubricated man on the other side. "I'm gonna drive you home."

"I'm twenty-seven," Pam says to him. "I got my whole life ahead of me. I ain't gettin' in no car with you."

"Mr. Oscar come in on Friday," Pam says when he leaves. Mr. Oscar buys the instant game in chunks. He's a legend around Lucky's. "I cashed a hundred for him the other day, four twenties and two tens, and he bought forty scratch-offs. Ended up buying sixty dollars. Won twenty-three. They be buyin 'em, though."

The printer squeals incessantly, the distinctive high-pitched squeak of the money machine printing out green for the state.

"We sell two thousand dollars on Sundays," Pam says.

Another man comes in and buys his tickets. A big man. He refuses to give his name. "Just call me The Man Unknown."

"I don't mess with the scratch-offs," he says. "You can't win with 'em. You can't win with 'em."

But they're paying for the stadium.

"They don't need a new stadium. Nothing wrong with the one they got. But they got it now. Nothin' we can do about it. We don't have a say-so on nothin'."

With the approval of instant lottery funds, a new hurdle immediately presented itself. The stadium's opponents mobilized quickly and effectively. By the ninth of April, a group calling itself Marylanders for Sports Sanity had collected twenty-eight thousand signatures to subject the stadium to referendum. If past performance in cities from Miami to Detroit to San Jose meant anything at all, the vote would have certainly spelled its defeat. Baltimore had already vetoed a stadium on the site: Hoffberger and Rosenbloom's most serious effort at building a multipurpose plant at Camden Yards in the early seventies was overwhelmingly defeated in a referendum.

There would be no such risks taken this time; in May, the secretary of state rejected the petitions, saying that the bill that mandated the authority was an appropriations bill, and appropriations bills could not be subjected to referendum.

In June, a *Baltimore Sun* poll found 39 percent of its readers against the stadium, 29 percent for, and the referendum proponents took the issue to court—where, to their satisfaction, in July, an Anne Arundel County circuit judge said the signatures were, in fact, legitimate. The state would now appeal in turn—to the highest appeals court in the state. The ruling would come in September.

In August, the *Sun* suggested without a hint of irony that getting legal clearance for the stadium could help the city get the St. Louis Cardinals.

AMERICA'S ARCHITECTS

NOW THE ORIOLES had a site. They had a baseball-only park. They had a state legislature willing to pay for the whole thing. All they lacked was a popular mandate, although the citizens of Baltimore and Maryland who didn't want a new park would no longer be a factor, not if the appeals court threw out their protest petitions in September.

But in the summer of 1987, Larry Lucchino didn't want to wait. The delay worried him, and with good reason. Ed Williams may not have been overly concerned about the way the park would look—Williams had, after all, already tacitly approved an HOK scheme—but Lucchino, who was taking on more of the club decisions each day and would soon be named its president, considered the design of the stadium a paramount concern. And he knew that the more time passed until the process began, the tighter the design restrictions would be down the road—and the likelier it was that the job would go to a cost-efficient architect better known for budgetary than design considerations.

In other words, the likelier the job would go to HOK, the state's de facto in-house architect.

The consequences of such a result were already on display all around the nation.

Think about the last stadium you visited; the chances are as good as even that it was designed by someone who works for, worked for, or will work for Hellmuth Obata Kassabaum. HOK people have designed or consulted on seven of the ten NFL stadiums built in the last fifteen years. They're doing the next one, too: a football stadium for St. Louis—a city that has no team, but does already have a football stadium, right downtown. In good condition. At the town's epicenter no less.

But then, Chicago already had a Comiskey Park, which didn't stop HOK from building them another one. The new Comiskey's construction marked HOK's first real foot in the door of the baseball business. Actually, it's more like they kicked the door down, because HOK is also designing Gateway Park in Cleveland, Denver's Coors Field, and they would have built San Jose's park if the people of San Jose hadn't voted the park down on their own referendum. For a while, it looked as if even that decision would benefit HOK indirectly, since the Giants were apparently headed to the monumentally unfortunate Florida Suncoast Dome in St. Petersburg—another HOK design.

"HOK," says Chicago architect Phillip Bess, a maverick butting his head against a brick wall, "has a choke hold on the business."

And not just the business of building stadiums—the business of baseball. As it dictated football stadium design in the seventies, it will shape the look of baseball in the decade to come. Heady stuff for a handful of midwestern engineers who caught the crest of the big business sports wave some fifteen years ago and have been riding it ever since.

Their story begins in the late 1970s. A small design firm in Kansas City called Devine, James, Labinski and Myers (DJLM) had assembled a group of young architects from midwestern schools who found they had two things in common: a love of sports and a desire to build stadiums. And who wouldn't want to? They're extremely lucrative—a quarter of a billion dollars' worth of contracts went out on Camden Yards. They don't take much design talent; they're virtually unchanged from ancient Greek times, save the addition of luxury boxes and club seats. And—most significantly—when you plant them out in the suburbs, or in a meadowlands, or amid a Miami Haitian neighborhood of one-story homes, or in the nothingness in suburban St. Petersburg, they're about as inconspicuous as a tarantula on a slice of angel food, to borrow from Raymond Chandler—which means that your work is extremely visible, all of the time. Which is just about every architect's dream, because, after all, there is no more frustrated artist than the architect, 90 percent of whose every creation has already been dictated by design restraints. Painters paint; writers write; architects plan the expenditure of large amounts of money. Other people's money.

A stadium is a project to stoke the most insanely inflated egos. It is the biggest thing America is still building. Future generations will gauge the culture by our ballparks—which is something of a disconcerting thought.

At any rate, the young turks at DJLM were anxious and eager. And when the state of Indiana prepared to accept bids on the Hoosier-dome, they saw their big chance. That contract went to the Kansas City engineering firm of Howard Needles Tammen Bergendoff, better known as HNTB, which had already worked on such notable goliaths as Giants Stadium and the Royals' complex. The crew at DJLM were crushed—until they got a call from HNTB, which had been impressed with their work and wanted to hire half a dozen of them to work on the Indianapolis bubble. Across town they went—Rick Deflon, Joe Spear, and four others. Within three years they'd won contracts to build Joe Robbie Stadium and the Florida Suncoast Dome, and to do additional work on Wrigley and Comiskey. Business was booming.

But Deflon and his friends were chafing. They were bringing in literally hundreds of millions of dollars, and not seeing much of it; sports was just a sidelight for HNTB, which brought in most of its business doing airport and highway work.

"It was pretty parochial," Deflon recalls. "We started thinking we should start our own firm. Then we got a call from HOK."

By 1983, Hellmuth Obata Kassabaum had made its mark on the American landscape, but had not yet ventured into the sports arena. Based in St. Louis, HOK was best known for the Galleria mall in Houston—a gargantuan space whose indoor skating rink earned it immediate distinction as one of the city's most compelling, if gaudy, tourist spots—and the National Air and Space Museum in Washington. Both were designed by senior partner Gyo Obata, a San Francisco native born of Japanese parents who had found his way to Missouri during the second World War in order to avoid the relocation camps. Obata landed a scholarship at Washington University, then went on to study with Eero Saarinen at the Cranbrook

Academy of Art in Bloomfield Hills. Back in St. Louis, Obata set up shop downtown in a renovated electric motor factory, across from the train station, with its minarets and distinctive stone work—the only building, it is said, that Frank Lloyd Wright liked in the entire town.

In the early 1980s, intrigued by the increasing willingness of cities and states to commit hundreds of millions of dollars to sports arenas designed either to keep their own franchises or to lure someone else's, HOK decided to branch into sports facilities. As Obata recalls, the HNTB gang made the first call. He was pleased to accept it.

"They felt the engineers [at HNTB] were not as sympathetic to design quality as they should be," Gyo Obata says now of the half-dozen renegades. "They wanted to join us. We felt they were bright young guys. We pitched in and helped them set up the office in Kansas City. They took off. They got to know all the owners of all the major leagues. They really know how to market that area."

This latter talent, say the critics of HOK's brand of stadium building, is HOK's most obvious one. Distinctive design would be far down the list.

"They're everywhere," says John Pastier, the former architecture critic of the *Los Angeles Times,* a frequent lecturer at various universities and a consultant on Camden Yards in the early stages. "They dominate for four reasons: They're everywhere—they even hand out HOK pins at the winter meetings. They have bowls of them! They come in on time. They come in on budget. And they do free work."

"HOK does do a lot of upfront work," agrees Phillip Bess. "I have several copies of [HOK] program work that's interchangeable. Done for free. That's not unusual—architects do use things again to get different jobs. But they have the volume of work to go in and do it for free."

Translation: A city or team decides to build a park. They put out some feelers at nine A.M. on Monday. By the end of the working day, an HOK rep shows up with the perfect park for your town. He can do this because he has generic blueprints in his briefcase.

"It's a lot of marketing," says Dale Swearingen, a vice president and director of architecture for the Osborne Company in Cleveland, the HOK of its time. Osborne built the Polo Grounds, Tiger Stadium,

Griffith Stadium, Municipal Stadium in Cleveland, Braves Field, County Stadium, Meulbach (Municipal) in Kansas City, and RFK Stadium. "They've gotten big quickly and they're extremely good marketing people. We butt our heads up against them all the time. We're behind on marketing. But we have a tradition of design going back a century. They have no tradition at all."

If Osborne is not getting as much work as their résumé would seem to merit, maybe it's a question of karma. It was Osborne that designed the sliding ground-level seats for RFK that changed the course of American stadium architecture by making multipurpose stadiums a reality. RFK begat Candlestick and Shea, which was built on a municipal budget for a World's Fair. Those three begat Busch, the Vet, Three Rivers, and Riverfront—all monuments to baseball's willingness to buy into the National Football League's sudden ascendancy into the American sporting fore, and to abandon all pretense toward putting art in stadium architecture. Among the four of them, there's hardly an architectural detail to be found, with the exception of Edward Stone Durrell's nearly kitschy arches that sit atop the rim of Busch; far removed from the visual experience of a game down on the field, they add no more real drama than the frosted flowers atop a birthday cake. All of the bare concrete that makes up these four parks is a reflection of the modernist movement that the nation's architects embraced from the fifties on.

By the time Indianapolis and Minneapolis and Pontiac and Miami and St. Petersburg decided to build, no one had thought of stylizing a stadium for decades. When Kansas City decided to flee its downtown in 1973, and had the good sense to build two parks instead of one, the first baseball-only stadium since County Stadium in Milwaukee was a Spartan monument to cost-efficiency. Designed by HNTB, Royals Stadium might as well be Six Flags Over Royal Land; twenty miles out of town, it is a chillingly symmetrical palace of polyurethane, the best seats in the place furnishing a view of an interstate highway. The hum of the semis highballing their way down the freeway beyond the outfield accompanies every game. Now, where Charlie Finley celebrated eccentricity downtown, Royals Stadium romanticizes the America of the interstate, and celebrates the highway engineers' greatest achievement—the road with a view of nothing, from which no part of the country can ever be seen.

It was with the construction of Royals Stadium that traffic flow became the overriding factor in stadium construction. And efficient flow of both cars and people is what HOK is best known for. The HOK trademark is the ramps. If the ramps are attached to the outside of an arena, it's an HOK-HNTB job. Giants Stadium, Joe Robbie, and the new Comiskey all share this distinctive trait: Circular, looping pedestrian ramps are stuck onto the outside of each park at regular intervals, ameliorating ingress and egress—and severely marring any architectural integrity. This is much of the reason HOK's stadiums are all so big; in the old parks, the vertical movement of the fans was confined to ramps and stairways that were contained within the stadium itself. HOK put them outside. And in addition, in stadiums without columns, the upper decks have to be cantilevered back, which allows for broad concourses beneath them, which makes for even bigger stadiums.

"The result," Bess explains, "is that there's this huge increase in the footprint. And in the height. HOK doesn't give a shit about it. Or they don't have a clue."

Phillip Bess, it should be noted, has a stake in the debate. Phillip Bess designed Armour Field. Armour Field wasn't built; the New Comiskey was. Chicago wasn't ready for Armour Field, and neither were the White Sox. Armour Field would have been built to the north of the old Comiskey, thereby (1) preserving the Armour Square neighborhood to the south instead of uprooting 250 households, and (2) preserving the field of the old Comiskey Park as a park, instead of the parking lot it is now.

Armour Field was a stunning proposal, aesthetically exciting. Perhaps inadvertently, perhaps not, in the updated version of *Green Cathedrals*, Philip Lowry's handbook on America's baseball parks, there are illustrations of Armour Field—and none of the new Comiskey. Bess's park featured columns that afforded intimate sightlines from the upper deck; they blocked fewer than one half of one percent of all of the seats. It had a lovely façade, bricked and windowed. It was a symmetrical park, because the plot on which it stood was symmetrical, and Bess saw no reason for fake assymetricality. His outfield nonetheless featured odd angles and quirks, and plenty of places for a caroming line drive to prove elusive.

Bess, who earned his masters of architecture from the University of Virginia in 1981, has a private practice in Chicago—Thursday Architects, from the G. K. Chesterton short story, "The Man Who Was Thursday." He is the unacknowledged leader of the new, unheralded salon of baseball-park architects.

"There are several of us—myself, Pastier—maybe we're aggressive in talking about theory. We would be on the cutting edge if we were getting anything built."

But Bess is not just a fringe player preaching impractical theory. He is a paid consultant on two current jobs in major-league cities exploring the feasibility of new stadiums. And he knows whereof he speaks when he says, "HOK blows people out of the water on the basis of their track record, appealing to clients who are not very sophisticated in terms of aesthetics and the stadium's impact. . . . They market themselves as the cutting edge of stadium design, but the work is quite clearly formulaic. It changes according to specific circumstances and makes minor variations, but they don't change the scale and character of the facility. It's not HOK's fault; HOK Sport is a service firm, which is a nice way of saying they'll do whatever the client wants for a fee."

It was Henry Hobson Richardson, the lauded nineteenth-century designer, who said that the most important part of any job was getting the job. And while no one has ever compared H. H. Richardson to HOK, in this respect HOK is right in step with the old master.

"HOK," says Richard Ayers, of the prominent Baltimore design architecture firm Ayers Saint Gross, "has been successful in dominating an industry from ground zero. . . . You've got to admire someone who is able to dominate the field the way they are. And ambitious, somewhat arrogant decisions are made within that context. HOK has a reputation, well-deserved, of doing things their own way."

Gyo Obata freely admits that the Kansas City branch of the firm, HOK's Sports Facility Group, is allowed to operate strictly within its specialty.

"In terms of design, over the years we have sort of helped them, too. We have always been known as a design firm, and we wanted to keep the quality of the design."

Some of them, of course, have been less than distinguished.

"We've done some bad ones," Gyo Obata agreed.

He didn't want to elaborate. He didn't have to, not to anyone who's visited the new Comiskey.

On a warm July afternoon in 1991, as forty-five thousand Chicagoans trooped into their new palace, a glass-and-concrete concoction of decidedly confused aesthetics, they were treated to the disconcerting sight of Comiskey's old shell across the street. It lay halfway razed, with its innards exposed, like an eel split down the middle. Wires and pipes hung out like entrails. The field was already overgrown, the grass resembling a parched midwestern prairie.

Comiskey Park wasn't even being allowed to die with dignity.

"You'd have thought [team owners Jerry] Reinsdorf and [Eddie] Einhorn would have torn it down by the time the season began," observed a Chicago architect, embarking on his first visit to the park, who had requested anonymity because of his own firm's associations with HOK. He spent his graduate years a few blocks away, earning his degree at Mies van der Rohe's Illinois Institute of Technology; it was van der Rohe who coined the phrase "Less Is More," but on this day the architect was quick to note that, in the case of the new Comiskey, van der Rohe was wrong.

"This is depressing," was his first take, as we examined the façade behind home plate. "They took the elements from the old one and made them flat, and cast them out of concrete. It looks fake. Concrete has its natural limits in terms of beauty. When you try and make it look like an historic building, it looks completely flat and fake."

We had some scalped box seats behind home plate, but before settling into them, we decided to ascend to the top of the park, alone, having been unable to locate any Sherpa guides at short notice. Because of the White Sox's decision to incorporate three decks of luxury suites, our walk from the first-level concourse to the upper-deck concourse behind the left-field seats seemed endless, and took on the feel of a march up one of those endlessly twisting parking-garage exit ramps. We were rewarded with a view of the carcass of the old park.

My companion remarked, "You'd think the last thing they'd want to do was remind people of what they'd done."

What Jerry Reinsdorf and Eddie Einhorn had done was standard operating procedure in late-twentieth-century sporting America: They'd threatened to move their team to another city if the state didn't build them a new park.

And in fact, the Illinois state legislature failed to approve the funding for a new stadium by the end of the legislative session in 1988; at midnight, the White Sox were officially tenants of the ghost town of St. Petersburg, where HOK had already built a $140 million dome to flash at prospective suitors.

Illinois Governor James Thompson, though, twisted a few arms, and when the bill to fund the stadium finally passed, a few minutes after midnight, they turned the clock back to make it legal—a curious thing, considering that in so doing they were forever and finally turning their back on real history, on the oldest park in baseball, opened in 1910.

In the final agreement, the state of Illinois and the city of Chicago agreed to build a stadium at the state's expense by floating some bonds and paying off their interest with a 2 percent hotel tax and direct subsidies from the city and the state—a tad less taxing than Maryland's tactics; the people paying would be visitors to the city, not its citizens.

The owners' tactics had surprised no one; the two men had a track record of treating the city in cavalier fashion. In 1981, when they bought the team from Bill Veeck, they immediately insulted him by promising to restore some "class" to the South Side—thereby alienating much of their new constituency, which held Mr. Veeck in some high regard. In 1982, they induced the city to give them sky boxes financed with city industrial revenue bonds, while making it plain that the old Comiskey was not in their plans. In a discussion of its future, Reinsdorf remarked, "I have no sympathy for preserving buildings that are unprofitable."

When the Sox installed more luxury boxes in the mid-1980s the inner decay of Comiskey's infrastructure became apparent. Structural engineers hired by the owners said it was hopeless; structural engineers for the city disagreed. When, in 1987, a report said that it would cost $70 million to make Comiskey "state of the art," public sentiment began to turn away from the preservationists, although the latter protested vehemently: We don't need a state-of-the-art facility, was the mantra of Save Our Sox; we just need a facility. Tax money should go where it's needed, they said.

Few listened.

"There was so much deterioration, the engineers told us the upper deck probably would have collapsed within a year or two," Reinsdorf told me in 1990.

"That wasn't true," one of his limited partners told me. "They just didn't want to keep it up."

"If there was a pivotal point," Reinsdorf insisted, "it was not during our ownership. Prior ownerships failed to take the proper preventive maintenance."

That was the truth. Renovating Comiskey would have been costly—although not as costly as building a new one. Almost from the moment Charles Comiskey laid the first brick, a green one for luck, he let it go. While the Wrigleys poured money into their jewel up on the North Side, the Comiskeys did little to keep the place up; there was little demand for it. According to a study commissioned by Bill Veeck in the 1970s, Comiskey could have been fixed up and brought to a state of good health for $4 million. But that was $4 million more than the Veeck budget.

It had been originally designed by Zachary Taylor Davis, a Chicago architect named for the man who was president when he was born. When Zachary Taylor was born, George Washington was the president. In other words, Comiskey Park, at its birth, was just two lifetimes removed from the birth of the nation itself. And sometimes it looked it. In one year Bill Veeck's coffers were so empty that the only maintenance he could afford was painting of the underside of the upper deck—black, the better to obscure some of the loose wiring. Another year, an opening day, one section of the lower concourse had to be cordoned off to protect the fans from falling concrete.

The Comiskey denizens were not the kind of people who effected

Chicago policy. These were found at Wrigley Field to the north; Comiskey was the blue-collar park, hard by the stockyards—the single most crowded neighborhood in the entire nation at the turn of the century. The Jungle, Upton Sinclair called it in his graphic exposé of the meat-packing industry.

Comiskey offered an antidote to the daily jungle. It was one of the first parks to install lights. In fact, Comiskey was a better park for watching baseball than Wrigley. It was small, and built on a human scale, for a human-scaled game. Its upper-deck front rows were forty-five feet closer to home plate than Wrigley's. Down in the street-level concourse, the scents were shellacked onto the walls, adhering to the brick like the very soul of the game made manifest: cigar smoke, Old Style beer, sausage, cooking oil.

While Comiskey crumbled, Wrigley became the focus of a "preservationist" fight over the installation of lights. Neighborhood groups in the well-off areas surrounding Wrigley objected to the Cubs' efforts to bring their park into the second half of the twentieth century. The Wrigley lights imbroglio may have doomed the efforts of Save Our Sox; the city, in love with its Cubs (up and down Michigan Avenue, bookstores are full of Wrigleyana, with virtually none of Comiskey), spent more time yapping about the cosmetics of one park than the salvation of another. The implicit message was: Protect our jewel and don't worry about that wreck on the South Side. By the time Rick Sutcliffe served up the first night-game pitch at Wrigley—and the second was smacked for a home run because he'd been blinded by all the flashbulbs during the first—Comiskey was dead.

The new owners were not wholly mindless of the passing generations. Although they did not attend the ground breaking—they were in Cleveland for a Bulls game—the day that the bulldozers had to raze McCuddy's pub across the street, the bar where Babe Ruth would sip a beer between games, they found the grandson of the original owner and put him in the seat of the cab. They took pictures.

The kid was crying.

Reinsdorf and Einhorn marketed the passing of the old park, of course, selling off individual bricks—including the bricks that, arranged by the dozen, fashioned the letter *C* in the wall of the park

in dozens of places. It was never a beautiful park, Comiskey, but the
C's were its most distinctive ornaments. Each *C* was several square
feet in size. When I asked a front-office type in charge of stadium
issues whether any of those letters would be preserved, he laughed,
and said, "It'd be a miracle if we could keep those together," and, of
course, they didn't.

They let Comiskey rot for its final season—all the while mounting
a heavy and insistent campaign urging folks to come out to the old park
before they turned out the lights. It was a little like a governor selling
tickets to an execution he had ordered. In the final year it looked as
though they spent no money on the park, as if to try and prove to the
people of Chicago how sorry a state the old girl was in. They didn't even
give it a coat of paint for its final year—perhaps so that the "authen-
ticated bricks" they'd be selling would seem authentically old.

Instead, they trucked a bunch of memorabilia across West 35th
Street: the fireplace from the original Bard's Room, Joe Jackson's
original contract (discovered, quite by accident, by Mike Veeck one
day when he was cleaning out the shaft of Comiskey's private
elevator). But to lift pieces of Comiskey and take them across the
street was more an evisceration than a transplant. They did not take.
The new one bears no resemblance to the old. It has stolen the name.

On this sunny July afternoon, in the new Comiskey, the upper deck
cant—35 degrees, among the steepest in the majors—was enough to
induce vertigo. Its seats furnished a view of the Dan Ryan Expressway
and its caravans of trucks, and the aural accompaniment was the
incessant hum of rubber tire on highway. We also heard a train, but
we couldn't see it.

The steep upper deck was required to furnish sight lines; without
columns below, the upper deck in a stadium has to be set farther
back. With the extra height forced on it by three decks of luxury
boxes—they are wincingly prominent, like the prow of a ship, the
staterooms looking down on steerage—the upper deck up top has to
be cantilevered even more.

Down below, in our seats behind home plate, the view of the
baseball game was fine. But the view to center field furnished no clue

about what city we were in, since the stadium had been inexplicably planted to face away from the city. The park is self-enclosed. Its arms wrap around so that the game is sealed off from the city, much as the high-rise public housing to the east was sealed off from Richard Daley's Bridgeport neighborhood by the construction of the interstate.

In fact, the new Comiskey is designed so that visitors by car will be able to drive in from the suburbs, park, cross the bridges, and never have to set foot in South Side Chicago at all.

What HOK had achieved was the perfect modern ballpark: no interaction at all with the surrounding neighborhood; no relation to the city; no view of anything. The antithesis of how the game began. The epitome of the modern profit machine.

Joe Spear and Rick Deflon, the architects, had not neglected to include some detail. On the precast concrete façade they'd etched an echo of the old arches—with plate glass filling them in, to hide the three-tiered private luxury level. In fact, much of the outside detail is obscured by HOK's trademark pedestrian ramps. Engineering super-ceded design. The façade is tinted precast concrete, with embellish-ment in pastel colors—Yup colors, in the trade.

"Dead historicity," said the architect on our way out.

And then he paused to point something out. On our concrete ramp, behind the left-field upper deck, yellow plastic tape had been strung across a large section, warding off pedestrians. We looked closely. A railing had come loose from the concrete. It was pulled right out of the floor. Where the railing had been was a rust stain, and the concrete had already chipped away. Two months after opening day.

Somewhere, Bill Veeck was laughing.

Larry Lucchino, not surprisingly, was no fan of the new Comiskey. In fact, he held it in something approaching derision. Vehement in his insistence that Camden Yards owes nothing to the new Comiskey, he would later say of HOK's intentions regarding Camden Yards, "Comiskey would have been the stadium they'd have built, given free rein."

In the summer of 1987, as he cast about for architectural input, Larry Lucchino's opinion of HOK was already well known. Ever since

HOK had done the twenty-two-site study for Mayor Schaefer in 1985, HOK was perceived as the Maryland Stadium Authority's architect— and, by inference, the architect the Orioles didn't want.

The perception was accurate. "HOK maintains the pretense that they're the architects. They're construction workers," is what Lucchino would confide one day in 1991, as Camden Yards was being built. But as far back as 1984, when a renovation of Memorial Stadium was being discussed, Richard Ayers, Lucchino's good friend and one of Baltimore's most respected architects, had suggested to Lucchino that they bring in HOK on the job; Ayers had worked with Rick Deflon on the renovation of the Baltimore Arena in 1983 when Deflon was with HNTB.

"You don't need those guys," Lucchino advised Ayers.

Lucchino's desire to keep HOK out of the Camden Yards project was a matter of more than the animosity between him and the firm. It even went beyond the knowledge that selecting HOK would put one more weapon in the hands of the state, whose overriding mandate, in a climate of fiscal restraint, was to build the park as cheaply as possible, while Lucchino wanted nothing less than a masterpiece.

No, Lucchino's strongest objections were rooted in aesthetic grounds. Lucchino's displeasure at the prospect of HOK landing the job was a direct reflection of the firm's work. They traditionally built their monuments to concrete in nonurban settings, and thus, the Orioles president figured, the firm was ill-prepared to take on a city project with its myriad urban-design issues.

"We were not," Larry Lucchino says now, "going to play in a ballpark we didn't want. And I was pretty skeptical about their ability to give us a ballpark we wanted."

Larry Lucchino wanted to build a park that would change the course of the river of precast concrete that had been poured into American stadium architecture. Larry Lucchino wanted to build a palace that would put the Orioles at baseball's epicenter. Lucchino's quick rise from the blue-collar streets of Pittsburgh to the Kennedyed cocktail parties of the District suburbs had helped him acquire a taste for the best. What Lucchino wanted was an all-star team of the best architects, urban planners, and designers he could find: Bill Pederson of the New York firm of Kohn Pederson Fox, a firm known as one of the nation's leading proponents of postmodernism without any cuteness, as lead architects. He wanted the urban planning team of Alex Cooper in New York, the firm that had designed Battery Park City, the dramatic cluster of buildings on New York's lower west side that had combined, with some success, the demands of the new with some of the warmth of the old. He wanted a designer named Deborah Sussman, who was responsible for the distinct and often effective graphics for the 1984 Ueberroth Olympics. Sussman had taken the L.A. Memorial Coliseum and bedecked it with pastelled filagree, a half-century after opening, that rang strong and true—exactly the old/new effect that Larry Lucchino wanted in his new park.

Above all, Lucchino wanted his new and dynamic palace to be mindful of the past. In Larry Lucchino's dream, the park at Camden Yards would remind everyone of the baseball vision of their own childhoods.

And the best and the brightest would have to be building it. This was essential. Larry was a brand-name guy. Ed Williams had taught him that. Ed had taught him everything, which to some was quite a blessing; to others, it was something of a curse.

He grew up in the Greenfield section of Pittsburgh, a working-class neighborhood within walking distance of Forbes Field, one of the most storied of the wood-and-steel neighborhood parks, an asymmetrical arena that featured a right-center-field meadow so vast that the grounds crew would roll the batting cage out to the wall after batting practice and leave it in the field of play during the game. No batted ball ever reached it.

Lucchino's father owned a small grocery store named the Skyview Superette, although it featured no particular view of the sky. He remembers about his mother that, no matter how long or short the first half of the Steelers game on television, she would always have Sunday dinner ready at the end of the first half, to be consumed by the family in time for the start of the second. Law and Burgess and Mazeroski were the baseball heroes of Lucchino's childhood, observed from the upper deck of Forbes Field.

"They've replaced Forbes with the Pitt law school—the worst trade I can imagine," Lucchino said one afternoon over a slice of pizza in a neighborhood joint a few blocks from Memorial. The setting of the meal illustrates the dichotomy inside the man who now runs the Orioles' show and owns 9 percent of the franchise: He is consciously reminding himself—or trying to convince himself—that his material success hasn't gone to his head.

He was the second baseman on the high school team that took the city championship in 1963, but Lucchino's real talent was at point guard. He combined athletic versatility with a sharp and analytic intellect to land at Princeton in 1964, and he was riding the bench in 1965 when Bill Bradley guided the Tigers to the Final Four. He went to Yale Law, class of '72, and he immediately joined Edward Bennett Williams's firm where he was delighted, on his first day of work, to find EBW himself dropping in for a chat of several hours, about sports.

"We talked about football, baseball, and basketball," Lucchino recalled. "I thought, 'What a nice place this is—the senior partner comes down and sits around and shoots the bull about sports. Won't this be a walk on the beach.' "

Lucchino didn't work closely with Williams until Williams brought him in on legal matters involving the Redskins. They had a certain kinship: both blue collar by root, both worked their way up in law, both loved sports.

Impressed with Lucchino's litigation talents, Williams brought all of the Redskins' legal work to his firm and gave it to Lucchino. When Williams closed on the Orioles, it was Lucchino who was at his side.

"He functioned as the principal, and he expected that of me," Lucchino said. "He didn't keep me as a lawyer drafting documents. He asked me to negotiate deals, get involved in operational things as well."

In the fall of 1985, a further whim of fate brought the two even closer. Early that year, Lucchino had had a persistent cough. In August he took a solo motorcycle trip from Paris to the south of France, and the cough worsened on the way. On his return he had a checkup. On Labor Day he had an X ray. On Friday the 13th he got the diagnosis: Diffuse Histiocytic Lymphoma. Is it curable? he asked.

It depends on the stage, he was told. Further tests revealed more and more dismal news. Yes, it was in an advanced stage. No, they didn't know what had caused it.

Lucchino found himself quite unprepared to face a fatal cancer. Friends rallied. He welcomed their support. On the day of the diagnosis, Lucchino made no effort to hide the news from colleagues; he knew he was not strong enough to handle it alone. In particular, he knew that it would help him if Williams knew; his boss had been fighting cancer since 1977.

Lucchino found himself growing introspective and detached. And angry and pessimistic. The chemotherapy was not doing the job.

One afternoon, Williams, himself recovering from his latest operation, stuck his face into Lucchino's door. "Come on," Williams said. "We're going out for some real chemotherapy." Four hours of cocktails at the Metropolitan Club lightened the load. Temporarily.

Williams steered Lucchino to his own physicians at the Dana Farber Institute in Boston. They recommended an autologous bone-marrow transplant, at the time an experimental procedure. Lucchino was the thirty-second cancer patient ever to try it.

"There were plenty of times I'd envision myself dying," Lucchino recalls. "I remember being told by a former patient that the best thing was to not be alone and let those thoughts germinate. I tried to spend as little time alone as I could."

He was in the hospital for thirty-seven consecutive days, unable to leave the room, during which time he could not be exposed to germs. He had no immunity to anything. But a month on his back was proving too daunting a prospect. In the middle of the stay, he resolved to abandon it and leave: "I said to myself, 'I don't think I can sustain myself through this ordeal.' I said to the doctor, 'I'm leaving.' 'No you're not,' he said. 'Leave the room and you die.' "

The transplant took. It's been six years since Lucchino left the hospital, with no recurrence.

"I'm still cautious. I feel very lucky. I'm grateful," he says with little discernible emotion. "I don't want to declare victory. I don't need to make declarations."

"Larry, you'll find, is a very private person," Rich Ayers says. "There were a number of people who made overtures to him after he was ill. He wouldn't let you in. What motivated Larry after EBW's death was something he feels very strongly about."

To those who knew both, much of what has motivated Lucchino has been his understandable, and impossible, quest to, if not fill the shoes of his late friend, at least to squire the Orioles the way EBW would have—aggressively, with no indecision, and no regrets.

"There are a series of people in this life that held the same kind of relationship Larry did, in terms of being adopted by Ed," says a man well acquainted with both. "It's not uncommon that a person of Ed's stature would adopt a person he's attracted to, and put them in his back pocket for a number of years and then spin him loose. Because, after a while, all of a sudden they knew how he thought, what he did. They didn't have to even ask what he'd think. They'd even start to smell like him. Vincent Fuller, he got Hinckley off the hook. Brendan Sullivan got hooked on the courtroom.

"The thing that's unique is that Larry didn't leave. And in the process, Larry got hooked on baseball. That's not to say there wasn't a very powerful link between Larry and Ed."

"Ed saw a lot of Larry Lucchino in himself—a good, tough negotiator, a good lawyer," says Jay Emmett, a longtime friend and former member of the Orioles board. "He emulated Ed. Larry would come back from making the best deal he could make on some contract—television, say—the best he could do, and he'd sit there with Ed, and Ed would say, 'WHAT ARE YOU? THE LITTLE WHIPPING BOY? YOU GAVE AWAY THE FUCKING STORE! YOU LAY DOWN FOR THEM, DIDN'T YOU, LUCCHINO?' Larry could never win."

Was Williams being serious, or just giving Lucchino grief?

"A little of both," Emmett said. "I'll tell you this—Larry is a better negotiator than Ed was. Larry is the best negotiator now that I've ever seen. Larry is brutal and tough."

Too tough, according to some of the people who have had to negotiate with him, as well as some of his employees.

"I never knew Ed Williams," says Bruce Hoffman, the executive director of the Maryland Stadium Authority, the man hired by Belgrad and Schaefer to oversee the actual construction. "But my impression was that he could turn it on and turn it off. Larry can't turn it off. He'll

119

get so angry he'll start shaking. You never know which Larry it'll be. He was a yo-yo. I think it's a shame—I don't think he slows down to enjoy life enough."

More likely, having confronted his mortality face-to-face, Lucchino now has little patience for time wasted. It was said of Williams that on his regular trips to Holy Cross he would needle the administration if he saw no construction equipment on campus; for Williams, time during which nothing was gained was time being lost. Lucchino, likewise, has no tolerance for work done badly, or not at all. Among the Orioles employees his temper is the stuff of legend. His explosions with the Stadium Authority were so frequent that eventually, says Herb Belgrad, they lost whatever effectiveness they might have had.

As far as the daily press is concerned, Lucchino is patronizing at best, insufferable at worst: "He's weaselly with us," says one Baltimore newspaper writer: "He treats us like shit." This is another: "He has one agenda, and that's to make himself look as good as he can. Basically, he was Ed's valet."

"I don't think he means to be sarcastic or demeaning—I think he thinks that's what Ed was like," says a former Baltimore newsman who knew Williams well. "Only, he's not Ed. Ed could pull it off. This guy can't."

But if there are ways in which Larry Lucchino could never measure up to his mentor, there are others in which his talents reach beyond Williams's. It was Lucchino, by all accounts, who fastened onto the notion of building a stadium of distinction from the outset. And if his own training was not in the visual arts, one early episode spells out Lucchino's passion for perfection. It was the week in which he met Richard Ayers.

In the early 1980s, Ayers Saint Gross was selected by the Orioles to develop a tiny two-hundred-square-foot store in Farragut Square in Washington—Williams's first marketing foray into the Washington market after his purchase of the team.

"They put as much critiquing into that little store as they would a stadium," Rich Ayers said one day in his firm's offices atop the Tremont Tower in the center of Baltimore, thirty stories up. "There was a curved wall, and Christ, they were debating about whether the banner should hang here or there. I think Larry's a frustrated architect, to tell you the truth."

Ayers Saint Gross has been Baltimore's premier design architecture firm for more than seventy years: In the last six years they've won twenty-six design awards. For thirty-six years the firm has been designing various buildings at Johns Hopkins. With the sandy hair and the aristocratic look of an archetypal academic architect, Rich Ayers is carrying on his father's tradition. His father founded the firm.

"Anyway, the day before it's supposed to open—there's going to be this big celebration, the O's playing catch—the place is a disaster area. Larry and I are frantically putting together storage containers. We went out afterward to get some beer to bring back, and that cemented our relationship. The store ended up doing a tremendous amount of business.

"And after that, I was on the O's side. I was trustable. That's important to the Orioles. They let very few people into the inner circle. My relationship with Larry and his relationship with Williams always kept us in good stead with the O's. So HOK always felt it'd be better to stick with us."

Whoever the architect would be—HOK or HNTB or Skidmore, Owings Merrill—the Orioles would likely ask a local firm to join their team. An HOK-ASG alliance would have been a natural, after HOK's work on the Arena—except that Ayers was Lucchino's friend, and Lucchino didn't like HOK.

In the spring and summer of 1987, while the courts took their time deciding the fate of the antistadium petitions and the process was paralyzed, Lucchino decided he had to get things moving. He opened up an informal competition, with Belgrad's blessing, and invited various firms to come to Baltimore and pitch their ideas. For free. This was not unusual in an economic climate in which architects find themselves jumping through hoops to get a tiny commission, in a recession so severe that a firm would gladly pay three times as much to get a twenty-five-thousand-dollar job. Every firm now has a full-time marketing department. In a recent competition for a biotech complex in Maryland, ninety firms submitted requests to be interviewed, and twenty were invited to submit; three were chosen for the final design competition.

For the Orioles' informal audience, HOK sent Joe Spear to town. When he arrived at the Orioles' office for his presentation in the summer of 1987, he was surprised to see Richard Ayers sitting next to Larry Lucchino. Ostensibly, one would have expected the Orioles to be impartial: Ayers would eventually be allied with one of the firms parading in front of Lucchino. By having his pal at his side, Lucchino was saying up front that in his own mind, he had already selected Ayers—and, by inference, whichever firm Ayers would ultimately ally himself with. This was not good news for HOK.

Spear and Deflon held no illusions about what they were up against. After two years of doing advance work for the state of Maryland, they knew that HOK had put itself in an untenable position. On the one hand, HOK could never get out from under Lucchino's assumption that HOK was representing Belgrad and the interests of the state, and that anyone working for HOK couldn't possibly be a design architect—although, in Joe Spear's case, this was quite wrong.

On the other hand, if HOK began to try to entice the Orioles with promises of a sumptuous palace—a fancy stadium club, a steel superstructure, rich and distinctive detail—the Authority might be less likely to support HOK when it came time to choose an official architect. Belgrad, committed to an above-board selection process, had made it clear that all of HOK's prior work for the Authority counted for nothing when it came time to design the park itself. They'd have to earn that job on their merits. But the phrase *our architects* had already been uttered by officials of the Stadium Authority.

"There was distrust of us on the Orioles' part," says Rick Deflon, who parted ways with HOK in 1991 and now works for another firm, Ellerbee-Beckett. Deflon was the vice president in charge of getting HOK the Camden Yards contract. Depending on whom you talk to, Deflon had either a great deal or nothing at all to do with the design of Camden Yards. But all agree he was part of the all-important acquisition process.

"We became a little piece of the negotiations with the Orioles and the MSA. The O's were knee deep in getting what they wanted and Larry may have felt we were the MSA's architects, and not looking out for their interests ... and [would just] do what the MSA wanted. Which is not true."

"We got ourselves in a very horrible position at the beginning," Joe Spear would recall one day in Kansas City. "When the Stadium Authority was trying to get it through that initial honeymoon session of Schaefer's first legislature in the fall of '86, we'd been asked if we could build two stadiums for one hundred twenty million dollars— very spartan—and we said yes, we could. We weren't sure the Orioles would sign a lease, but we could. They approved a seventy-four-million-dollar construction budget for a baseball stadium. In the course of all of this, we expressed concern. We knew the Orioles were expecting more. We were fearful. And that's how we got ourselves into the role of the bad guys who were trying to build a facility that was less than it should be.

"But we were obviously concerned about shooting ourselves in the foot with the Stadium Authority. We hadn't been accepted yet. So we were obviously in a very uncomfortable position. We were trying to not arm the Orioles with a lot of negotiating tools when they did, in fact, finally sit down with the MSA. We were being asked some very specific questions by the MSA—[but still] had not gotten the job.

"We didn't show a steel structure because we thought it was cheaper to do concrete. We didn't show a building that was wildly asymmetrical because we thought it'd be more costly. So we had created a crude set of drawings about the spartan stadium. The Orioles invited us to look at the issue without constraints. But we still couldn't divorce ourselves from the Stadium Authority. They were watching everything we showed to the Orioles."

In fact, Spear concedes, "All of this was extremely painful to go through. Because of the circumstances—I was coming off Pilot Field with an open relationship with the owner, and [a mutual desire] to see it become a project that literally turned the city around."

Now you may like Pilot Field, and you may not. The purists don't. "HOK had the gall to say that Pilot Field was modelled after Ebbets Field," architecture critic and consultant John Pastier says. "Basically it's got a cute roof. The stuff on Pilot is bad postmodernism. Not done with the kind of wit good architects would build. Crude and simplistic. Terribly inadequate. It's insulting."

Buffalo, on the other hand, likes it just fine. And what it likes most are the crowds it now attracts. Buffalo hadn't had a ballpark to speak of since—well, ever. War Memorial, the ungainly fortress that had housed its Eastern league franchise for so many years, was never featured in anyone's architectural annals until it was chosen for the home park in *The Natural*. Soon after filming was finished, the park was razed.

But when the city decided to build a ballpark downtown, as part of an overall effort to get that once-proud port town back on its feet, HOK got the call. And while it is true that Buffalo had some say about the way Pilot turned out, Joe Spear wants it made perfectly clear that his role in Buffalo was substantial, and real—his pen acted of its own accord on this one. The hubbub in Buffalo about HOK coming in and trying to fob another flying saucer off on the city fathers, he says, was quite overblown.

Joe Spear grows weary of all this talk of HOK's aesthetic ineptitude, and, for all of his self-effacement—he is as genuinely modest a man as you'll ever hope to meet—is quick to clarify his own contributions in Buffalo. Joe Spear, as anyone who knows him will tell you, is often known to whip out his pad and start to sketch. Whatever your definition of an architect, Joe Spear fits it.

"In Buffalo we'd come to the conclusion in advance that any of three plans were possible: a domed stadium for forty thousand, an open-air stadium for forty thousand, and an open-air for twenty thousand," Joe Spear told me. "When we showed up, there were all these articles in the paper about this huge dome we were going to build across from the old post office. Buildings on two sides were on the historic register. So at the first meeting, arms shot up—people were very concerned. They were thinking of Pittsburgh and Philadelphia.

"But we were on similar paths. I remember working over a weekend, after they'd said, 'We want you to think about what we could do with the architecture.' We were thinking of Ebbets Field and Connie Mack. We wanted to convince the people of Buffalo it could be more than a stadium. So I worked over the weekend. I had been drawing a green peaked-roof building over the weekend. Then the mayor's director of economic development called me on Monday morning and said, 'You know, we have to pick up on the old theme.'

"Well, the hair stood up on the back of my neck. It was an eerie feeling."

I had met Spear in the foyer of the Sports Facilities Group of Hellmuth Obata Kassabaum; the room is adorned with helmets from all of the NFL and Major League teams for which the HOK Sports Facilities Group has done stadium work—which, according to the helmets, is just about everyone. The wall is adorned by a picture of San Diego Jack Murphy Stadium at halftime of the Super Bowl. A field-sized American flag is visible.

A model of the multipurpose stadium HOK first designed for Baltimore sat in the lobby.

Joe Spear had come out wearing a blue blazer. In his left lapel was an HOK pin. Among his office decorations was a baseball cap with the legend PIGEON BUSTERS on the crest, sent by a company that designs products to keep pigeons from fouling steel girders. It is not, it is true, the kind of accessory you'd have expected to see on, say, Walter Gropius's shelf, but then, Joe Spear never pretended to be Walter Gropius. Besides, how much did Walter Gropius ever actually build?

"All of my clients are public clients," Joe Spear said. "And, by virtue of that, you don't have the opportunity to come in and be an unbending artist."

It is an unusual avocation in this respect: The architect is artist, but more beholden to his client than virtually any other artisan. The architect must subsume the purity of his art not only to the wishes of his client, but the mandates of physical laws that govern just how a building stands and functions. A stadium comes with an even more stringent set of requirements; its parameters are as rigid as any building built. It must hold forty-six thousand people, and give them the best possible view of the playing field, which makes experimentation on any scale other than the miniscule an absolute impossibility.

"I've heard famous architects say, 'I don't design to a budget,' " Joe Spear said. "Well, I'd only say that once in this business."

And the budget was paramount in Baltimore. It dictated HOK's approach even when the Orioles told them not to worry about it.

Of the three firms making presentations in the summer of '87, the real long shot was Skidmore, Owings Merrill, which had built the Metrodome and Oakland–Alameda County Coliseum—neither design likely to give SOM much credence with Lucchino. In fact, SOM came in with some wild designs, as Richard Ayers recalls: "SOM came across as being the academics. They presented a seven-tiered stadium. It was absurd, but they showed it anyway. Intellectually, they felt they had to."

(Curiously, this was not the most futuristic proposal ever made for the site. As far back as 1967, Jerold Hoffberger, in concert with Carroll Rosenbloom, had commissioned his friend Bo MacEwen to draw a stadium for the exact same site. The result was a wild and fanciful plan that, had it been built, would have drastically and radically altered Baltimore's urban profile for all time. It had the world's first retractable dome, soaring arches, curving concrete planes. Another feature was a huge replay scoreboard—unheard of at the time. It was, in fact, quite stunning. It would have done for Baltimore what the Opera House has done for Sydney. Sort of.

"The stadium at Camden Yards," MacEwen says now, "was a four-martini job."

That doesn't mean Bo drew it after four martinis—not literally. Bo liked to categorize his ideas in terms of their creativity along a martini scale. One-martini was sparse. Two-martini showed some artistic integrity. Three-martini was a plan that probably wouldn't fly with the client, overfull as it was with frilleries and flights of aesthetic fancy.

Camden Yards '67 was a four-martini job.)

Back in the real world, the only two serious players were HOK, which held so many cards, and HNTB.

On the side, Lucchino had asked for Richard Ayers's advice. They can both give you a good job, Ayers said. But his own preference was to lean toward HNTB. He trusted them more. Ayers realized that his own firm had to finally make a decision; HOK was being simultaneously solicitous and standoffish, wanting to stay on Ayers's good side but not wanting to give away too many of their own ideas, lest

Ayers Saint Gross would decide to go with HNTB—which is exactly what they did, over the objections of Adam Gross, Ayers's partner.

"Adam said, 'Let's go with HOK,'" Ayers recalls. "I said, 'Yeah, we can get the commission, but hate ourselves in the morning.'"

According to Christ Delaporte, Belgrad's assistant on the Stadium Authority, HOK did not want to ally itself with any Baltimore architects at all. They felt there was no need; they'd built stadiums in cities before. But at the Stadium Authority's suggestion, they took on the Baltimore design firm RTKL Associates, Inc. as a partner, and empowered RTKL to go to work on the master planning—the details of how the stadium itself would fit into the site. Though they are Baltimore's most oft-used firm, RTKL are not known for their artistic prowess.

Ayers Saint Gross and HNTB began work on their presentation. Ayers had a bad feeling from the start. HNTB was not giving it their all, he felt. They seemed to be lacking enthusiasm for stadium work. In fact, of the three ballparks being built after Camden Yards, HNTB landed only Texas.

On September 8, 1987, the highest court of appeals in the state cast its overwhelming vote, 6–1: the petitions to challenge the sports authority and put the stadium on a referendum were invalid. The private citizens of Maryland, said the jurists, had no power to challenge the expenditure of funds. In essence, in siding with the state and against the opposition, the appeals court decided that the bill funding the stadium authority was an appropriations bill—like a tax bill. In other words, the court ruled that the stadium funding was a necessity to maintain the operation of the state. The governor, of course, agreed wholeheartedly with the interpretation, even if some of his constituents—those without jobs, those trying to learn in a Baltimore school system that ranked among the nation's lowest in reading test scores—did not see a ballpark as a necessary ingredient of state government.

With that final ruling, the door was opened. The stadium would be a reality. That left two things to be immediately resolved: the selection of an architect, and the signing of a long-term lease with the Orioles. These were not independent actions, and between them lay all of the important factors that kept Camden Yards from becoming another Comiskey.

THE WAREHOUSE

◆

ON A FEW DETAILS about the park, Larry Lucchino and Herb Belgrad agreed: The park was to feature sky and grass. The rest of the aesthetic detail was still up in the air.

Clearly, one issue had to be addressed as quickly as possible: the warehouse. HOK's initial presentations had not included a warehouse. Nor had Richard Ayers's first ideas, shared with his friend Lucchino.

Both HOK and Ayers Saint Gross, in retrospect, suggest that this was not so much an aesthetic decision on their own as it was a response to a clear signal from the Orioles that they didn't want the warehouse.

"As I recall," Rick Deflon says now, "there was a lot of opposition to the [warehouse] . . . from Lucchino: 'No way. This is stupid. You don't want this ugly old building.'"

Joe Spear: "I remember we did have to spend a good deal of time with them on the warehouse issue. They never came out and said it should be torn down. . . . It was more a case of the Orioles saying, 'You want to save the warehouse?' We did a whole study of keeping it and a whole study of removing it."

In the fall the Maryland Stadium Authority had sent out to the finalists a twenty-two-page document outlining the Authority's desire to have an old-style stadium. The document was produced with help from the Orioles. It included the request from the Authority and the team that prospective architects think asymetrically.

As Deflon remembers it, the HOK team responded to that

document by holing up in a Baltimore hotel where, according to Deflon, it was he who hit upon the idea of saving the warehouse.

"The thing I feel most responsible for," Rick Deflon says now, without being asked, "is saving the warehouse. And I feel responsible for leading the site selection to that site."

Deflon was one of the authors of the original twenty-two-site study, and had a right to feel proud—except that the Camden Yards site had been considered by Hoffberger and Rosenbloom in the sixties, by Bill Veeck in the seventies, and again in August 1980 when Schaefer had suggested it to Williams in Williams's box during the Yankees series that drew a quarter of a million people. Deflon had been unaware of the previous plans for a park. But on the subject of the warehouse he is clear and emphatic.

"The warehouse," Deflon said, "was a building that was a problem. We had a site that was right for access and availability. We thought, 'If we could bend [the warehouse] and build seats it'd be a great ballpark. We were already doing Pilot Field. One night, at our hotel in Baltimore, there was talk of return to the past, and Comiskey was starting to be that."

Still, what would have changed the thinking of Lucchino, who had opposed the building? Renovation could be costly. Fire codes would make it difficult. Previous attempts at renovation had fallen by the wayside. And invoking Comiskey would hardly be effective. Deflon continued:

"The reason the warehouse was to be kept was twofold: It appeared to me we could take some space into the warehouse to save money. And asymetry? Here's a way. It went from, 'Gee, we got to tear it down,' to 'Here's two reasons to keep it.'

"Also, at about that time, there was this young guy floating an idea," Deflon volunteered. "The Orioles were excited about it. He may have had the warehouse shown in his model."

Was his name Eric Moss?

"Yes."

This was a gracious concession by Deflon. The only principal in this entire tale whose design for the park started with the warehouse was Eric Moss. And history has done its best to wipe his breakthrough plan off its pages.

It was hardly a notion without precedent—a warehouse in the outfield of a baseball park. In the Huntington Avenue Grounds, home of the Boston Pilgrims from 1901 to 1911—before they became known as the Boston Red Sox—the eight-story Boston Storage Warehouse watched the game from just outside the park, down the left-field line. More recently, a brick warehouse peered over the left-field fence of Baker Bowl in Philadelphia, home of the Phillies until 1938.

If they wanted an old-style park—and from the beginning, Lucchino insisted on that—it was necessary for the new stadium to be familiar with the brick-skinned textures of America's machine age. Most of the old parks were true to the industrial rub of their cities. A home run out of Sportsman's Park could break the window of the car dealer across the street; a foul ball out of Comiskey could carom off the Southern Illinois tracks, travelled by endless freights whose lowing lent a sweetly mournful counterpoint to the buzz of the White Sox crowds. In the old Yankee Stadium, the blue-steel screech of the Number 4 train lumbering from right to center filled the grandstands with the ozone smell of the rails. In Exposition Park in Pittsburgh, home of the Pirates and Burghers and Rebels, the diamond furnished the full panoramic view of bridges woven of cable and steel. (The park on the same site today, named for the three rivers those bridges spanned, is another enclosed featureless shell; from no seat in the house can you see any of the eponymous rivers.)

When the Orioles revealed their intentions to build an old-fashioned-feeling ballpark, keeping the warehouse would have seemed a natural instinct. It was, after all, a landmark of some distinction—nothing less than the longest building on the entire east coast. But when the deal was struck, and Camden Yards was going to become a reality, Lucchino didn't want it. Three years later, in an apparent effort to rewrite history, he handed out to the press a mimeographed question-and-answer session with himself that included the question, "Why did the Orioles want to retain the B&O warehouse?"

At the time, however, according to several sources, he wanted it removed.

The real question is, did *anybody* want to retain it?

The architects had several plans at the ready, but none of them showed a warehouse. The city's most influential and high-visibility sports columnist, John Steadman, mounted a loud and persistent campaign to knock it down. The mayor-turned-governor—the man who found the site and fought for it for a decade—assumed it would be torn down. And why not? After all, the railroad had intended to tear it down for years.

As for the people of Baltimore, well, most of them had never even seen it. Until the I-395 extension was finished, the most-used entrance to the city from the South was farther west, onto Russell Street, from which the warehouse was hardly visible.

In truth, no one cared about it. The warehouse—so oddly disproportioned and squat, so antithetical to the new harborcity, with its glass-and-steel miasma of a downtown profile—was like the other ingredients of Baltimore's once-delightfully eccentric skyline, fine for the legend, but not right for the new age.

Captain Emerson's Tower, for instance, had a seventeen-ton replica of a Bromo-Seltzer bottle on top of it, lit by six hundred lights—a steel sculpture to make any pop artist proud. It was ten thousand times bigger than the bottle you could buy for ten cents at the pharmacy. Captain Emerson, the chemist, had named his remedy for an active volcano in Java. The tower could be seen twenty miles at sea. They tore the bottle down in 1936, and pummeled it into scrap. Then they tore down most of the building, so that now just the tower stands, with no bottle, awkward and alone.

At least it's still standing. The McCormick Spice building isn't. It used to be the building that kept the harbor in scale. At some point in the city's history it had been decreed that no buildings on the harbor should be taller than the McCormick Spice building—until it was torn down. Now it's been replaced by a park, peopled at night by the homeless, a terrifying border between the evening glitter of

Harborplace and the rest of downtown, which hollows out each day at five.

Farther up Charles Street, the Washington Monument stands tall, but, after all, not very tall; when citizens of other states hear about the Washington Monument, they don't think of Baltimore's.

And who could forget the building with the RCA Dog on the top? Everyone, apparently. A man in Virginia bought the dog, legend has it; there doesn't seem to be a record of it. There's no trace of it—or the McCormick Spice building—in *Bygone Baltimore,* the official coffee-table pictorial record of the old days.

Then again, the book makes no mention, and shows no piece of, Camden Warehouse. Truth be told, the passing of the warehouse would have provoked little concern—no more than, say, the passing of Mister Diz. (Mister Diz was known around town as a greeter, to just about anything you might show up at. He was a man of particularly Baltimorean stripe, an odd figure who used to show up at parades selling balloons, or parking cars free-lance at Orioles games, or leading you to hog-calling contests—the last good vestige of the Guys and Dolls aura the town used to strut.) But without the warehouse, they would have been left with a nice ballpark just trying to look old, asymetrical when it didn't have to be, at the expense of bad sightlines for several thousand fans.

With the warehouse, though, Camden Yards is something more than a paean to the old; it *is* old. The oldest ballpark in America, as well as its newest.

With the warehouse, the beauty of the ballpark's steel-and-brick confines has a context. It's the 'house that makes Camden Yards a home.

It was finished in 1905, the year that White Star began planning the Titanic, and they had much in common—long, lean, horizontal, massive beyond human scale—with this difference: While the warehouse was as tall as the luxury liner, it was 230 feet longer. It was eight stories high, big enough to store one thousand boxcars full of merchandise: four hundred thirty thousand square feet of floor, elevators to hoist five tons. The center of each wooden floor was pierced by a huge, twisting iron chute that resembled a massive, oversized corkscrew, or a twisting child's slide—down which the crates would tumble to the loading docks below.

It was a goliath, built for an era in which architects had not yet comfortably turned to the vertical, a time when greatness was still measured by mass, and engineering feats were judged by bulk. It was huge and impassive, as indifferent as nature itself, until you looked at it closely and discovered that it was full of subtle touches, from the arches set into the wall up on the third floor down to the rusticated stone base—a symbol of strength and solidity and permanence in the architecture of the time. It was distinctive to the trained eye, but not unusual; any architect designing a building of such stature in the 1890s, even one as functional as a railroad warehouse, would adorn it with design touches, although the designer was likely an in-house architect whose name history has declined to reveal.

Baltimore needed the warehouse. The city of Baltimore had had a rough decade. The depression of 1896 brought on by the Democrats' Free Silver scare had sent the B&O into receivership, and the railroad had to sell 40 percent of its stock to the hated Pennsylvania.

Then, on the night of February 6, fire wiped out half of downtown. Like just about everything else that has happened in Baltimore, somebody always did it bigger and fancier, and that went for the Baltimore Fire, too. Chicago's blaze took the press. But Baltimore's inferno ripped out its architectural heritage: One of its most promising industries in the final decade of the nineteenth century—and one of its distinctions known nationwide, although not quite as prominently as Wee Willie Keeler's National League champion Orioles—was its cast-iron building business. Not only was the city taking on a dramatic and significant cast-iron look, but the city's foundries had gained global acclaim, and were shipping building fronts as far away as the state of Washington—until the fire.

So the completion of the warehouse was no small thing. Rising just a few blocks from the grand old red brick B&O roundhouse, which rose above the tenements in Pigtown a few blocks away in 1883 as a repair shop for the passenger cars, the warehouse became the first thing that passengers coming up from Washington—and the rest of the South, and the West—would see: a giant, red-brick dock to usher them into town, pointing South, the city's natural orientation.

It was the greeter. It was a Diz kind of place.

It was a merchandise storage building, a classic railroad warehouse, just bigger. The boxcars were stacked on sidings five deep to the east, and on the west side, on Eutaw Street, the trucks would root at the loading docks before departing for points north. Or workers would cart the stuff a few feet to the B&O track that ran up the spine of Eutaw, to intersect with the tracks on Pratt. Lexington and Howard had always been the commercial hub of the city, a half-mile up the hill, and now, with the warehouse anchoring the scene down below, the neighborhood west of the harbor was a beehive. In the early years, receipts from the warehouse could be used to borrow money anywhere in the city. In the first quarter of the century, the Camden Yards were as busy as Camden Station, which had been, for fifty years, the hub of railroad America.

The warehouse's usefulness outlived the station's, but not by too many years. Its commercial heyday was the fifties. "Here we have everything from toothpicks to refrigerators, from dried coconuts from the Philippines to artificial snow bound for the Hawaiian Islands," manager C. M. Wrightson told the B&O monthly magazine for the October 1957 issue, as he led the railroad's in-house reporter through each bay—household appliances in A, paper products in B, down to E, where they stored the Christmas ornaments fifty weeks a year.

Clearly, its architecture was not Camden Warehouse's main attraction—not to the railroad, anyway. The cover of the magazine depicts several employees standing in front of a wall of brick. There is no effort to convey its size or its look or its impact on the city's texture.

In the sixties, the C&O and B&O affiliated, with the C&O taking control of the B&O's stock. In the seventies, they merged with the Western Maryland to become the Chessie System. Then the Chessie System merged with the Seaboard Railroad to make the CSX, and by the mid-eighties, CSX started making changes. Track was abandoned, jobs lost. Finally, in 1988, the CSX pulled its corporate headquarters out of Baltimore, in favor of Jacksonville.

In 1976 the president of the B&O suggested selling off the

warehouse. In 1978 it was suggested the railroad donate the place outright to the city for an industrial museum. In 1979, the Oliver T. Carr Co. proposed developing Camden Station Inner Harbor West—the warehouse to be converted "into residential units." It never happened. Washington developer Morton Mack bought it, but never developed it. He would sell it to the state for $11 million.

"There wasn't much you could do with it," said Hays T. Watkins, the president of the C&O, now retired. "To the railroad it was just another piece of property. We tried to develop it. But a building that big is just not very adaptable."

Hays T. Watkins never met Eric Moss.

Eric Moss's name is nowhere to be found on any official documents pertaining to the construction of Camden Yards. But Eric Moss deserves as much credit as anyone for saving the warehouse. Probably more.

"When I hear someone now saying something like, 'Paul Newman stole my recipe,' I begin to understand," Eric Moss said one day over lunch. "I feel a little violated."

Moss had arrived at lunch with his portfolio. When he opened the book, the first page revealed not a plan for the stadium, or a picture of his model for the park, or even a sketch of his warehouse. The first thing in Eric Moss's portfolio was a slightly out-of-focus black-and-white picture of a kid pitching in a Little League game.

"I was eleven. We had three pitchers who were twelve, so I hadn't pitched all year. I gave up a huge home run. But we won, seven to two."

He said this with a smile, the same smile everyone uses when they're talking about the way they used to be really good athletes, except that on Eric Moss's face it's a little startling, because he has this round face that hasn't really aged in the twenty years that have elapsed since that city championship game, so it's as if the kid himself is talking to you. There's a tangible wistfulness to the smile, though. Moss took his baseball very seriously as a kid. So did his dad, the sculptor, himself a former semipro catcher. Moss's dad taught his son such a serious curveball, in fact, that Moss can recall vividly the day his father climbed out of the stands and pinned the umpire against the backstop after the official had called a ball on an Eric Moss curve that broke so sharply it knocked the batter on his backside.

"How can I call it a strike," said the umpire, "when it knocked the kid down?"

Whereupon the father grabbed the umpire by the lapels and pushed him up against the backstop.

"So my dad says, 'If they're strikes,' " Eric Moss remembered, " 'call 'em strikes.' " And he laughed at the memory.

"The next year, when the family moved to Delaware, I stayed behind and lived with the catcher so I could finish out the season and pitch in the all-star game. I was the MVP. I got a signed ball from everyone. Then, when I was thirteen, before the season started, I fell off my neighbor's bike and fractured my skull. I was out for twenty-four hours. I missed the last eight weeks of school. I couldn't play baseball after that. The doctor didn't think I should be getting hit in the head with baseballs."

Moss's voice drifted off, and the echo of his words made it eminently clear that, in the big scheme of things, not getting credit for the warehouse may in the long run have been no worse than not being able to reach the major leagues.

"Oh, no question," he said.

Then again, not getting credit for the warehouse, not getting credit for anything—that was pretty tough.

"I don't know if anything was legally incorrect," he said. "I do know that I came to town with something of potentially considerable value, and didn't know what to do with it. I always wonder if I could have profited better. I feel like . . . a lot of people saved it . . . but I don't think there's a single category I can be cut out of.

"And there's a certain pride in knowing that my ideas changed the direction of the stadium."

Eric Moss has always had an eye for stadiums; when he was a young child in his father's sculpture studio on the campus in West Virginia, he'd lean out of the studio on a Saturday afternoon, and, through the trees, he could glimpse Mountaineer Stadium, hearing the ebbs and flows of the cheering, the waterfall-rush of sound when the home team scored a touchdown. After the family moved to Delaware, the father would drive his sons up to Veterans Stadium in Philadelphia for baseball, and Eric remembers nothing particularly wrong with it; it was odd in tone and color, yes—the green of the carpet was no color that occurs in nature, the red rubber warning track a most peculiar skin indeed—and in its empty reaches, sounds echoed eerily. But it was baseball.

In the five-year architecture program at the University of Syracuse, Moss remembers all too vividly his first basketball game in the cavernous precast-concrete carapace of the Carrier Dome. He remembers climbing to the top of the bowl and taking his seat, far behind the large curtain that slices the place in half for basketball games. To see the basket, he had to stand.

In Italy for his junior year, searching for a thesis topic, Moss toured the Colosseum, and first thought of designing a football stadium. But the notion was somehow not intriguing enough. For football the field requirements are specific.

But right after he came back to the States in the early summer of 1986 he saw his first baseball game at Fenway, and something clicked. For baseball, he reasoned, only the infield is absolute. Foul ground and the outfield can be manipulated.

"Fenway was perfect! Because in our school we were taught primarily urban projects—how to respond to an urban condition. Here was Fenway, which due to a site pressure of having a road too close to home plate, built this tall wall, and that became the thing that made it place specific. Then you stop and think about Philadelphia for a second. There's no site response. It's just a machine to get people in and out as quick as you can."

Moss decided to design his own urban ballpark. But he needed a location. A friend from Washington told him they were going to build a ballpark in Baltimore. So Moss called a classmate working for Ayers Saint Gross, who told him to come down and drop by the offices.

"I pull into Baltimore off of 395 and I see the B&O warehouse," Moss recalled. "And I think, 'Aldo Rossi, eat your heart out.' Long bar, very repetitive, very strong urban condition. Here is the urban condition to respond to. What could be better? It's downtown, near the harbor. What could be more perfect? I admired it, and kept driving."

When he reached the offices of Ayers Saint Gross, Moss was told that Hellmuth Obata Kassabaum had done a feasability study for the city just a few months earlier—HOK's five-pound, twenty-two-site tome. He examined the document and was delighted and surprised to discover that one of the sites adjoined the warehouse. Whereupon Eric Moss went back to the University of Syracuse and closed his door. For the entire school year. When he came out he had a model of a baseball stadium in Baltimore built around a warehouse.

And one day in June, along with the other two-dozen fifth-year students, Moss mounted his project for presentation down in the auditorium. He was up in the studio when a friend told him of a man down in the auditorium "going crazy when he saw your stuff. He couldn't believe it." Moss went downstairs and saw a tall man scrutinizing the model, admiring its numerous startling details: the gentle slope of the seats, the discreetly tucked-away luxury boxes, the height of the place—not a foot higher than the warehouse—except for the delightfully bold radio tower, a salute to the game's radio history, with its scoreboard to broadcast the score to the city without.

And the warehouse. In the model on stage, right field lapped up right against the wall of the warehouse, which had a restaurant sunk into it so that diners would look right out onto the field.

The field was asymetrical. The landscaping reached out to the adjoining neighborhood of Ridgely's Delight.

Eric Moss approached the man.

"Hi," Adam Gross said, offering a handshake. "Put these plans under your arm. We're going to fly you down to Baltimore. You're going to work for us."

Adam Gross of Ayers Saint Gross had also earned his architecture degree at Syracuse. When he was asked to serve on the jury for the class of 1987, the last thing he'd expected, up in New York State's Leatherstocking region, was to come across plans for a baseball park in Baltimore.

Eric Moss flew down a few days later, stunned and flattered, with his plans rolled up under his arms. He left his plans with Ayers Saint Gross.

*   *   *

In the meantime, some of Lucchino's informal presentations were not being held in the Orioles offices. They were held in the offices of Ayers Saint Gross. When that happened, Richard Ayers recalls, he and Gross hid Moss's model—not just so the big firms couldn't steal the thing, but also because Ayers didn't want the Orioles to see it. Adam Gross loved it. Ayers, though, loved the idea of his firm getting the project even more. And Lucchino, according to several sources, didn't want a warehouse as part of his ballpark.

"Truthfully, it was a radical idea when I came down, to keep the warehouse," says Moss. "There were times when the firm didn't want to be associated with it. They did not want to alienate themselves from the O's who . . . did not want the warehouse.

"Adam had me present it to Richard, who was going to give the O's what they wanted. He was upset because he'd be fighting with Adam. Here was something contrary to what the O's wanted. They waited until I left the room to sort out their differences.

"They had their own politicking. They made presentations without my being there. There were other times it was considered politically correct for me to be there."

Eric Moss recalls being asked to present it to Herb Belgrad. He recalls being asked to present it to Larry Lucchino.

Adam Gross then threw a new ingredient into the gumbo. He went to Eric Garland, the writer for *Warfield's*, the city's small but highly respected business magazine, and told him about Moss and Moss's model. In Garland he'd chosen the right man. As a reporter for the *City Paper* in 1979, Eric Garland had covered the World Series—with considerable delight—and to this day owns the pair of spikes that Bill Robinson of the Pirates wore in the seventh game; in the chaos of the winning locker room, Robinson just gave them to him. Garland cherishes them.

Garland likes baseball. He loved Eric Moss's model. And he wrote about it—with an accompanying photograph—in the August 1987 issue of the magazine: "A highly original and inviting model of a baseball stadium—with the B&O warehouse forming the right-field wall . . . engaging the city" is how Garland described it.

Three months later, with the final design competition still two months off, Ed Gunts, the highly regarded architecture critic of the *Sun*, did a story on Eric Moss's model. He praised it to the hilt.

Twelve days later, the *Sun*'s editorial page echoed him—with an editorial entitled "A True Baltimore Stadium." The paper had embraced everything about Eric Moss's concept. The editorial was accompanied by a photograph of Moss's model. It bore little relation to the drawings and models that HOK and HNTB had provided.

Moss went on the radio and talked. He talked on sports radio. He talked on the local public-broadcasting affiliate. Although he had been hired in September by Ayers Saint Gross, he was not mentioning the firm.

"And all of a sudden I was being asked by Adam, 'Why aren't you talking about our firm?' I knew I'd arrived when early morning deejays were mocking it, guys making jokes about what a stupid idea it was to have a warehouse near a baseball stadium."

In December, in his look back at architecture in Baltimore in 1987, Ed Gunts cited Moss's model as one of the highlights of the architectural year, for keeping Baltimore in Baltimore—even though no one had been selected to design the park yet.

In January 1988 *Baltimore Magazine* featured Eric Moss and his warehouse.

It was a heady time for Moss. The last heady time—because his idea now belonged to everyone.

For two days in late January 1988, in a suite at the Omni downtown a blue-ribbon panel—Lucchino; Carmen Turner of the Washington, D.C. Metro system; Jay Brodie, the former director of planning for the city, and then chairman of the Pennsylvania Avenue Redevelopment Agency; and Walter Sondheim, a prominent Baltimore businessman—heard presentations from the prospective architects. They ranged from the amusing and the fanciful to the tedious.

On the former end was John Burghee, representing himself and Philip Johnson. Burghee came in unencumbered by models or plans, and sketched his ideas for the group. The mundane end of the scale was represented by the Bechtel Corporation, best known for being Peter Ueberroth's in-house architects; during the Ueberroth days, anyone planning to build a stadium could call the offices of Major League Baseball and get a set of the Bechtel plans.

Lucchino found himself shaking his head as HOK came in with their plumb lines and their pedestrian ramps. He was impressed by Robert Pederson, who spoke at length of the need for urban design. Everyone was.

HOK's model showed a symmetrical park. With outside ramps. Concrete ramps. And half a warehouse.

The team of HNTB and ASG and Alex Cooper showed a symmetrical park with a gracious and stunning series of parks and plazas leading from downtown into the park. The warehouse was kept.

Between the various presentations, Lucchino found himself raising his famed temper in the direction of the now-deceased Turner, the D.C. metro expert who had never seen a game in Memorial Stadium. She was concerned that Lucchino's assemblage of all-stars would not be able to work as a team. Lucchino, as is his style, let her know what he thought of that fear—in no uncertain terms.

But it was all too clear that Lucchino was fighting a losing battle. For all of the glitter on their own team, Ayers recalls, HNTB had not been as aggressive as he'd hoped they would: "They didn't put in the kind of effort we expected." HOK's bulky résumé, their past history with the city, and above all, their reputation for coming in on time and under budget, were clearly swaying the panel.

Furthermore, a key minority engineering firm, Delon Hampton from Washington signed on with the HOK team.

After the first day of presentations, Lucchino knew his all-star team wouldn't make it.

"Larry said to Ed, 'We're in a bind,'" Ayers said. "Ed said, 'Go with what you think.' Larry held out for everything he could get out of the group."

HOK won. The papers reported a 4–0 vote. In fact, it was 3–1.

His philosophy of "save only what we need," is how Deflon defended the decision to knock down the south half of the warehouse.

"I was the leader of the orchestra," Rick Deflon told me, when I asked him about who should get credit in the end. "Joe [Spear] was a technician who had a solo."

"He said that?" said Gyo Obata. "The guy [Deflon] was a nut. . . . He was an ornery guy. A nasty guy. And he was not . . . The HOK family tries to work on real teamwork between various offices. He was not a team player. He had a lot of other problems, frankly."

Did he design Baltimore?

"Rick was not a designer. . . . He had really nothing . . . very little to do with Baltimore. He was involved in the contract negotiations for which he was operational guy. After that he didn't have much to do with the project."

Rich Ayers recalled Lucchino's disappointment at the competition: "Afterward, we were sitting at the DH lounge and he said to me, 'I always think how things might have been different with your group.' "

The DH Lounge is not a cloud-scraping haunt of the wealthy and powerful. The DH Lounge is where the Orioles' Designated Hitters relaxed in Memorial. The Designated Hitters are the businessmen who came together in 1980 to persuade people to buy more Orioles' tickets to save the team.

The club was modelled after the Kansas City Royals' ultramidwestern Royal Lancers. It is not the sort of activity you expected Rich Ayers, Ivy League and suspendered, to be part of. But in fact, he is one of the most successful ticket sellers in Memorial and DH history.

"I did it literally out of my love for baseball," Ayers said. "I heard them say they were taking applications, and I figured, you appealed to the nationalistic fervor of Baltimore—here's a Washington lawyer [Williams] with a lot of bucks and an empty stadium."

These days, incidentally, you're likely to find Rich Ayers down in the Eutaw Street concourse, admiring the street at the foot of the warehouse, before he goes into a game. "The greatest public space in America," he'll tell you, enthusiastically, embracing with a sweep of his hand the thousands of nightly strollers and shoppers and browsers and chompers, all milling beneath the waft of Boog's fragrant smoke.

It's an odd exhilaration, Ayers's delight, considering the ultimate resolution: He didn't get the commission. He didn't design a brick of it. Losing the competition, he said, "Broke my heart. A stadium comes along once every twenty years."

How, then, do you reconcile his unabashed delight in the result?

Because Richard Ayers, of course, is a Baltimorean first, an Orioles fan second, and an architect a distant third.

Such is the way in Baltimore.

LEGACIES

◆

THE SIGNING OF THE LEASE was all that remained before planning and construction could begin. Both sides hoped to announce it on Opening Day of 1988.

But the Orioles were in no hurry. By now, Williams saw that they had a chance to build a park that would leave an architectural legacy. His interest in the park's design had increased.

"Dad was very, very concerned," remembers his son, Ned Williams. "He didn't like the ultramodern. He really liked the old-time stuff. He sort of wanted a simple thing. It's hard to call anything that costs that much money simple.

"But he said, 'Build it with a sense of the past.' They wanted a feel for Baltimore. That was the real idea. That you wouldn't be able to take this stadium and put it in Milwaukee. It should be a product of its surroundings. The gist of the conversations was, 'Create one with ambience, and the feeling that you were in a special place.' They wanted a feel for Baltimore. The warehouse and the feel of the city—it was all sort of fortuitous, but that was the real idea.

"He was getting sick at the time. He was so excited about it initially when he thought that he'd be around to enjoy it."

But if his passion waned as his health declined, Williams still had no intention of giving an inch to the state. This was to be his last major negotiation, as both attorney and sports king, and he was not going to go out knowing—in his own mind—that he had been anything less than his hard-nosed best. There were more than thirty meetings.

"[The negotiation] was long and painful," Belgrad recalls. "These were intensive, sometimes aggressive. I make my living as a labor negotiator in the nth hour of strikes, [but] these were the most difficult I've ever been involved in. There were a number of conflicts. Sometimes there were personality problems.

"Williams only appeared about three times—when he did, he was an imposing and controlling figure. Larry has a more bombastic style. He tends to lose control of his temper, more often, more easily. After a while it doesn't have impact. You get used to it. They could be hard-assed because they had the leverage."

"As we got into our negotiations in early 1988 we established for ourselves the opening day of '88 as the day we'd like to announce the lease. That would be a Monday. I had Seder, as did Eugene Feinblatt, our attorney. Lucchino had Easter. In between our services we met in a motel on Route 32. But it became clear we couldn't do it. It was a big, big letdown. When you've set a goal for yourself—well, I was so disheartened I didn't attend the Opening Day reception. We lost our momentum."

On the field, things were even more depressing. The beginning of the 1988 season was a nightmare.

Under the management of Cal Ripken, Sr., 1987 had been no better than Earl Weaver's desultory 1986 farewell. When Weaver left, the city drafted Ripken with a ground swell that Williams could not ignore. He did act in the executive suite, though, relieving his payroll of general manager Peters and farm director Giordano, bringing in Roland Hemond and Doug Melvin, and promoting Frank Robinson to the front office.

Ripken was considered a good teacher but not a good manager. Still, it was not all Ripken's fault that the 1987 season was nearly comic. When Cal Senior took over, he had on hand the likes of Eric Bell, the pride of the farm system—who threw 82 miles per hour. The stopper was Tom Niedenfuer, who gave up home runs to three consecutive batters in one game. The club had an ERA over five—the first time it had happened in baseball in twenty-five years. In one game they gave up ten home runs.

In April 1988, then, when the Orioles lost their first eight games,

Williams axed Cal Ripken, Sr., to the general dismay of the entire state; eight games was a term of unprecedented brevity in baseball. It was a typical play by Williams, who had only months to live and wanted to see results immediately. To no one's surprise he replaced Ripken with Frank Robinson.

The team took a road swing through the Midwest, but even under Robinson they shrugged from town to town—and, to the gathering pity and interest of the nation, continued to lose every game. Roland Hemond took to wearing for luck a rumpled, gray pinstriped suit that had been soaked in champagne and hadn't been washed since the night his White Sox clinched the 1983 Western Division. But still the Orioles lost. Now the national press had hopped on the funeral train, documenting the record. Robinson was, by turns, resigned—this was not his team, and he could not be expected to right it quickly—and furious; after one loss in Kansas City, by a margin of several runs, his yelling could be heard out in the corridor through the thick, closed door of the visitors' clubhouse, loud and pointed enough to make impartial eavesdroppers wither in fear.

The team would lose its first twenty-one games—a major-league record. Four years earlier it had won a Series with remarkable ease. It was one of the quickest descents in modern sporting history. The baseball Orioles were the laughingstock of organized sports.

Back in Baltimore, where both sides were growing desperate for an agreement—anything to counter the horrible performance the city's fans were reading daily in the box scores—momentum picked up: Both sides had decided they might as well aim for a date to give the fans something—anything—to cheer for. The team was due to come home on May 2 for—of all things—Fantastic Fan Night. There was no assurance the team would have even won a game by that point.

Nor were there assurances, as Belgrad and Eugene Feinblatt travelled down the Baltimore-Washington Parkway, that they'd have a lease agreement that night. But this was just the third time Williams had intervened, and his presence heightened the sensation that things would get done.

As Belgrad and Feinblatt sat down in Williams's office, Williams straightened up and buttoned his suit jacket, but he had become so thin that the jacket slipped off his shoulders. He pulled it back on, and they began to talk.

"He cut right to the core," Belgrad recalled. "It was as if he was an arbitrator instead of an interested party."

For once, Williams had reason to give in if necessary. He knew his days were limited. He would not allow himself to die without seeing this accomplished.

Belgrad: "That session ended with us being very close. Close enough that despite the physical effort, Williams himself left for Baltimore around two, so that if an announcement were made he would be there. Arrangements were made for the governor to be there, too."

"We got closer and closer and all of a sudden we came to the realization that it was close to five, and if we didn't get the six o'clock Metroliner we wouldn't be there. We ran for the Metroliner, and when we got to the station, a couple of us stayed upstairs to get our tickets. Feinblatt went down as the train was about to pull out. He physically stood with one foot on the steps and one on the platform so it couldn't pull out."

In the club car they continued to negotiate over *force majeure*. As they pulled into Pennsylvania Station, Lucchino and Feinblatt worked out the agreement, wrote it on the back of the club car menu, and signed it.

Up in Memorial, Williams sat behind his desk in the Orioles' offices. "Larry came in and briefed him," Belgrad said. "I briefed the governor. Williams wanted an announcement made before the game. The governor was opposed. The governor told me over the years in all his dealings with the Orioles every time he thought there'd been an agreement it always turned out there wasn't. He wanted to make sure everything was in writing."

In the tweed coat, his face thin but his eyes alight, Edward Bennett Williams assured William Donald Schaefer, for the final time, that he was an honorable man, and that he would live up to the terms of the agreement.

"Williams always had a dominating influence over the governor," Belgrad said. "And the governor went along."

Williams refused to go onto the field. So Schaefer did. He

announced to the sellout crowd that the Orioles had agreed to a fifteen-year lease to play in a new stadium to be built downtown in Camden Yards.

Memorial Stadium thundered with an ovation more resonant than the cheering it traditionally bestowed on rallies and home runs. It was a rich sound, and a sad one.

In his owners' box, Williams stood and watched, and let it wash over him.

It was the last game Edward Bennett Williams ever saw at Memorial Stadium. He would die two months later and never see the stadium his last negotiations made a reality.

At Larry Lucchino's insistence, the lease agreement that was signed in May incorporated two words that, in retrospect, make every fan of Camden Yards beholden to the Orioles' president and CEO: *Design concurrence.* In other words, no design decision could be made without the Orioles' agreement.

Now the stadium was a reality. The architect was in place. The funding was in place. But all of the specifics were on hold. The owner of the team was near death. The first priority for everyone was finding a new owner.

It did not take long.

At a cocktail party at Ethel Kennedy's house in McLean, Virginia, in early June 1988 Bobby Shriver, a private investor in Manhattan, is talking with his father about the Orioles. R. Sargent Shriver had been a lifelong friend of Ed and Agnes Williams, and it's only natural, two months before Williams's death, that Shriver would be wondering about buying the team.

Also in attendance is Larry Lucchino. Larry's connection to the crowd is twofold: He had once dated Maria Shriver, and he and Bobby Shriver had met when the younger Shriver interned at Williams & Connolly in 1980, and became friends.

That man over there could buy them, Bobby says to his father, pointing to a tall, ungainly fellow, a big guy who sort of looks as if he's listing to one side, with a facial twitch and oddly unstylish glasses.

That's Eli Jacobs, Bobby says. Of Jacobs, Inc. LBO king—leveraged buyouts. He's said to own controlling stock in companies worth $5 billion.

Jacobs is in attendance because he'd known Bobby Kennedy since the latter's term as a U.S. Senator from New York, and, more recently, has been known in Washington circles as a man to whom Ronald Reagan turned to chat about national security issues. National security has been Eli Jacobs's hobby since 1980. Before 1980, it had been architecture.

"Sarge, because of Bobby, went to Ed and said, 'If you ever want to sell I'd like first crack at coming in,' and Ed kind of gave him a commitment," Jay Emmett recalls. "Then Bobby did some negotiating. Eli's guy came in. Bobby introduced Eli to Larry. Agnes came in. There was a major rush. A major rush. Within a month they'd made an offer."

Agnes Williams, EBW's widow, liked the offer, primarily for the presence of Sargent Shriver and Larry Lucchino; now she terms their presence a "definite factor." Agnes Williams had agreed with her husband that she would sell the team, and they would not look for buyers who intended to move it.

Agnes Williams didn't know Eli Jacobs. She had never met him. She had no idea he had a certain passion about architecture. In fact, she didn't meet him until after she'd sold him the team. When she last saw him, at a party at George Will's house before Opening Day at Camden Yards, he talked to her about architecture.

"As we talked," Agnes Williams said, "it became obvious that he had a real passion, an authentic passion for it," she said.

There was an odd symmetry to the closing. Just as a last-minute offer had nearly clouded Jerold Hoffberger's sale of the club to Williams in 1979, this time the late offer came from Hoffberger himself. A decade after his family had convinced him to sell the team, the old brewer's son was now quite anxious to get it back. Determined to keep it from being sold to Jacobs, a Bostonian who spent his professional life shuttling between New York and Washington, Hoffberger began to mobilize a local group. By now, however, the price was not $12 million; by now it would be eight times that amount—$95 million, twenty more than the announced purchase price, according to Bob Flanagan, because of assumed debts.

Hoffberger would later tell the press that Flanagan had not allowed him to bid, and vilified him in the press. Of course, had Hoffberger regained control of the team, Camden Yards would not have resembled Camden Yards.

"It was preposterous," Flanagan said of Hoffberger's explosion. "My approach was to ignore the name-calling. He's respected in the community for what he did.

"But I had a personal commitment from Ueberroth [then baseball commissioner] before and after Ed's death that he'd do everything he could to get it over the political hump. I didn't think I could wait until spring [and Bart Giamatti's regime] and I thought I'd not get the commitment from the new guys.

"I had to get to the winter meetings with a candidate in Atlanta in the first week of December. Hoffberger'd been flirting with the idea. He spent some of his own money to look at it. One of his lawyers spent some time with it. Hoffberger calls me at home the night before Thanksgiving. He said he was going to Israel for a week—with Schaefer—and do I care. I told him, we wanted the offers by Friday. I said, 'You've got forty-eight hours to get something to me.' Monday came and went and we didn't hear. The other problem was he was depending on a plethora of parties as well as Japanese money to pull it off. I didn't think it'd fly."

Hoffberger's complaints notwithstanding, the sale to Eli Jacobs's group was approved. The Orioles had a new owner, one infinitely less compelling than Edward Bennett Williams and far more reclusive, but no less influential in determining the course of the stadium.

"I think Baltimore is the best baseball city in the country. Baseball is more than just baseball in Baltimore. It performs this kind of community function. One ought to find ways to give it a spiritual sense."

This is Eli Jacobs talking in his office in the Seagram Building on Park Avenue in Manhattan. The shades in the window behind his desk are drawn against the snow flurries that, because of the height of his office and some weird air currents in the canyon of Park Avenue office buildings, are drifting upward. He is sitting at his desk eating half of a roasted chicken and a pasta salad.

He had said we should have lunch. We are. A door opened and two of his staff members came through carrying two trays, each bearing half of a chicken and a bowl of pasta salad. The cutlery is silver and very heavy. When I drop a fork onto his desk by mistake, the sound resonates eerily.

In Baltimore media circles, Eli Jacobs has taken on the aura of myth—a strange, quiet, quite-larger-than-life sort of guy. An outsider, capable of acting in fell swoops. In fact, Baltimoreans are largely scared to death of him.

When Major League Baseball told Jacobs that it preferred he have a Maryland residence, Jacobs bought a home for $2 million—the largest sum paid for a house in the entire state that year. When Eric Garland wrote a profile in *Warfield's* suggesting that Jacobs's leveraged-buyout holdings were faltering, Jacobs promptly sued the magazine—whose total assets were in the hundreds of thousands of dollars—for $36 million.

Where Edward Bennett Williams's aura welcomed virtually everyone and anyone into his presence; Eli Jacobs's seems to reject them.

In the lobby of the Seagram Building is The Four Seasons, the power-lunch seat of the city. Eli Jacobs last visited the quiet cavern in 1985. "It's not my style," he says. "And the prices offend me. And you don't find me at the Regency for power breakfasts. That's not my scene. I dine in my office. You have more privacy."

On matters of Orioles finances and leases and business, he defers to Lucchino, which has endeared him very little to the writers. On the subject of his hobbies, though, Eli Jacobs is positively effervescent. *Hobbies* is probably the wrong word. Eli Jacobs attacks his hobbies. After his de rigueur tour of fourteen European countries after completing his education, at Andover, Yale, and Yale Law, one of the first things Eli Jacobs did after moving to New York was to call Philip Johnson and say, "You don't know me, but I'd like to get to know you."

Eli Jacobs does not think it is odd to call up a famous architect out of the blue. Eli Jacobs thinks it's odd not to.

From the moment one enters his office's lobby, it is clear that the way things look matters to the man. It contains a dark-green, rich, leather-upholstered chesterfield sofa. Quarter globes of glass are set into the wall. The floor is marble, of green and black, and graced by oriental rugs.

"Remember the old Savoy Plaza Hotel? There was a great street wall on Fifth Avenue—all the buildings related to each other," he said, his voice rising, between somewhat inelegant bites of his chicken.

"Fifty-ninth Street and up was one of the great blessings to the American skyline! You replace it with the GM building? Highly destructive of the skyline. We were allowing property values to destroy the theater district—an important part of the critical mass that makes New York unique.

"And there was no mechanism to even raise these issues. We asked the city to give consideration to the quality of the architects it chose on public buildings."

Soon after his arrival in the city—having also befriended Mayor John Lindsay and Senator Jacob Javits—Jacobs was asked by William Paley, on Johnson's recommendation, to serve on a panel to discuss the future of New York's architecture. Paley needed Republicans; he already had Johnson and I. M. Pei. Jacobs, of course, had no formal training in architecture. His vocation was, and would always be, the buying and selling of businesses.

"I taught myself," he says. "Not like a serious student of architecture and urban design. But how cities work is self-evident. I've taught myself to hear, too. I've taught myself to hear classical music."

It was New York's Senator Kennedy—"I had known him before," Jacobs says—who asked him to put together a group to study the future of housing in the blighted Bedford-Stuyvesant section of Brooklyn: "I ran the Bed-Stuy project. I was intimately involved in developing Welfare Island. It was my idea to set up the organization to develop it. [President Gerald] Ford appointed me to the Commission on Fine Arts; I went off that in 1980. The last twelve years I've been involved in national security. I knew nothing about it. But make no effort to link them [i.e., architecture and national security]."

This is the way Eli Jacobs talks: There are no random words, and no out-of-place ones. Jacobs, figuratively and literally, means business. It is not hard, after a few hours in his presence, to believe that his net worth is astronomical. On the other hand, it may not be at all, as Garland suggested, and as have a few national business publications since. Jacobs's holdings are private. He wants them to stay that way, along with all details thereof. But at the mention of any of this, at the mention of any of the articles that have attempted to chronicle his current business health, he is quick—and heated—in pointing out that he has sued before, and could quite likely sue again.

All this tends to put the line of questioning back in matters of his stadium, to which, eventually, he added considerable design input.

"I was thinking of the concept of the agora. Where do people convene? The baseball park is the gathering place, the meeting place where fifty thousand people can convene. If you can look at this as a place where everyone convenes, you have to go back to ancient history to see it as a place of bonding.

"Ed and Larry wanted a traditional stadium," Jacobs continues. "Larry's view of a traditional stadium is different than mine. Mine was something that interpreted the great lessons of architectural history— but does it so it's something that has its own integrity. It can't be eclectic. You can't repeat. You have to learn. You have to reinterpret into a new synthesis that points to the future. Don't let the past straitjacket you. Learn what worked then, then create your own expression of that. Be mindful of what went on in the past. But don't take the character of six old stadiums and patch them together. Give some contemporary expression to it."

Jacobs reads ten newspapers a day. His current passion in reading is military history. Ask him if he's reading any twentieth-century novels and he says he's still getting through Tolstoy.

Ask him if the chance to have input in the stadium design was an important part of buying the team.

"It was in the equation. I'd be exaggerating to say it was a critical factor."

But his input was immediate and heavy. Within two months of the agreement to sell to his group, before it had been approved by baseball's owners, Jacobs met with Joe Spear in the Orioles offices in Memorial. Spear revealed his model.

"It sickened me," Eli Jacobs says, with something like a sneer. "It physically sickened me. They unveiled a plan for something that looked like a spaceship. It was clearly not what the doctor ordered. Not what this doctor ordered, anyway.

"Spear turned to me and said, 'What do you think?' expecting me to be some philistine, and sign. I said, 'This won't work. This isn't acceptable.' I walked out of the room.

"Larry came out into the hallway, and I said, 'Larry, I won't insult these people to their faces. But this is totally unacceptable. This is not what I thought the contract [provided] for. I'm going to reject this design.'

"I went back in and said, 'I'm sure that working together we can find a solution that will make us proud.' Spear did not look happy. It was clear to him that I was taking charge of the global design process."

Bruce Hoffman, Belgrad's chief on-site lieutenant, remembers the meeting well.

"Jacobs walked in, and after ten seconds he said he didn't like it. He said it as if he'd been studying it for three months. It took him ten seconds. Someone asked why. He said, 'The upper deck is too steep.' I said to myself, 'My God, how the hell does he know that?' We knew it was too steep. But with a model that small, you can't tell. But he could."

"Eli's passion for architecture," Agnes Williams said—"that certainly turned out to be good for Baltimore, didn't it? That was very fortuitous."

Within weeks of the closing of the sale that gave Jacobs the Orioles in December 1988, the warehouse decision had to be made— immediately. In retrospect, it was fortunate that it was even still standing.

Richard Ayers deserves some of the credit. Eric Moss and Adam Gross had convinced him of the building's value, while, on the HOK side, RTKL's master plan recommended saving the building as well.

("I think what happened," Ayers recalls, "is that [ASG] may have by force of will kept the warehouse issue open. Larry was not convinced at all. I don't think Larry was ever convinced we should save it.")

When Jacobs first saw the warehouse, on a trip to the site before he bought the team, he remembers thinking "it had real possibilities." He recalls telling Lucchino, as Lucchino went off for the meeting with Belgrad at which the final warehouse decision would be made, that the Orioles should be "strongly'" in favor of saving it. Bruce Hoffman attended the meeting, and he confirms that Lucchino had been against saving it: "By then, he'd accepted [the warehouse]. But he knew he was doing something wrong. He didn't know what." Lucchino's instincts were to raze the warehouse, but the negotiator in him knew well enough in this case to let the majority rule. And the majority did want to save it.

Belgrad said he wanted it. Belgrad got it. The warehouse would stand.

"I was responsible for saving the warehouse," Belgrad said later. "Larry said from the beginning that I was the historic preservationist. From the beginning I felt there were two things that had to be saved: the warehouse and the station."

Even Eli Jacobs concurs: "I would give Herb a lot of credit on that."

But what convinced Herb Belgrad, of all people, that the warehouse should be saved?

When the question is posed to Rich Ayers, he smiles. Ayers remembers the conversation he had with Herb Belgrad after Belgrad was privately shown Eric Moss's model in the summer of 1987.

"Belgrad told me it wasn't until he saw Eric's model," Ayers said, "that he was convinced it could work and needed to be saved."

On December 16, 1989, at the opening of a show of stadium models at the Babe Ruth Museum, Janet Marie Smith, the new Orioles vice president in charge of stadium affairs, told the assembled guests that she appreciated all the work that had been done to date by local people in helping them come up with the design.

And the Orioles, she said, would be interested in any more ideas from the public sector.

A few feet away, Eric Moss stood next to his model. He didn't really expect her to mention him, though he would have appreciated it. After all, when Janet Marie Smith came through the ASG offices in 1988 as a friend of Adam Gross, in preparation for an interview with the Orioles, Adam had asked Eric to show her the model. Eager to please, Eric Moss showed her everything he had.

Now he sort of stood there. And stewed.

A couple of people sidled up to his model. One of them said, "That's the stadium scheme that Richard Ayers did."

It's easy enough to understand why the man who'd made the comment was a little disconcerted when the young, baby-faced blond guy a few feet away turned on his heels and shouted, "That's the worst thing you could have ever said!"

"He thought I was crazy," Moss remembers.

Eric Moss's model went on tour with the rest of them. When the tour was over, the model was returned to him. So he hung it on the wall of his apartment. He hung up the plans, too. Eric Moss's apartment became a small shrine. He would sit and look at what he'd done.

On Opening Day, when he saw the stadium on television, he had to turn away. He remembers feeling physically ill and wondering if he'd ever be able to enjoy a game at the park.

Eventually he would. Eventually he would sit behind home plate for a night game and look up at the warehouse, its windows lit, the field lights atop the building making it a workable, tangible part of the park itself.

"A friend of mine," Moss recalled, "said to me, 'I hope you don't end up as a drunk at the end of your life standing outside this place, saying, 'This place is mine! This place is mine!' "

Eric Moss laughed. Sort of.

"[HOK is] now taking credit for the design that wasn't theirs," says Eli Jacobs. "Just as they wanted to give us a replica of the several they've already done. HOK's design record speaks for itself. Let's just say that the original relates to the final design model in a one-hundred-seventy-nine-point-nine-degree change."

At hearing this, Joe Spear sighs.

"I'm sure all of these people—the Orioles and Eli and Ayers—will claim they authorized the design. That they were responsible for HOK not missing the boat," Spear says, in the Savoy Grill in downtown Kansas City. The walls are covered in dark green tiles, heavy and lovely things. The wood trim is dark and rich enough to be ebony. Western paintings evoke Remington, lit in subtle fashion, displayed as if in an art museum. A gas lamp illumines each leathered booth. The waiters wear white coats, each of which sports a metal badge with a number on it; the lower the number, the longer the waiter's service. The Grill has been in operation since the 1920s. The ghost of Harry Truman dines in the very next booth. It was his.

I tell Spear that Rick Deflon has described himself as the man responsible for just about everything.

At this, Spear hesitates. He hates to take credit, he really does.

He toys with his salad. Then he speaks. "I did ninety-five percent of the design. Deflon was the principal in charge of the project. What Rick tended to do was pay more attention to the contractual side, assembling the teams. I've seen him quoted as saying he was the principal architect. The truth is, yes, he was, but in terms of design, the park . . . that was . . . uh . . . that was . . . me."

And the warehouse?

"It'd be hard to pin down who had that idea, to save the warehouse," Joe Spear says. "You talk to the Orioles, they want to say it was all their idea."

Spear sighs.

"I don't know. A good idea is a good idea, isn't it?"

DESIGN CONCURRENCE AND THE WOMAN OF STEEL

◆

SOON AFTER HOK HAD LANDED THE JOB, Larry Lucchino walked into one of the first meetings with HOK carrying a pile of brochures. He dropped them onto the table in front of Joe Spear. Spear glanced at the folders.

They were sales brochures—for Yugos.

"The Orioles don't drive Yugos," Lucchino told Spear, "and we won't play in one."

It was the kind of flair for drama that Ed Williams might have appreciated. But Joe Spear didn't think it was all that clever. Spear had just come off a Pilot Field project free of tension and long on celebration and backslapping, during which just about everything he'd sketched had been built.

Now he found that everything he had drawn was being derided, and not even by the client—by the client's *tenant*. Already, Joe Spear was wondering what it would be like to design Camden Yards with the same cast of characters—without any of the baggage.

And already, Joe Spear was asking himself why he was representing a building that the tenant thought of as a Yugo.

Lucchino was not optimistic about the road ahead. He knew there was going to be an inordinate amount of friction—the selection contest had driven that home. He'd presented some of the best designers and architects from New York to the blue-ribbon panel— he'd given these people the chance to build an award-winner, for

Memorial Stadium in 1988.

◆

Edward Bennett Williams (arms outflung) exults in receiving the 1983 World Championship Trophy. William Donald Schaefer is in the baseball cap at right.

Bo MacEwen's "four-martini" drawing of a futuristic stadium (including a retractable roof and a video board for replays) and commercial complex for the Camden Yards site—drawn up in 1967.

◆

4

*One of Memorial's memorable moments: Earl Weaver waves goodbye
after losing the pennant on the last day of the 1982 season.*

◆

Cal Ripken, Jr. and Sr., in 1983.

HOK's bid-winning design for Camden Yards, 1987. Note the symmetrical dimensions, the curved grandstands, the exterior walkways, and the truncated warehouse.

◆

Joe Spear, senior vice president and principal in charge of the design of Camden Yards for HOK.

Eric Moss and his model, from Warfield's, *August 1987.*

Governor William Donald Schaefer's first pitch is outside as he aims a wrecking ball at the likeness of Herb Belgrad, June 28, 1989.

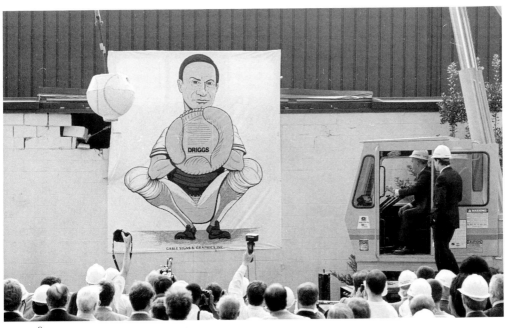

Janet Marie Smith.

◆

Construction workers pour concrete for the bleacher supports, July 1990.

At the dedication of Schaefer Circle at Oriole Park: from left, Bruce Hoffman, William Donald Schaefer, Larry Lucchino, and Herb Belgrad.

◆

Eli Jacobs, front, at an Orioles game with then–Supreme Court nominee David Souter (in Red Sox cap) and then–baseball commissioner Fay Vincent.

An aerial view of the final product, Oriole Park at Camden Yards, on opening day 1992.

◆

God's sake—and not only had they opted for the engineers from the West, with their pedestrian ramps and plumb lines, they'd opposed his choice unanimously. He'd offered them artists, and they'd voted to ally themselves with construction workers.

Just as ominous was a situation involving Chris Delaporte, Belgrad's lieutenant at the Stadium Authority. A veteran of the Carter administration, where he'd directed the Heritage Conservation and Recreation Service of the Department of the Interior, doling out the funding for parks and historic preservations on their grounds, Delaporte had been brought in by Belgrad to oversee the construction, to make sure the project came in on time and on budget, this in addition to fulfilling his duties as the head of Baltimore's parks.

It was Delaporte who represented the MSA while Belgrad was out of town during the two-day selection process, during which Lucchino asked Delaporte for his opinion. Delaporte protested that he was supposed to be neutral, but the panel pressed him. So he admitted that he'd go with the HNTB team—because, he said, of the design experience of the group: Kohn/Pederson/Fox as architects, Alex Cooper and Associates as master planners. Delaporte agreed with Lucchino, he said, that any good architect and any good urban designer could learn how to build a stadium—after all, with the exception of a few outfield wall measurements, the whole thing was quantifiable—but that sports-facility engineers accustomed to dropping their concrete spaceships into the exurbs were not likely to be well versed in the problems and solutions of either urban design or good architecture—sports architects from Missouri least of all.

"[HOK] wanted to [just] build a ballpark," Delaporte said later. "I wanted to build [one] in the eleventh largest city in the nation, in the old part of town, and link it up to the city. It had to be set right."

In speaking his mind, Delaporte allied himself with a lost cause—making it appear as if the state was going against HOK. "Belgrad was not happy," Delaporte recalls. "He raked me over the coals for it."

Within a couple of months, to Lucchino's discomfort, Delaporte would be replaced, leaving Lucchino without a key ally. Delaporte was his only sympathetic design voice on the other side. Now Lucchino had no one but himself—and he'd already burned most of his bridges—and an owner holed up in a Park Avenue office, a man whose public persona was so elusive and enigmatic that he might as well have been Howard Hughes to the citizens of Maryland.

Lucchino knew all too well that if the Orioles were going to oversee the design of a stadium that evoked baseball's past, they were going to have to put someone else on their side of the negotiating table—someone who came unencumbered by any prior attitudinal baggage—to translate their vision while simultaneously convincing HOK and the Stadium Authority to build it.

When the application crossed Larry Lucchino's desk, passed on down from football Hall of Famer and Orioles' director Calvin Hill, Lucchino's first impulse was to send polite regrets. But the combination of details on the résumé made it impossible to ignore. "I thought it was interesting that a woman was available who was an architect and urban planner," Lucchino says. "I was convinced we needed someone to shepherd the project. I remember saying to Eli, 'I'm going to hire this woman.' He said, 'Absolutely. What we're doing will be around for fifty, sixty, seventy years. We have to do it right.'"

"We don't think," Lucchino said at the time, "this whole thing should be designed by a couple of Kansas City architects and some state officials."

"I wanted someone on our design team to give us parity," Eli Jacobs says. "I am not an executor. I'm not a technician. We needed a professional. If we'd sent to central casting we couldn't have improved."

In fact, Jacobs's thumbnail assessment of the entire park was this: "It was Janet Marie and I. It's my basic vision, and Janet Marie's attention to detail—luck was shining on us the day she appeared on the scene. She's just remarkable. The strategic part—the large part—is mine. The technical is hers."

The résumé spoke of a Southern woman armed with degrees in architecture and urban planning. What it didn't reveal was the personality: a Dixie façade slathered in Southern syrup, but reinforced by a soul of steel. Janet Marie Smith had never designed a thing in her life—which makes it all the more impressive and curious that, before it was over, a few of the Orioles' employees would be calling it Janet Marie Smith Stadium. For very good reason.

By Opening Day 1992, her critics would be nearly as legion as her admirers. Her distinctive no-nonsense demeanor would come to incite wildly divergent reactions. For some, Smith's work would forever endure as a manifesto for women in the workplace—the story of how a furious work ethic and a headstrong attitude could triumph in the notoriously masculine arena of steel, concrete, and sport. For others, hers would be a far different, more sobering tale—of a person driven so hard to succeed, for whatever reason, that no matter how grand her actual achievement, its significance is forever colored by both her somewhat cavalier treatment of so many in her supporting cast and her inexplicable need to inflate the degree of credit she was due. She was due a great deal, but she always seemed to need more.

It is probably most accurate to see Janet Marie Smith as one key member in the ensemble—nothing more, nothing less. But that characterization, somehow, comes up short. Because the truth is that something happened to turn HOK's original plan, which would have evoked nothing more than a yawn from baseball's historians, into a jewel of a park that will forever resonate throughout the hallways of baseball history.

That something was Janet Marie Smith.

"She was unbelievable," said one Orioles' official. "She was all over [the architects and the authority]. All the time. On everything. Baseball should kiss her feet. She's responsible for them being able to build stadiums for the next twenty years."

"It's one of those stories that in a way, Peter, is too good to be true," Janet Marie Smith says one day, maneuvering her black BMW in search of a parking space near the construction site. Smith likes to use people's names in conversation even when she doesn't know them—a reflection of her Southern courtesy, or her seemingly patronizing manner, or both.

The stadium's carapace rises around us, the steelwork of the upper deck completed. The usual cloying choke of loose dirt and cement dust tossed by the whirls of wind is shut out by the airtight seal of her car as Smith maneuvers it up the dirt road that will become the stadium's main entrance.

"They say timing is everything, and my letter arrived on their doorstep just about the time they were getting concerned about how they'd manage it. I was finishing up a project in Los Angeles, and wondering what I'd do next, and then it hit me like a lead balloon—that they couldn't possibly have someone on staff who was in the business of design management. So I wrote a letter to Larry. And one thing led to another—my fantasy come true."

None of the principals here—not Smith, not Lucchino, not Jacobs—ever volunteer how it all really came about: how Chris Delaporte was the key. How Smith had first called him and sent samples of her work, because Delaporte and her first husband, of whom no one speaks—friends go off the record simply to mention she had a first husband—had known each other back in the District in the late seventies. Maybe everyone's avoidance of how Smith first showed up reflects how symbolic she's become of the Orioles' interests, as well as the Orioles' insistence that the park be etched into history with their own name all over it; perhaps they want to erase even the notion that Smith might have ended up on the other side of the table.

In retrospect, it would have been an intriguing notion: Janet Marie Smith working for the enemy. Because before it was all over, the Stadium Authority had had quite its fill of Janet Marie Smith. On the other hand, it would have ultimately made little difference. Either way, Janet Marie Smith's indelible stamp would have molded Camden Yards into the ballpark that stands today.

It is an odd thing, really, that the woman so responsible for getting the park to look the way it does is not a design architect at all. What she is, this woman who so piqued the press, who daily strode so conspicuously across the construction site, is a translator. Others have visions; Janet Marie translates them into reality. That's what design management is about: managing design, not creating it.

"They could bring me all the specs and drawing and models in the world, and yet it's not a vocabulary that I speak," Smith says. "[But] I can react to it. What I do on the job is act as a funnel for a lot of things. Someone coordinating. Someone to take this dictum of the old-fashioned old-time stadium and quantify that and work on the day-to-day stuff."

There's no question of her being qualified in dealing with matters of city design. Her dad is an architect, now practicing privately in

Jackson, Mississippi. Her paternal grandfather was a railroad man, track boss on the old Gulf, Mobile and Ohio—which, of course, qualifies her automatically for Camden Yards work.

Smith stayed in public school in Jackson in the late sixties while many of her white friends were being enrolled in private schools—an experience that, she has said, helped forge her lifelong belief that people of influence should remain in the inner cities: "My ability to shape the framework of the projects I'm engaged in," she told the *Chicago Tribune,* "doesn't get at the heart of some of what's troubling our cities today—socioeconomic problems."

Her father was a Yankees fan. On a family vacation, he introduced his daughter to her first major-league baseball game—in, of all places, the Astrodome, Judge Roy Hofheinz's monument to excess. Perhaps that initial dose of Plasticine baseball—the peculiar way the dome transforms traditional baseball sounds and scents and sights into sterile and muffled sensations—turned Smith toward the traditional view of the game that would inform the Camden Yards aesthetic. At the time, as a young girl, she had no idea that she was sitting in the brainchild of one of sport's most controversial visionaries, the home of the first luxury box (the judge's own quarters, which included a bar with a tilted floor and a bowling alley), and the antithesis of everything she would come to represent on the part of the Baltimore Orioles two decades hence.

Smith recalls being most impressed by the way she could use the empty popcorn containers as a megaphone. And one design feature stuck in her head: the enormous dot-matrix scoreboard.

There was never any question she'd go to college, or that it would be anywhere but Mississippi State. The question was what her major would be: either art or engineering. At the time, the architecture school was just being set up at Mississippi State, and her dad was on the advisory board. One day he insisted she go to the campus and see both schools and then meet him at the architecture school, which had been set up in an old masonry dairy-judging pavilion out at the edge of campus in Starkville.

"I swore I'd never do what my father did," she says as we circle the park. Out the windows of her car lies the landscape of construction chaos—cranes, steel, ironworkers astride deep beams. "But I spent the morning at the art school and the afternoon at the engineering school. At the art school there were all these still lifes, people doing these wonderful things that were very selfish, in a way, a very personal kind of thing. Then engineering couldn't have been more boring and staid. The architecture building had all these drawings up everywhere, and music was playing, and people talking, having a great old time."

She enrolled in the architecture program. But it wasn't a love of the look and fit of buildings that had drawn her, and it wasn't the love of the art that would lead her into the career. It wasn't the design that hooked her; it was the process.

"I was as intrigued by the business and communication electives as the other things. I always felt like I would do something other than conventional architecture. I suspected at the time I'd do business or marketing."

After earning her degree from Mississippi State, she was awarded a grant from the NEA, then spent a year working for the NEA in Washington before going to New York to work on the master plan for Battery Park City, as the coordinator of architecture and design from 1982 to 1984. By night she earned her master's in urban planning from City University of New York. By day she foraged through New York neighborhoods from Riverside Drive to Bed-Stuy looking for details in the city's architecture that could make the development's size and scope a little less intimidating.

Smith's work ethic was clearly as formidable then as it is now. Cite a random block in a random neighborhood in Brooklyn and Smith will be able to tell you the kind of trees that are growing from its sidewalk as easily as she'll be able to tell you how many bases Boog Powell stole in 1968.

"What I learned very quickly was that the things that go into making a city culminate in the architecture," she says, over a salad at a restaurant near the park. The words carry the Mississippi lilt as softly as dogwood petals drifting to the ground, but her voice has no affect, no emotion. Smith is a handsome woman, but very little detail animates her features, and her eyes do not smile. On the other hand, her absolute steeliness, her resolute demeanor, is far more intriguing.

"But all the political, economic, and social decisions that go into determining how a piece of land is zoned—how the transportation feeds to it, what the developer's economic requirements are, the way the bank dictates things, the building codes—by the time an architect gets around to doing things, it had little of the kind of urban character I was interested in. So I had chosen consciously to back up in that process. I was looking for some place I could deal with this myriad of factors. I also had a fondness for the public sector.

"I never expected to end up working at baseball. Baseball was a diversion."

She'd go to Yankees games and Mets games with friends; there was something more enticing to her about Yankee Stadium, planted in the middle of the throbbing streets near the Grand Concourse. Although her hometown of Jackson had acquired a Double-A Mets farm team, she preferred the Yankees, for a simple reason: A night at a Yankee game meant a night in an urban environment—she'd meet friends at a local tavern in the Bronx, have a meal, walk over to the park. At Shea, she remembers with some disapproval, you had to meet at your seats.

"One of the wonderful things about baseball is the city culminated in a sport. The field, the fans, the food tend to reflect the city they're in. An embryonic version of wherever you are. I came to love it as much for that as for the game itself."

There were down sides to the city, too, of course, and they revealed themselves to her regularly—drunks and homeless men sleeping in the lobby of her building on Murray Hill. She was attacked one time in her elevator. Any notion of fear, she remembers, was overcome by outrage. She ended up chasing her accoster out of the elevator and onto the street.

"I ended up chasing him out of the building with a Fresca can."

This is not a boast. There is no doubt about the truth. You can tell from the look in her eyes, which is no look at all. They get a little harder when she's asked to expand on her impressions—the girl from Jackson living in Manhattan, amid the squalid modern fray, scraping up against the underbelly of the inner city that is the focal point of her career.

"The times I had to step over the people in the foyer in Murray Hill," she says, ". . . it made the human race look pathetic."

It is a curious take on one of the nation's greatest social ills, especially from a woman who is devoting her life to the cityscape, and who has professed concern for our neglect of the American city's socioeconomic problems. There is a hint here of a woman who had come to trust the buildings more than the people who fill them.

When the Battery Park project was over, Smith crossed the country with her husband, whom she had met when he was supervising design competitions for the NEA in Washington and who had been hired to head a design school in Los Angeles. Smith landed a job as the president of the Pershing Square Management Association, where she conceived a design competition to renovate the park. The winning plans were never implemented.

It was in Los Angeles that baseball began to lure Smith. Her offices downtown were a mile from Dodger Stadium, her home in Silver Lake not much farther. She started to attend games regularly, on her own and with a few friends.

"I loved watching baseball at Dodger Stadium. That was a personal experience. I saw baseball by myself at Dodger Stadium. I lived a mile and a half away in Silver Lake. It was a big thing for me. Leave the office at seven-fifteen and slide over. It was a thing that made me feel like part of a bigger community."

One day back East, after she'd given a speech in Philadelphia, Smith decided to take the train to Baltimore to catch an Orioles game, where she first learned of the team's intent to build a new park. Back in Los Angeles, she called Delaporte to see if she could work for the state of Maryland.

She had a fairly acceptable fallback if the Orioles didn't bite: She'd been accepted for a Loeb Fellowship at Harvard, one of a half-dozen professionals awarded a free ride at one of the nation's best schools for a year—the most prestigious academic fellowship in the field.

"She called me," Delaporte recalls. "I would have hired her in a minute. She sent me a book of all of her things. I looked at that. I continued to talk to her, [even as] I saw myself getting to leave. I called the O's, or I told her to call them and recommended her simultaneously. I felt like someone of her talent should be somewhere.

"I'm very proud of it. Tough woman. Raw talent. And the one thing men don't like—a lot of ambition."

In her letter to the Orioles, she did not ask if they needed anyone. Instead, she wrote, "You need me."

And they did. In February 1989, she came aboard.

"My first real day on the job, there was this big meeting with all the attorneys," Smith recalls. "I was being introduced to these people for the first time. HOK was there, the Stadium Authority was there, this thing was sitting in front of us. This round thing. We were talking about what changes should occur. I said something, and Larry, who had this wonderful manner of challenging things so that you have to defend them the best you can, he asked me somewhat rhetorically, but challenging nonetheless, 'What is this, Planning 101?' "

Smith took no offense. She immediately sensed an ally—someone as hard-eyed as herself.

"What makes you think you can do a stadium?" he asked her.

"As I understand it, you don't want a stadium," she said. "You want a ballpark."

Right then, she became a voice for Lucchino and Jacobs.

Janet Marie Smith's mandate was clear: Find a way to quantify the vision that Jacobs and Lucchino had articulated. It was not going to be easy. In fact, it was somewhat daunting. To start with, HOK had given the Orioles something tall, steep, curvilinear, and entirely unrelated to the surrounding cityscape—spartan and practical, a structure dictated by HOK's generic vision and a severely restrictive budget. In the spring of 1989, huge underestimations on the cost of land acquisition made it clear to Herb Belgrad that the $74 million allotted by the legislature was not going to suffice. Not only had the Orioles already angered the architect with their arrogance, but the state was not prepared to tolerate any costly whims in the new park.

To ensure that the budget and the design stayed in line, Belgrad hired Bruce Hoffman virtually the same week to replace Delaporte. Hoffman's family had for decades run an Albany construction and development business with overwhelming success. With a reputation for coming in without nonsense and within budget, Bruce Hoffman came into town with no aesthetic preconceptions. Unlike Delaporte, whom he was succeeding, Hoffman was a man of few words and little taste for theorizing. Hoffman's forte was practicality. As far as the

MSA was concerned, he was to be the immovable force to meet Janet Marie's irresistible object.

Janet Marie Smith, then, had to use her expertise in architecture and urban planning to find ways to personalize the park without spending much money. She had to find a way to make the ballpark intimate.

She called John Pastier, a friend in Los Angeles with a passion for ballparks.

The call, the chance to have input into a live, already-on-the boards stadium represented something of a dream for Pastier. As a child, Pastier recalls, he visited a friend in his apartment building and found the man sketching Yankee Stadium. Something about the shape of the place fascinated him. But it wasn't until a couple of decades later—after he'd earned an architecture degree at Cooper Union and done stints as a city planner for Los Angeles and as the architecture critic for the *Los Angeles Times*—that Pastier found the idea of ballpark design gnawing at his frontal lobes more and more frequently. A free-lance critic for various professional publications and a frequent visiting teacher at schools around the country, he'd hooked up with Phillip Bess while researching a story about the University of Illinois architecture school. The two became friends and co-idealists. Bess calls Pastier one of the few visionaries in the business, but, of course, visions are all they have, save Bess's plans for Armour Field.

It was in the planning for Armour Field that Bess had quantified the sight lines in some of the old parks, noting distances from home plate to various seats in the parks. Pastier did him one better, compiling numbers for as many old and new parks as he could find. He then tabulated them in graphic form, spurred by his fascination with ballparks—but toward what particular end Pastier was unsure. His proposal to write a book on the old fireproof ballparks of the pre-1915 era had captured no publisher's interest. And while he and Bess agreed they ought to be able to come up with something revolutionary for the antiseptic arenas that housed modern baseball, they were lacking in concrete avenues.

In high school in New York Pastier had worked as an office boy with Janet Marie's first husband, and later attended Cooper Union with him. When they meet again in Los Angeles, Pastier was already talking about his plans for the book. Pastier soon discovered that he and Janet Marie had the game of baseball in common. He recalls a game in the late 1988 season, in Anaheim, that he attended with Janet Marie.

"She called and said, 'Feel like going to a game?' " he recalls. "We explicitly did a lot of talking about stadiums. She might have already been working on the idea [of Camden Yards]—I don't know. She doesn't divulge a lot. She was very explicitly asking me about good stadiums and bad stadiums, and why isn't this good, and why is this good. That stuck in my head. It was a funny kind of thing.

"Early in the next year she sort of disappeared from L.A."

John Pastier tries to keep the frustration out of his voice. He fails.

In March 1989, Janet Marie Smith asked John Pastier for some help. He began work immediately.

"I gave her the use of my slides—a visual history of the evolution of ballparks," Pastier said. "I reviewed the plans. I drew a couple of cross sections as alternatives to what HOK had. It was crude—trying to get things a little lower and a little closer to the field. I cantilevered three or four rows from the back"—in other words, by redistributing the weight through redesigning the superstructure, he knocked off some of the back rows and put them down lower.

In truth, his advice was a little more specific. On March 21, 1989, Pastier wrote this to Janet Marie Smith:

"Assuming that intimacy and proximity to the field are important, the current [HOK] scheme does not come out well in these comparisons. In fact, it usually does the worst of the ten parks under consideration. In many respects it is a regression from Memorial Stadium. This analysis involves a location behind home plate. If sections behind first and third are analyzed, the current scheme might compare even more unfavorably. Making the park more intimate would probably require several changes of structure, geometry and client expectations: (1) Reducing the number of rows in the upper deck. (2) Increasing the cantilever dimensions. This may necessitate a change from concrete to steel. (3) Moving the column line forward. (4) Tightening up the legroom. . . .

"I raise the issue of intimacy at this early stage of my involvement, because it is important and frequently overlooked. In an urban setting its importance increases. It would seem appropriate to build a new park of greater intimacy than other recent stadiums, rather than one possessing less intimacy than its contemporaries."

On March 24, Janet Marie Smith's files show, she returned to Baltimore from a trip to Kansas City to consult with HOK, and her memo to Lucchino reports a successful meeting: "The building mass itself now takes on the shape of old ballparks. The four rows in the upper deck will be moved to the outfield corners. This should help our intimacy issue immensely by creating a sense of enclosure around the foul poles and reducing the scale of the upper deck. And, most importantly, the façade of the building can assume an historical character."

Subsequent memos detailed the appeals of the sunroof on Cleveland's League Park; the parallel-to-the-street orientation of the old Wrigley in Los Angeles; the façade of Ebbets as a street-building façade; the advertising in various parks (in Cleveland: "Nightly Steamer to Buffalo"); the steel truss of the Fenway roof and its artistic integrity; the right-field inner-pointing seats in Fenway. Attached copies of pictures of old stadiums revealed the world Smith was now immersed in. The aesthetic was coming together: She felt most strongly about wrapping the outfield seats around to face home plate; the integrity of the signs and the design of the sunroof were not far behind on her list of priorities.

Janet Marie was on her way.

Pastier, however, was finished.

"It turns out I never did as much as I should have," he said. "It's been very frustrating. This is the first time she's ever mentioned my name to a journalist. . . .

Pastier originally expected to work on the project for three phases. "We did the first phase and some dribbling around with the second. But I don't think she wanted to get me involved too much because she wouldn't have looked good—she would have been paying someone and people would have said, 'This is what we hired *you* for.'

"For someone who is so charming she is very private," John Pastier says. "She doesn't divulge a lot. She is a very eccentric person, at the same time a very in-control person."

In Baltimore, Smith took control immediately. Prodded by Jacobs, and immersed now in the data and schematics, postcards and slides, Smith began to chip away at the ungainly mass of HOK's spaceship.

In the next several months, armed on the one hand with Jacobs's and Lucchino's blessing—and "design concurrence" leverage—and, on the other, with her by-now vast knowledge of ballpark design history, Smith managed through perseverance, prodding, and not-so-gentle persuasion, to mold Camden Yards. Element by element, foot by foot, she re-invented a baseball stadium. One of Smith's first targets was the circular ramps—in particular, the one Spear had tacked on to the north side of the stadium, facing the city.

"Ramps must be hidden to avoid the appearance of sterile stadiums," she instructed HOK in a memo in the spring of 1989. "The design of stair towers should be given special attention so they do not seem tacked on . . . compatible with the warehouse and Baltimore's historic civic buildings in terms of scale, configuration, and color."

Other memo excerpts from the next two months show Smith revising everything from the number of toilets to the design of the trash baskets—and everything in between.

"The outer wall of the upper roof concourse should be designed so fans can see the city . . . Move the upper deck closer to the playing field. Reduce the height of the second deck. Reduce the height of the third deck . . . Flatten the upper deck so it is not so steep . . . Extend the left-center-field grandstands down Pratt Street so that they wrap around the field . . . Reduce the number of curvilinear forms to get away from the boomerang form . . .

"Turn the upper deck seating where it abuts the warehouse to face home plate. The rail at field level should be ornamental iron work . . . Trees, plants and other greenery are critical to designing this facility as a ballpark, not a stadium . . . Seeding is preferred over sodding . . ."

One by one, the improvements were implemented. Lucchino and Smith, together, chopped several yards off the scoreboard, bringing it down in size. Jacobs's Tall Wall scoreboard, an homage to Fenway's

Green Monster, was sketched into the right-field wall, and Jacobs suggested a private club in the warehouse.

On May 19 the new schematic form from HOK showed an upper deck at an angle of 30.5 degrees—a full 4.5 degrees flatter. It also showed three decks now instead of four.

Piece by piece, to the delight of the purists, the park was becoming Janet Marie Smith's.

The most important question left to be decided was whether to construct the frame out of steel or concrete. The warehouse had been saved; asymetry was assured. But for the Orioles, a precast concrete frame would be intolerable. Herb Belgrad declared this decision "was expected to be made within two weeks." In reality, the question had been stewing for well over a month, and resolution was not weeks but months away.

HOK's engineers had told them that steel would cost $8 million more than concrete. But to Jacobs, steel was nonnegotiable.

"I was very definite about what I wanted," Eli Jacobs says. "I was prepared to wait until hell froze over to get it."

In the matter of steel, Jacobs's—and Smith's—insistence was grounded in logic. Steel's only drawback was maintenance costs; rust on steel can grow like a cancer. But its advantages in a ballpark are several—not the least of which is its ability to evoke the old-time game because steel is far easier to work with in designing asymetrical frames.

HOK's preference for concrete, the firm now insists, was grounded strictly in monetary concerns. Steel was prohibitive in cost, according to the engineering firm HOK had hired, Delon Hampton of Washington. DH was a Minority Business Firm—the state had required a certain minority presence—the plum MBF engineer in the business, and, interestingly, the same firm that Richard Ayers had wanted so badly for his own team.

The Orioles, though, strongly suspected that Delon Hampton had been working from a far-too-conservative configuration, likened by Tom Rogers, the construction manager on-site, to a plan to accommodate "forty-five thousand fat people in the stadium during a hurricane wind and a two-foot blizzard." They'd based their cost estimates on a steel structure designed for one hundred pounds per square foot—far in excess of practicality. The Orioles hired their own architectural engineers, Lehrer McGovern Bovis of Manhattan, and an independent New York structural engineer, whose own drawings showed a substantial reduction in required steel tonnage—26 percent. When all of the interested parties met to discuss the issue in June, it became clear that one of the greatest misunderstandings could be attributed to a predictable disagreement: aesthetics. HOK's engineer had designed heavy steel posts and beams in order to alleviate the need for highly visible trusses and webs of steel—which was exactly what the Orioles did in fact want. It was the lacy gridwork of steel that had so dramatically enhanced the feel of Wrigley.

Janet Marie Smith remembers an HOK engineer telling her that they could do it her way—"but it would look awfully old-fashioned." At one point in the meeting, one HOK representative "expressed concern" that the Orioles did not fully understand the "look" they were getting with the structural steel system. Smith, of course, understood that look very well. At another meeting, Bob Wyatt, the construction manager for Barton Malow/Sverdrup, the chief contractor on the job, asked John Palmer of Lehrer whether the Orioles were aware of exactly what look they were going to end up with. Palmer told Wyatt that Janet Marie Smith had made it quite clear to him: "I know what we're getting," she had told Palmer.

Soon thereafter quite fortuitously for the Orioles, problems with the concrete structural design in the new Comiskey—also designed by Delon Hampton—had popped up, which then caused HOK to question their Baltimore figures. Now HOK brought in another engineer, Bliss & Nyitray of Miami. In retrospect, Spear admits that Delon Hampton's numbers were off: "The engineer came back with something conservative in steel and not as conservative in concrete. Maybe the guy felt comfortable in concrete—it's easier to design."

Still, even with Nyitray doing the engineering, the numbers were still much too high for the state's liking, and Hoffman and Smith squared off. Hoffman knew that there wouldn't be a single penny more coming from the state. And he was sure the Orioles weren't going to offer to chip in too much, either. On May 20, Hoffman wrote to Smith: "We agree with the recommendation of our architects that the $3.5

million in additional expenses required to incorporate steel into the project does not offset the aesthetic benefit."

Hoffman demanded the Orioles comply within the week. They didn't. The Orioles' engineers keep working at coming up with wholly different figures, and by early August, they'd convinced HOK that the steel would cost less than $1 million dollars more. And the longer they delayed, Smith figured, the likelier she'd win out; a steel frame would take at least three months less to construct.

In early June 1989, a new complication arose: Herb Belgrad began to realize that he was about $100 million over budget. Land acquisition alone was going to cost $40 million more than budgeted. Belgrad huddled with his advisors, and in two days he'd cut the overrun in half: The state abandoned plans to acquire a building south of the site; Belgrad then induced the Orioles to agree to cut out twenty-five hundred seats, and expand the capacity of the luxury suites; they figured out ways to get revenue from on-site parking.

But he was still considerably over budget. Belgrad called William Donald Schaefer. Schaefer was not pleased, but told him to do whatever he had to. The legislature reluctantly approved another instant lottery and made it clear that the bank was thereafter closed.

On June 22, rather suddenly, the Stadium Authority announced that the stadium alone, apart from land acquisition and interest payments on the bonds, would not cost $78.4 million, but $105 million. Seventeen million extra dollars would be spent on "design work"—the fifty-five-foot brick and multipaned window façade, with each brick laid by hand instead of being laid in sheets off the site then trucked to the site and assembled. An advanced drainage system. Seven million dollars for extra design details: expensive field lighting, the sunscreen roof, the deluxe sound system.

"When we talked to the legislature originally we were talking about a no-frills ballpark," Belgrad explained. "Along the route we paid more attention to the fact that because of our location we were the gateway to Baltimore, and we wanted our ballpark to be a signature of what Baltimore is all about—a combination of traditional and state of the art. The stadium we ended up with was not the one we began talking about."

On August 16—months after the steel decision should have been made—Hoffman wrote Smith: "The Authority has authorized HOK to proceed with the design on a concrete-framed ballpark."

Smith answered the same day: "Every individual involved with the design of the new stadium prefers steel if the cost differential is not prohibitive. MSA initially told us a steel superstructure would cost $8.5 million more. It has revised that estimate to $611 thousand. We could shorten the time needed for construction by 2–4 critical months. Clearly, such a minimal cost differential is a small price to pay to ensure that the ballpark will be completed in time."

Three days later, Hoffman answered back: "We are in no way convinced that a concrete frame will detract from the function or success of the ballpark. We believe the Orioles have unreasonably withheld their concurrence on this issue. I have instructed HOK to proceed."

The next day's response from Smith had a new tone: "We have been advised by our attorneys to inform you that these letters do not comply with the requirements of the May 2, 1988, agreement. These letters impose no obligation on the Orioles to respond to the arbitrary deadline set forth."

Design concurrence had struck again. On every significant point in the process, those two simple words gave the Orioles a club to wield in order to get what they wanted.

Four weeks later, after the Orioles had agreed to pay for half of the annual maintenance, the state agreed: It would be a steel frame.

The tone of Smith's letter, it was later suggested to Bruce Hoffman, sounded like a threat.

"They'd threaten us all the time," Bruce Hoffman said.

"Bruce could have filled a room," Herb Belgrad said, "with his daily correspondence from Janet."

The Orioles take full credit for the steel, and without their insistence, Camden Yards would indeed have been supported by massive columns of concrete. But Stuart Smith, a young architect who worked under Spear, is adamant that HOK always wanted steel, too; they were just constrained by the budget.

"Joe really wanted a steel structure from the start," Smith said.

"We were in Hoffman's office talking to John Nyitray one day. [Nyitray] said, 'What do you guys want?' We said, 'We want to do a steel structure.' They went on about signing contracts while we knelt on the floor of Hoffman's office and sketched what the building section would look like. I still have one of the sketches. It was very near to what happened in the end."

It is not hard to believe. Pilot Field's superstructure is steel. And, after all, Joe Spear's first two stadium jobs for HOK were Shea and Wrigley. During the renovation at Shea, where the rest of the world saw a bowl of inexcusably tacky adornment, Joe Spear saw wonderment in the design on the connector plates for the steel beams. At Wrigley, where he designed a rebuilt concourse for $10 million early in the eighties, he saw everything about which Eli Jacobs waxed so eloquent.

"When you look at the steelwork in Baltimore, the years of working in Wrigley are part of what that is," Joe Spear says, "—a wonderful elegant structure."

"Everybody knows they like the older facilities, but people aren't able to quantify what it is exactly they like about them," Janet Marie explains over lunch one day, offering the short-form summary of her work—the quantification of the old into something new. There is not even a hint of didacticism in her voice, although she is speaking from rote memory.

"But if you try and pick out what they have in common you'll see some fairly simple urban design and architectural rules: The buildings were always very civic in appearance. They could easily have been a library or a city hall. They held tight to the building site. The block dictated not only the seating, but the configuration of the field dimension, and you found on the exterior they'd build up the block. They had traditional street walls that came right up to the sidewalk. The field dimensions were always dictated by the site. When you ran out of real estate horizontally, you put up walls. Of course, that's the wonderful thing about baseball—you have guidelines, but not rules.

"The seating wall was almost always contained within the building profile. They were low buildings. And that was taken into account in the choice of building materials. They were always steel, and not just post and beam, but steel trusses. The seats always had slats and cast-iron standards. The facies of the roof at Yankee Stadium, the decorative end to the grandstand of the Polo Grounds, you get a sense of the attention to detail.

"The advertising was a part of the architecture. It was never stuck on afterwards. It was thought of in terms of how it was part of the outfield fence, how it was part of the scoreboard. Now every marketing department will tell you you have to stick an ad where the camera will catch it—the catcher, the pitcher, and the ad. It wasn't thought about that way. The roof design over the upper deck was often very flat. The colors were often very parklike—usually green, but not always. The most important thing was the fan's relationship to the game—not only did you have a minimal amount of foul territory, since you weren't trying to squeeze yourself into a football stadium, but you were completely surrounded."

She takes a bite of her salad.

"We've tried to think about some of those things."

Certainly, baseball has always belonged where American people gathered. Baseball in the cities has always mattered in America; for as long as men brought the game with them from the farmland, they dropped the meadow into the cityscape wherever it could fit, and a lot of the time where it fit gave it a shape and personality. In Crosley Field, left field sloped upward to the wall, steep enough to confound opposing fielders: "You couldn't play in the middle or on the top," Frank Robinson recalls, "because by the time you got up there and [the ball] hit the wall, it's back down again. The visiting teams would come in for three days, it was see you later—they're on their backside. Even the best of them, the terrace got 'em."

In all of them, baseball rubbed up against commerce and life, so that a fly ball out of Sportsman's Park could land in the auto dealer's lot—or, if Ruth hit it, on the roof of the YMCA. Old parks were local. They had local advertising. In Brooklyn, it featured Abe Stark, the tailor—HIT THIS SIGN, WIN A SUIT. At Huntington Grounds, the Red Sox's home until they moved to Fenway Park, it was the Boyle Brothers—THE WORLD'S GREATEST CREDIT CLOTHIERS. In Crosley it was Hudepohl Beer and Tenderay Beef—all of them strengthening the sense of being part of a specific place, the opposite of the effect in the current parks, where the same half-dozen companies—Coke, Budweiser, Pizza Hut—simply reinforce our loss of place, and thus of self. Local advertising fueled rivalries; an Iron City sign in Pittsburgh would raise the hackles of a Philadelphian who frequented Shibe Park, with its Schmidt signs. Now, a fan in Philly will see the same Bud sign he sees in Three Rivers.

In the Bronx, it was DeNito's Bread, the logo painted in red, green, and white on the tenements behind the elevated tracks that ran beyond center field. Now, baseball as displayed in Yankee Stadium features $4.75 beers, an army of security guards, and the bleating of commercials from the huge scoreboard in right-center field—loud television commercials one hundred feet high, so that the effect on a Bronx night with a sparse crowd is like watching television in your basement.

It is true that the old stadiums were not nostalgic per se; they used available technology, just as the concrete domes of the seventies used theirs. But it so happened that the materials used in the early technology—wood, steel, rivets, brick—were easily fashioned into the angles and attitudes that allowed the game of baseball to be grafted onto them. Like the game itself they were asymetrical, and full of odd angles and nooks and crannies, and isn't that same asymetricality what makes baseball so appealing? Follow the baselines away from home plate—they diverge forever. The game's geometry, like its extra innings, has no closure at all. Neither should its homes. Steel webs create a sense of depth and space; concrete presents a closed face.

These are the issues that surround the decisions that were being made every day on Camden Yards. Yet it is fair to ask how well Janet Marie Smith understood them. Some of the old-time elements she insisted on were originally present not for their aesthetic value but for another purpose altogether, and the ardor with which she pursued them displayed remarkable attention to detail, but uncertain judgment.

On June 28, 1989, William Donald Schaefer climbed into a crane for the first demolition ceremony.

"This was the right spot," he pronounced, on a Brigham Youngish note; few begrudged him the moment. Although in his short gubernatorial tenure a state budget surplus of $412 million had become a deficit nearly as huge, he was about to start building something for his city again. And, after all, this was the site he'd championed for nearly twenty years, and a moment of which he had dreamed for just as long.

Several hundred workers, city officials, Orioles officials, press, and spectators assembled. On the cinder-block wall of the Ramcor company had been painted a large caricature of a catcher, designed to resemble Herb Belgrad, with a catcher's mitt awaiting the kiss of the wrecker's ball. Schaefer donned a hard hat and tried to work the crane. His first three swings failed to touch the building, but they did come awfully close to the heads of some of the workers. His fourth hit the wall and dislodged a few cinder-blocks.

His fifth swing landed square in the catcher's crotch.

By January of 1990, demolition was complete. And five days after Opening Day up the hill at Memorial, beneath a brilliant blue sky, a second Opening Day was held downtown. The tableau of decay that Baltimoreans had become accustomed to seeing at the construction site—the windows of Camden Station shattered and gaping, its window frames rotting under the eaves, the grass tufts sprouting up on the warehouse's roof—was now graced by the addition of a huge, red crane sitting on the northwest corner of acres of sandy yellow soil.

From its 250-foot-long arm hung a shaft of steel two hundred feet long, an impossibly large black needle with a massive drill bit four feet in diameter attached to its bottom tip—a sculpted piece of steel weighing nearly a ton, sprung from some Machine Age artist's wildest imagination. Like some giant divining rod, the needle swung over the dirt. Finally, the crane's arm stopped; the nose of the bit was guided to its spot.

The dirt beneath it had already been loosened by a huge hollow steel cylinder that had burrowed into the ground with its nasty serrated edges. Now, turned by a motor attached to a platform on the front of the crane, the drill lowered into the dirt and began to churn. Soil climbed up through the bit, like the sawdust piles of a carpenter's hand drill.

The earth had begun to move, concrete and steel to take its place. Camden Yards was officially born.

Over the next several days, several more shafts were dug straight into the earth, and the caissons were poured into the shafts, deep into the ground—vertical roots of concrete, each reinforced by ten steel bars, each caisson hardening into a column whose bottom tip rested on solid rock; each might as well be resting on the crust of the planet.

Next came the concrete beams, laid horizontally, at grade—on the ground—from the top of one caisson to the top of the other, until a giant grid had been laid into the ground, protecting against nature's shifting whims. Memorial Day saw three of the caissons already poured. The ends of ten steel rebars poked out of the tops of the caissons, the steel bars all bent and twisted in different directions, like snakes poking their heads from the ground.

By late May, it was already clear that the Orioles were going to play dismal baseball in 1990. Baltimore's more significant baseball sounds were rising from the new site just east of the harbor—the heavy, purposeful tones of a landscape being altered. On top of the concrete beams laid horizontally across the tops of the caissons was assembled the steel infrastructure, rumbling onto the site in flatbed trucks, hoisted vertically by the cranes, and assembled in nearly humorously logical fashion—each beam locked into the next, joined with two dozen rivets, like a giant Erector set. Precast concrete walls were placed between the steel beams, and it was clear that something was rising from the wasteland west of the warehouse.

In the first week of June lights were mounted on the warehouse so work could go on at night, and the site, filled with hollow caisson casings, buzzing beneath a canopy of construction noise, took on the look of the monolith dig on the moon at the beginning of *2001*.

By the Fourth of July, out in left field, the first real sign that this would be a ballpark had appeared: a maze of walls of thin precast concrete, standing on edge, cut at a sloping angle. Only one thing could be put into place atop such a base: a sloping bed of seats. These would be the left-field field-level seats. By the first week of August, more bleacher supports had risen, and the concrete floor that would hold the seats behind home plate had appeared. Now all of the white concrete was beginning to wrap around the acres of dirt, enclosing and reining in what, until then, had been a random dozen acres of sand.

In September, rains resulted in a new feature for the downtown geography: Camden Lake, a body of rainwater that filled the area where the field had been dug dozens of feet below ground level. And on the morning of September 10, for a fleeting moment, nature reclaimed the site: Beneath the raucous sound of steel being hammered and riveted into a framework, a white egret skimmed Camden Lake. But the lake was surrounded by the unmistakable shape of a stadium's skeleton.

On the final day of the 1990 season, the balance of baseball power had shifted in Baltimore. Up in a quiet Memorial Stadium, the Orioles marketers were already promoting the final season, the air having drained long ago from the penultimate one. Down the hill, the park's shape was now clearly visible, a frame of dark green steel wrapping in a circular arc behind home plate.

The warehouse was sheathed in scaffolding, awaiting a complete repointing of every one of its hundreds of thousands of bricks, and a skirt of bright green grass had been planted at its base to stop erosion, lending a humorous nod to the real field, which for now consisted of a muddy excavation fifteen feet beneath grade.

On Christmas Eve, up on the eighth floor, outside the outer wall of the warehouse hidden by a huge plastic tarpaulin eight stories high, workmen outfitted in space suits sat on scaffolding and ground out the ninety-year-old cement grouting with drills that spun little circular saw blades three quarters of an inch into each crevice. Inside each window, massive iron shutters that had covered the windows for decades lay awaiting disposal on the floor.

By spring, as the trees budded down on the narrow streets of Ridgely's Delight, the residents of the ancient neighborhood found a new shape peering in at them from across Russell Street—the ninth baseball park in Baltimore history. And while it may have been clearly lacking in the intimacy of, say, the old Union Park on 25th and Greenmount, home of the world champions of 1894, 1895, and 1896, or Oriole Park on 29th, where housewives would come out their back doors at the sound of a particularly loud cheer to see who'd struck the home run, it had a certain stature of amicability. It spread to the sides. It showed them arches, and green steel, and brick, and above it, blue sky.

On Opening Day, 1991, the final opening day of Memorial Stadium, while the Orioles were going through infield practice up the hill, a 450-ton crane was lifting a large steel beam and truss assembly from the ground outside Russell Street. It rose slowly, this massive piece of steel, heavy enough to swing out of control and knock down a building, and, suspended by two cables, slowly and astoundingly came into the hand of an iron worker, a single man sitting astride another piece of vertical steel; it was as if one man had steered, with his hands, a freighter into dock.

He and another worker guided the end of the assembly into the slot between the first man's legs. It was a piece of the frame that would support the sunscreen roof.

"Baseball stadiums should be green," said Bob Wyatt, the construction manager for Barton Malow/Sverdrup, the chief contractor. A quiet, serious Connecticut native with a history in building hospitals, Wyatt kept checking his watch; he had seats up the hill for Opening Day. This would be a half day of work.

Wyatt is a practical man, and wary of all of the steel that surrounded and dwarfed us; it felt as if we were surrounded by a series of suspension bridges from the thirties. Where the trusses converged at 45-degree angles, they were anchored by huge steel gusset plates. The bolt pattern had been designed to give the feeling of the old days, when hot rivets were thrown straight into the steel plate.

Wyatt reached out to caress a steel gusset plate—not with a great deal of affection, either.

"Every time there's a scratch or a spot of rust," he said, "you have to scrape it or paint it. It's like cancer. If you let it get started, it'll kill you."

Where the steel had been painted, it gleamed darkly, like the depth of a forest. Where it hadn't been painted, it was rusted in some places. In others, the bare steel was more evocative. Across one cross beam that anchored the upper deck in left center had been painted the legend SHERI, COLLEEN, TERESA, WE LOVE YA.

"The day before we had to start painting," Wyatt said, as the huge steel beam hung motionless in the air, "we still hadn't selected the damned color. We had black. We had red. We had blue. I asked the sales rep of the painting supply company for green. They gave us two chips. I said, 'Come in with one in between. And we need it painted on steel.' She said to me, 'But we don't paint.' I said, 'I don't care if you don't paint. Do you understand what I want to do?'

"The next day," Bob Wyatt said, "we had a sample. It was painted."

They called it Camden Green.

Far above us, the first hammer blow echoed out. The man with the hammer astride the vertical beam had aligned the horizontal steel beam with the top of the beam he straddled. He began to pound the first of the four rivets. It was not the sound of a hammer hitting a nail; it was the sound of pieces of iron being pounded into permanence.

Bob Wyatt excused himself. The first pitch was thirty minutes off, back up the hill.

Forty-five minutes later, Jay Ballard had given up four straight singles in the first inning to the White Sox, and Chicago won, 5–1, behind Jack McDowell.

"I'm not worried about the last season, or the last game," Frank Robinson said, in his luxuriously panelled and padded office. "I'm worried about Wednesday's game."

On Robinson's desk sat a hard hat with his name on it.

He'd be using it sooner than he'd hoped.

By June, as the park took shape and the Orioles foundered up the hill, the city had divined the war of wills between the state and the team, and as details of the new park emerged, the newspapers filled with letters and commentaries. *Sun* columnist John Steadman was nearly daily decrying the decision to preserve the warehouse, and the old-style tone in general—"Now the official blueprints have been drawn, and it's downright ugly. The public deserves to be forewarned. As incredulous as it seems, Baltimore is the only city in America that is actually trying to create an old stadium. If it's being built to look old and rundown, we already have one of those . . .

"The Orioles have obviously had too much to say about the

building. Isn't it enough that we are putting it up for them to play in, and paying for it, without their telling us how it's going to look?"

On June 20, a letter appeared in the *Sun* from a woman in Baltimore: "I became ill when I saw the design of Baltimore's new stadium. Who told these designers we wanted to go back to the old days?"

Three days later, another offered this: "A stadium with an all-brick façade, a real grass playing field, a scoreboard, advertising panels in the outfield. Isn't there already one up on 33rd Street?"

A visitor from Seattle wrote, "Why? You don't realize what a gem you have in Memorial Stadium."

At the same time, a *Sun* writer pitched in with the first of what would become the avalanche of profiles of Janet Marie Smith. Two days later, the paper printed this missive from a man in White Hall: "Now we know why this stadium is such a hokey, screwed-up mess. It's being done by women from Mississippi who know nothing about baseball. Great job, Lucchino. You really know how to pick 'em."

In August, Queen Elizabeth visited Memorial Stadium. Her helicopter flew over Camden Yards.

"Why do you need another one?" she asked.

Janet Marie Smith bounds into the room holding something that looks like a right-angled iron boomerang. In fact, it is a section of the railings that will separate the box seats.

But it is much, much more than a piece of iron and a ball joint; where Bob Wyatt might see an unneeded piece of metal that may rust and need painting, Janet Marie Smith sees a work of art. Now the box-seat railings will look exactly like the box-seat railings in the old parks, and to Smith, anything that looks the way it used to is a work of art.

Of course, art is not always practical; this particular homage to the good old days will ensure that the box-seat holders in the lower deck, while being fortunate enough to watch a game in an historically correct setting, will also have to twist and turn to get into their seats, bumping the knees of the people closer to the aisles, because the railings will eat up a good six inches of walking room.

In fact, there is no reason to have railings at all; they are a holdover from the days when the wealthy preferred to be separated from the other wealthy, if only symbolically. But they are pretty. And they signify another Janet Marie Smith victory in her ongoing battle for historical detail.

"The contractors said we couldn't get them!" she says. "But we found a foundry in Kansas City that can get them."

She is smiling a mile wide. She is smiling more widely than, perhaps, she has ever been seen smiling before.

"I think I'm just going to hold on to this for a while," she says, settling into a seat in an office trailer on the site, ready to look at the blueprints for the outfield wall. She and Frank Robinson, now a former manager who has been reassigned to stadium detail, are concerned that the wall is too close to the seats, so that a line-drive home run might appear to have hit the wall and stayed in play, when, in fact, it may have cleared the wall by an inch, hit the concrete, and bounced back in. The agenda for the day is clotted with other details: inspection of the showers. Inspection of the bull pens. Examination of the Camden Green canvaslike plastic material that will cover the outfield wall.

Within a minute or two, Janet Marie's smile has waned. Truth be told, she is not in a great mood. On this day the state is still talking about building a right-angled extension onto the south end of the warehouse to house the state highway department, against the Orioles' strident opposition.

In addition to which, the last few weeks have seen the announcement that ticket prices are going to be high—in all, a 25 percent increase over prices at Memorial, the biggest hike in the majors—and that reserved grandstand tickets have been eliminated, so that lower reserve moves to the outfield and some terrace boxes that had been slated for $7.50 are now $12.

The papers continue to be full of speculation over the naming of the park. Jacobs is vehement about Oriole Park. Governor Schaefer is vehement about Camden Yards. The lease agreement says they have to agree. They can't. It is getting ridiculous, and everyone knows it.

On top of which, the day before, the *Post*'s Jonathan Yardley has called it a rich people's park.

"Rich person's park? This is hardly a rich person's park," Smith says, before we begin. "It was Mr. Jacobs's idea to keep the slope low, for the fans' comfort. *That's* hardly a rich person's park."

At the table, blueprints spread in front of him, Frank Robinson has to smile. That's the exact, literal truth: He *has* to smile; she's a coworker. He'd prefer not to, though. Janet Marie Smith had left him waiting for forty minutes, waiting outside his car on a dusty road on the site—no surprise, she is never on time, and by now no one expects her to be—but this was forty minutes in the middle of an afternoon during which Frank Robinson could be back in the Orioles' offices finding ways to market Sam Horn's swing, which produced a sweet home run the night before, to the rest of the league. Frank Robinson had been a manager not long before, with full expectations of extending that tenure into the new park. In his third time behind a manager's desk, he had once again done a good job in his first two years, bringing a sense of professionalism, class, and cool to a franchise sorely in need of identity.

But his tenure was not to be. Ultimately, his major failing caught up with him—"No rapport with the players—none—the *worst* manager at rapport with the players I have ever seen—*please!*" was the assessment of a long-time Oriole, now retired. Lucchino (or, just as likely, the spirit of civil-rightsman Edward Bennett Williams, channeling through Lucchino) had kept Robinson on to both help with the stadium, ostensibly lending a player's point of view, and to help with the general-managing duties. But since the stadium was clearly Janet Marie Smith's (if Robinson had to give out the quote about how the quirky outfield would produce more triples, one of the "most exciting plays in baseball," one more time he would scream, as would the journalist obliged to hear it), what he really wanted was to make his mark as a GM. This was difficult enough, what with Roland Hemond being the real GM and Doug Melvin the assistant.

And here he'd squandered forty dusty minutes, a man in a suit without a hair out of place, his shoes so polished they reflected the morning sun, out here in the dust and the wind and the scraps of paper from the lunch cart blowing up in little tornadoes, forty minutes during which time he had to endure various workers looking for autographs, people with less than a great deal of tact ("Could I get your autograph? I couldn't get Brooks's the day he was out here"). When, finally, Smith pulled in in her black BMW, and jumped out of the car in a black-and-orange jacket/skirt ensemble, visible at three miles, and jammed the hard hat on her head, neither exchanged glances.

But now Smith has come in with her cast-iron ball-jointed box-seat railing, the one she's been looking for for months, and Frank Robinson has to smile. It's a slow developing thing, that smile, but once it gets going, it gains momentum, until Robinson is shaking his head while he's smiling.

Soon the Frank Robinson dry humor—it's his favorite mode of social interaction—is in full stride. She leaves the office for a moment and returns with a swatch of the material that will cover the outfield fence.

"We have a Camden Green swatch here," she says. "Isn't it beautiful?"

"What if they call it Oriole Park?" Robinson asks, with a Frank Robinson smile.

"It's still Camden Green," Janet Marie says, and the expression on her face begs no further discussion.

Now, when Frank has finally loosened up enough to see humor everywhere, Janet Marie's smile is waning.

It is often difficult to tell whether Janet Marie has heard you or not. When they leave the trailer to tour the site, when Janet Marie puts on her hat, it appears to be too small.

"Your head's gotten larger," Frank says. Janet Marie appears not to hear.

Down in the showers, down in the still-nascent locker room, Robinson the player has a chance to turn the tables. Even in its half-baked state, this is clearly a players' place. Robinson sees that the shower heads are too high up, and—worse—are of a design that will spray needles of water instead of gentle showers. With stunningly short words, as if he's biting off pieces of a radish, Robinson snaps, "The tile is beautiful, but the shower head is all wrong! You put that up here? We talked about this."

"I know we did," says Janet Marie. She is not trying to get out of it, although she does admit making the mistake. It seems an uncharacteristic concession but it's prompted by one of the wisest philosophies she has held on to throughout the project: Always defer to a player in baseball matters.

They poke their heads into the manager's shower stall, which is still under construction. Janet Marie notices several numbers written on a few tiles, a couple of square inches. She wets her thumb and rubs them out. Robinson points out, with a smile, that she has erased the workman's specifications. Janet Marie allows herself a smile at her manic attention to detail.

Above us, the field is still a parched prairie, half the seats have yet to be installed, the lights haven't gone up and there is no scoreboard, yet she is agonizing over three square inches of a manager's shower stall.

In the Orioles' locker room, Smith explains, the mirrors will give an open feeling to the space.

"Mirrors are a good thing," she says, "when you use them wisely and well. The mirrors beneath the bars in the luxury suites give a reflection of the warehouse. In the locker room, men like to pretend they don't care, but they do. You can bet your bottom dollar they stop to straighten their tie."

Well, yes, except that none of them wear ties, I offer. But she seems to perceive even this mild jab at humor as an effort at contradiction, and her own retort is quick and impatient:

"Have you seen the men's rest room at 30th Street Station in Philadelphia?" she says.

Well, yes, I have.

"Then you don't have to ask me about mirrors," she says, as if annoyed.

"Wait a minute," I say, hoping to lighten the mood. "What were you doing in the men's room at 30th Street Station?"

Frank Robinson smiles.

Janet Marie doesn't.

End of conversation.

We pass a room that was going to be used as a green room for national-anthem singers and pregame performers. She explains that they have decided to use it for child care.

What, then, will the rock singers get?

"What they deserve," she says, and there's no use pursuing that. Or asking what in the world she meant.

Out in the outfield, I ask her why she asked for an office on the other side of the warehouse, behind everyone else's.

"My job isn't to have a good view of the game," Janet Marie says. "My job is to get a good view for forty-eight thousand other people. It's hard to tell people what to do when you're in front of them."

"I'll take the view," Frank says.

Janet Marie appears not to have heard. This last exchange actually sums up Smith pretty well: She genuinely doesn't care about having a luxurious office, since she'd rather watch a game from the stands any day. But when it comes to the concerns of those average fans, she is not so in touch with them that she would abolish box-seat railings in the interests of comfort, or insist that the third-base seats curve toward home plate instead of facing the outfield; she'd rather the park adhere to the street grid. While she makes every effort to consider the viewpoint of the common fan—both in the stadium design and in her daily life—she never loses sight of who's signing her paycheck.

"It's taken on the look that she wanted." Robinson says in his car as we drive up Charles Street. "Not *similar* to what she wanted. What she wanted."

I observe that she can be tough.

"She doesn't hit you WHAM!" he says. "She hits you BOP. You say to yourself, 'Did she just hit me?' She comes on all soft and gentle, but she means business. She knows her business, too. With all the travelling she's done, I've gotten to know her chair more than her."

He does a quick pantomime of himself sticking his head into an office and saying hello to an empty chair. And he laughs.

"And you call her Janet Marie Smith. Not Janet. You call her Janet Marie."

In landscape architect Kent Sundberg's car, en route to a New Jersey nursery, Janet Marie is talking about the fringe nature of her neighborhood in Baltimore—Butcher Hill, a gentrification zone marked by the insistent tugs of white and black, poor and not-so-poor.

Like Silver Lake in Los Angeles. She has put her domicile where her philosophy is.

Perhaps it's the prospect of an afternoon spent strolling in a nursery, away from the site, away from the Orioles, away from the phone calls and the dust and the workers and the bricks and the cinder blocks. Perhaps it's the neutral environment of Sundberg's car. Whatever the cause, on this morning Janet Marie Smith uncharacteristically agrees to volunteer an episode of a personal nature.

Sundberg, an associate with Wallace Roberts & Todd, the Philadelphia firm, remains quiet, and drives.

"Getting mugged didn't bother me that much," Smith says. "The incident upset me, but it didn't bother me philosophically.

"It was one of those classic nights. One of my best friends is in town, a reporter turned attorney in Nashville. I've been three days out of town, looking at Candlestick, Busch, the Skydome, and I have one day in town in Baltimore before leaving on vacation for a week. She was going to be in Washington for one night. I said, 'Come on up, but I'm going to have to work.' So she said, 'Don't worry. It won't be a problem.' Then I got asked if I'd sit in a box with Jesse Jackson during that night's game. I said, 'Yeah,' being a Jesse Jackson fan. So we went to the game with Jackson. He left in the seventh.

"Then we go to a club. We're the only white people there. It turns out to be ladies' night. Men dancing around, the women are putting dollar bills in their . . ." and the sentence trails off.

It is nearly impossible to imagine: Janet Marie Smith at ladies' night in a black bar with her girlfriend. Then again, there are so many shadows in Janet Marie Smith's personality, it's just plausible enough. And it is true that small clues hint at another side to Smith, like her Polár beer key chain, a Brazilian brew favored in Miami. Or the night a colleague spied her in the lounge in the Baltimore train station playing a video baseball game. Or the times, John Pastier recalls, when she and a girlfriend would pile into her car in Los Angeles on a Friday and drive to Mississippi for a long weekend.

Janet Marie as Thelma! But Janet Marie doesn't need a gun; a Fresca can will do.

Which is the point of the story.

"At two we left. We went home. I was driving around, wanting to park close to my house. My friend is afraid she's going to get sick. The police pull us over."

Here, it is easy to imagine Janet Marie laying the Mississippi lilt atop her best blue-steel-eyed look, for the Luke Skywalker Force-Be-With-You effect: *"We're fine, officer." "You're right,"* says the cop, *"you're fine." "You'll let us go." "You can go,"* says the cop.

"Ten minutes later we find a place. I jump out and a guy has a knife at my throat. He came from nowhere. I say, 'Is this about money?' He says, 'Yeah.' I say, 'Okay, my purse is in the trunk.' I have a trunk where I can lock the door with my trunk key, so I open the trunk and lock my friend inside the car. I get my purse. I keep my bills ordered in my purse. I have several hundred dollars—I'm going on vacation. I took advantage of it. I pulled out two twenties. He said, 'This isn't enough.' I pulled out two ones and said, 'This is all I have.' He ran."

I ask her if she's wary now when she parks.

"Now when I come home late at night I park at the bus stop and take the ticket. It's worth the seventeen dollars."

It is quiet and calm at the Millington Nursery in Millington, New Jersey. The day is full with the scent of summer meeting fall. The wind is whistling through the red spire pears, and the sun pokes through the branches to skitter across the ground in odd patterns. The landscaping at Camden Yards, Sundberg explains, includes silver lindens for the east side of the warehouse, ginkgos for the pedestrian spine—female ginkgos, of course—honey locusts for the picnic area, and flowering pears for the perimeter on the west side and London Plane on Russell Street.

Janet Marie walks on ahead. Kent rubs the trunks of various trees affectionately. He envisions the way they'll look ringing Camden Yards. He is worried for them.

"When you take them to urban areas, they'll go through a period of shock," he says. "We recommend a special soil mix, trenching the entire tree, mixed with peat moss and organic fertilizer. The paving design can't limit the moisture. It's difficult to get air and water. There will be potential compaction problems because of the roots. It's not ideal for the roots to be in an urban environment. Irrigation rings for every tree."

Janet Marie Smith is walking from tree to tree, choosing some, discarding others. Beside her is Betsy Gulick, a personable young woman who works for Millington. She is holding a pile of yellow tags. Every time Janet Marie sees a tree she likes, Betsy hands her a tag, and Janet tags it for transportation down to Baltimore.

Besty is trying to rein in a whole lot of excitement. She spends her days dealing with landscape architects. She has never spent her day with people building a stadium.

"Did you guys design the stadium?" Betsy Gulick says.

"We're helping," Janet Marie Smith says.

"My kids aren't going to believe this," Betsy says, to Janet Marie and Kent and me. "My kids saw a television show on that place. They said, 'Mom, you gotta take me down there.' They *hate* to watch the Phillies. They're not going to believe this. When they saw it on TV it really hyped 'em up."

Janet Marie is looking at the trees, closely, skeptically, with the trace of a frown. This is not her favorite nursery. It is nothing like Angelica, where they found their ginkgos, down on the Eastern Shore, with its long driveway lined by Dawn redwood and American Holly and Blue Star Juniper and burning bush and—their own tree— Angelica, two thousand acres of perfect green. One hundred and fifty migrant workers live in dormitories, working forty-hour weeks, with free child care and full health insurance. But Millington is better than the one on Long Island where the dog at the gate had fleas and they were unable to bring themselves to buy a single tree.

"Wow—a woman's in charge of this project? You'd think baseball, it'd be all men," Betsy Gulick says.

"I think it amuses the Orioles," Janet Marie says. "I think they like it . . . perversely, because it seems so different."

It is the first and only time she says anything like that.

Smith pauses in front of one tree.

"I thought they had a pendulous form when they got older. These are pyramidal."

Then she says, "What'd your kids find so impressive?"

"The grass," Betsy says. "You know, my kids eat, breathe, and live baseball."

They walk on. Then Betsy says, "How did you get the job?"

Janet Marie frames the answer in her head first.

"The Orioles have an agreement with the state to let them be involved," she says. "They wanted it to look old. They felt that the best way to do it was to hire someone who's worked on these projects before. It wasn't like baseball was a new thing. I'd done it as recreation. Not as a job."

Janet Marie is walking ahead of Betsy.

"I'm ready for another one," she says to Betsy without looking at her. Betsy hands her a tag. Smith never says please, but there's no condescension intended. It's as if she doesn't see the other woman at all.

"My son," Betsy Gulick says, "won a contest to meet the Phillie Phanatic. But you step on that Astroturf, and it feels so weird."

"Did you know that physically you couldn't have built the pyramids the way they did in those Cecil B. DeMille movies, on those platforms? You would have used more man-hours than there ever were. What they did was put rounded things on the sides of the blocks."

On a hot, windy July afternoon, wind swirls dust on the site, and Tom Rogers is patrolling the park. Born in Worcester, Massachusetts, the son of a wire salesman and a Romanian gypsy, Rogers is a walrussy kind of man, and he's just about always smiling when he's on a construction site.

"See that pile of sand there? That's what I'd play in as a kid. I had the giant Erector set. With the motor. I had the giant set of Lincoln Logs."

Several piles of sand dot the field; they are being brought in to lay down beneath the turf; the stadium itself is nearly in place now. On this day, some of the final concrete is being poured down the first-base side, the base for some of the best box seats; in the upper deck, clusters of seats cover some expanses of concrete, like Christmas-tree farms, while other expanses lay bare.

Tom Rogers works for Barton Malow/Sverdrup, the chief contractor. He is the on-hands supervisor for the entire project. But part of him belongs at a lectern. It seems to be that way with a lot of the men on the site, as if, in working with their hands, their brains are starved for engagement.

"The traditional park started where it started because the city streets told it to," Tom Rogers is saying. "The streets said that was where it was going to be. The city park was bounded by streets that didn't have buildings on them. When they went suburban, they took a big piece of land, found the center, and said, 'Okay, this is it.'

"We wanted to go back to where it grew organically."

Tom Rogers didn't design any of the park, but like a lot of people at the park, he speaks of the place as his. As well he ought. He has stopped in front of the cement that has just been poured on the first-base side. It appears to be slightly warped.

"Is this your work?" he demands of the man from Greenwald Concrete. "I'm not going to pay for it. It's the worst I've seen"—and turns his back and walks away. There is no question that Greenwald Concrete will redo the concrete.

Tom Rogers earned his master's from Missouri in civil engineering, and that's what he does: he engineers civilly.

"We have seven hundred guys out here. We'll have several thousand of man-years time spent on the job. Between the factories making the stuff, and HOK, and the design, two thousand hours a year, I figure four hundred thousand man-hours overall."

We are standing in what will soon be Eli Jacobs's luxury suite. Right now it consists of a couple of planes of precast concrete. The view is of a field covered by white plastic and PCV piping.

"Prescription Athletic Turf," Rogers explains. "First you lay the sheet goods."

The sheet goods?

"The plastic. Then thousands of feet of PCV piping with slits so narrow they allow water molecules through, but not dirt. Eight inches of sandy dirt will go on top, then the sod. It'll absorb seven inches of water in twenty-four hours. One rainout represents five hundred thousand dollars in lost revenues.

"It's all dollars and cents. But the Orioles did the right things," Rogers says. "They could have said, 'Fuck it, let's bulldoze the warehouse.' Or, 'Let's build a concrete doughnut in Glen Burnie.'

They did the right things. The cheap seats here are better than the cheap seats in Memorial. And the [luxury] boxes aren't going to be shoved in the faces of the forty thousand people who can't afford them. They won't have signs saying, 'Rich people here, assholes and groundlings here.' You're going to have to know how to get to them. They could have had the boxes sticking out, but it wouldn't have worked with what they were trying to accomplish."

The view from the box does not seem dramatic. The suites seem to be set back, inconspicuously, not at all annoying; like the boxes at an opera, in effect. Mostly, the warehouse looms, gently. The steelwork is no match for the brick mass directly in front of us. Rogers notes the differing shades of brick in the old building.

"They had hot spots in the old kilns. The darker bricks have more iron oxide. And maybe he couldn't pay the kickback, and they didn't deliver the rest of the batch. The walls of the warehouse are thicker at the bottom, you know. In the warehouse, nothing is level, or plumb, or flat. There's a lot of disparity in floor elevation. It slopes three feet. It was supposed to. I worked in an old B-17 factory in Ypsilanti. Everything rolled downhill."

I ask about the extension to the warehouse.

"We worked with HOK on that. We even worked with the Historical Society," Tom Rogers says. "They liked it. But Janet Marie Smith didn't like it. So it was out."

He shakes his head with a smile. Janet Marie will do that to people.

"This is being done as well as anything I've ever seen. The collaboration between the city and the agency and the architects. But I'm not saying we don't get angry at the Orioles. They've been a pain in the ass."

Janet Marie is working her way through the maze of cement deep in the half-finished basement. A few walls of cinder block signify what will soon be the team dentist's office in the middle of the locker-room complex. On this day, Janet Marie has decided she doesn't like the dentist's office. She thinks it would be better served now as a foyer into the players' lounge.

"One of the things we're concerned about, because the space is so huge, is we could lose the camaraderie of the clubhouse spirit," she says. "I don't want to segregate the environment and make it feel like a schoolhouse. See, I don't want to lose the sense of openness."

She walks back to the trailer. She asks an MSA assistant to find her the keys to the luxury box that's been finished; in a few minutes, she has to choose carpeting colors. No one can find the keys. Smith bites back her impatience.

In Tom Rogers's office, Janet Marie sits down with Rogers and Bruce Hoffman. There are stray ions shooting about the room. But everyone seems accustomed to the tension, long grown used to it, like a nagging cold that won't go away.

Smith tells Hoffman that she wants to knock down the cinder block wall of the dentist's office. It would be a good idea to do it today, she says; the appropriate work crew is here on the site. If they wait, they may have to wait months.

As usual, Rogers senses the need for levity: "It's just another nail in my coffin, that's all."

Hoffman isn't smiling. He doesn't like it. A moment of heavy silence. The door to Hoffman's office is closed, although the sound of people clomping in and out on the other side is as loud as if it were open. It's one of the oddities of construction sites that men and women building permanent structures do their work in structures that would vanish in a serious sneeze.

The pause is filled by a sense of a showdown. Janet Marie's mouth is set in a straight line, and her eyes are at their most blankly impassive; they are bottomless, entirely empty. Quite suddenly, this is not Janet Marie Smith and Bruce Hoffman; it is the Orioles versus the state of Maryland.

"We're backsliding," Bruce Hoffman says.

"It's player related," Smith says, playing a trump card; player-related changes are a priority.

"So's not having a stadium," Rogers says.

Point, Rogers. A pause.

"We're tearing down finished work?" Hoffman says.

Smith nods.

"It's demoralizing," Hoffman says.

He and Rogers exchange glances.

"We'll do it later," says Hoffman—whereupon Janet Marie Smith's face hardens still another degree. She appears to be contemplating a response, then thinks better of it, and jumps out of her chair, pivots, and whips out of the room, so quickly that she leaves a tangible empty space. It's a prickly void, too; its very silence is like a scream. Hoffman and Rogers exchange a careful glance.

In the adjacent trailer, Smith tracks down the assistant empowered with finding the suite keys. The keys cannot be found.

"I'm leaving," she barks, making it clear that they have failed. "I'm gone."

As she walks to her car, someone on the site whistles. If she hears it, she doesn't indicate it.

CHAPTER 9

RED AND GREEN

◆

"EVERYBODY THINKS because a guy's a bricklayer, [and] you work with your back, you're stupid," Charlie Smith says with a shake of the head one August day, and while it is true that he is broad backed, and possesses a handshake that features bunches of muscle and tendon born of decades of hefting the hardened-clay blocks, Charlie Smith is also not lacking in intelligence. He talks a great deal, of a great many things, most of them made of brick, in the confident tones of a man giving a lecture. Men will do this when they've practiced one craft for thirty years and have had ample time to think about it.

Charlie Smith speaks in logic as unassailable, as carefully assembled, as the wall of perfect red Maryland brick in front of which he is standing.

"When a house burns down, what's standing?" It is a riddle not unlike the Sphinx's. Charlie Smith seems to endow it with a great deal of significance. He has an earnestly ruddy complexion born of three decades of bricklaying in the sun and wind.

He waits for an answer, can't wait any longer.

"The chimney," he says, with a satisfied nod. And he's right. "See, the beauty of brick is *it's there*, and it's there for all time. It gives you this individual pride. Instead of boxed walls . . . When you drive by the site, you say, 'I worked there.' You can't take it away."

Charlie Smith stops.

"Unless you blow it up."

We are strolling the grounds of the park on a warm and windy July afternoon. We are on the Russell Street side, the third-base side, where the wall of brick has been finished. On this day, Smith's crew is working on the wall on the other side, down the right-field side, heading inexorably, a dozen feet a day, toward the warehouse. Charlie is showing me the work they've already done. Charlie's talking brick. It's his favorite subject. He backs up his talk too; in his basement room at home Charlie built a fireplace and put brick on each side of it, up to a height of four feet, and then laid wainscotting above it. The opposing wall is mirrored, so it looks as if it's brick too. Charlie puts his brick where his mouth is.

Charlie Smith is the on-site foreman for Baltimore Masonry. Since 1963 he's been a member of the Bricklayers and Allied Craftsmen of Maryland Local One. It's a brick town—used to be, anyway. Camden Yards, with all of its bricks being fired right over in Westernport, has brought back a little of the glory.

And there is glory in brick, certainly in Baltimore. If you doubt it, ask Charlie Smith. It doesn't take a fine eye to see that there is glory on this job. When it's finished, Camden Yards will feature 600,000 bricks—most of them ornamental, like a curtain hung flat in front of a wall, but inspiring nonetheless.

The job is full of detail; thirty different kinds of custom brick were fired in local kilns to build this park—two kinds of bullnose (thumbnail and toenail), stacked bond, running bond, circle arches, jack arches. Thirty different bricks. That speaks of plenty of detail. That is a good thing for Smith's crews, for monotony is the mason's enemy. He was pleased to discover, he said, that the Camden Yards job was quite full of variations on the usual theme, which is generally, well, just a wall. That's how bricklayers refer to themselves when they're at work—"on the wall."

"I told them, 'Don't be afraid to design curved, serpentine,' " Smith says, of a conversation with the architects. "If you do this day in and day out it gets monotonous. If the bricklayer's got detail work to do, he's happy. Besides. If you do too much of one thing it's no good. It'll look like a fucking dungeon. But what if you come up with wainscotted brick? The distressed panelling? The arches? You break it up."

"This is a Roman arch," he tells me. "The same type of arch at Pompeii."

At our feet is an arched wooden mold. It is inserted into the opening, the bricks are laid above it, and when they harden, the mold is pulled out.

We continue our stroll. Charlie moves swiftly and surely, despite some girth. Everyone on a construction site moves with agility; there's always the chance they'll have to get out of the way of something quickly.

"Look at the houses today," he says. "They don't want to give you brick. A wooden porch, I had to paint it three times. Brick ain't like painting. You don't have to paint every year when you're using brick. Brick looks good with landscaping, too. When you got your green against your brick? When that brick gets washed, and they put in some grass and shrubbery—bingo."

I ask Smith about old bricks and new bricks. New bricks, he says, are generally wire cut now—a sheet of brick is cut up into its rectangles by a wire grid.

"Years ago," he says, "the bricks were softer. Now they're harder, and if you break them, there's a ragged edge. The new mortars are definitely stronger. You go over to Russia, they have façade nets. The bricks are all dropping off."

Charlie Smith lives for extolling the job, for extolling the union, but mostly extolling the brick. He has earned the privilege. He won a Building Congress Award for craftsmanship a few years back for his brickwork on the Fort Meade School, off state Route 175. The award means everything to him,

"Now they're gonna know my name," he says. And what more does anyone really want? No one knew his grandfather's name. His grandfather was a miner who lost his lungs and his life in the mines of northern England. His father welded warships in this town during the forties, when the docks in Baltimore turned out a ship every month. Charlie Smith has been a mason in Baltimore since 1963, and he believes in his work. He believes in his material. He bemoans the passing of his craft, and of brick itself.

"Everybody thinks a union is bad," he tells me. "In the meantime, we're taking a cut. Union-wise, this country, it doesn't take no genius to see they're knockin' down the unions. But if you want to get something good, you got to pay a few dollars more. The union guy is out here in the elements. Hot sun! He's got to work. People say, 'He doesn't work in cold weather.' It's because the mortar freezes!

"Also, you get your money's worth. [A mason] can't hide how much work he does. You can't scam me. I can walk away and come back and see how much work you did."

Across from the Russell Street side of the site, where the brick skin is finished, stand the brick rowhouses of Ridgely's Delight, and the Metropolitan Life Insurance Company, with its splendid brickwork, and its stunning stone quoins.

"Flemish Bond," Charlie says. "The bricks in that building. They're Flemish Bond. You see them on churches. Lemme tell you something about these buildings. They'll give you eight inches of brick. Look at those houses over there. It'd be a sin to build this stadium out of anything but brick. Look at that. That's design."

In three months Charlie Smith's crews have finished three quarters of the skin, starting down the third-base side at the eighteen line— the eighteenth steel girder away from home plate—and working toward home plate, then wrapping around and heading for the warehouse.

The job went to a union crew, Smith insists, because on a job this size, with public funding, under such intense scrutiny, "they're not gonna take no chances."

The brickwork called for skilled work. With 600,000 bricks to be laid, HOK looked into the possibility of precasting the brick into panels: putting the bricks into a plastic liner, cementing it to a precast five-ton concrete panel, removing the plastic after the whole thing dries, and shipping it to the park. But HOK decided they didn't want to risk the sides of bricks chipping off in the process of erecting a precast concrete wall; they opted for the more costly process of stacking the bricks, one by one, against a standing wall.

"They had to go with who they felt was going to give them a good job," Smith says. "Knott went in and his bid was higher."

Henry J. Knott Inc. is Baltimore Masonry's chief competition in the Baltimore brick marketplace. Knott is not a union shop. Knott was awarded the block-laying part of the job—something like stretching the canvas for the artist. (Worse. Cinder block is America's shame. Why else would we paint it? We don't usually feel the need to paint brick, do we?)

Charlie Smith could have gone to Knott, by the way—"I coulda been riding around in one of Knott's vehicles with a phone right now"—but he wanted to stay on the sites, laying the bricks. He wanted to stay union.

"This job was godsent. We've been hanging by a thread. This was godsent. 'Til this came along, we were getting a smaller and smaller percentage of the work."

Baltimore Masonry used to mostly build schools, but now they're losing so much to drywall: "The kids can push right through it," Charlie says. "We used to do more elevator shafts, too. In this building they're brick. But in the VA hospital? Stairwells and shafts are drywall."

Charlie Smith shakes his head.

"This town is a brick town. Local One! We were the first local! Now all you're seein' is precast and glass." Charlie isn't just lamenting the loss of work, either; his aesthetics are weighing in. Concrete looks terrible most of the time. It's heavy and it's ugly. Concrete in the rain, streaked and soiled, is ugly as hell. There's no question about the distinctly impermanent look that modern materials lend big buildings, or of brick's opposite effect.

As we talk, a fire truck passes on Russell. The driver bleats his horn. Smith waves. Union to union, workman to workman.

"Once in a lifetime you can build a stadium," he says.

Above us a bricklayer gives a thumbs-up sign. It is not because things are going well; it is because he needs a brick, and in the bricklayer's signing code, a thumb means a thumbnail bullnose. Ten fingers would mean he needs a corner slope for the quoin.

"Let's go lay brick," Charlie Smith says suddenly, with such enthusiasm and appetite, with so much emphasis that each word deserves to have its first letter capitalized. It's a startling proposition, not the sort of statement you'd expect to hear from the mouths of other workmen: "Let's go bag groceries," or, "Let's go write an editorial." It is the declaration of a man who would rather lay brick than talk about it. And it is the one way to prove to the world that laying brick is more than you think it is.

Laying brick is all rhythm: Dip the flat trowel in the mortar to scoop it up, slap the stuff on top of the last brick with your right hand, drop a brick onto the new mortar with the left, take the corner of the trowel and trim the excess mortar off, dip the trowel back into the barrow, start it up again.

"I worked on the Russian embassy," Smith says as he slaps a few bricks himself. "They had cameras on the wall. They were watching you all the time."

To get on the wall he'd had to walk up to the concourse level, crawl over the ledge down onto the rickety planks of scaffolding, walk out to the corner of the tower, and climb down five feet on the scaffolding. The planks supported a barrow full of mortar and stacks of several thousand bullnose (fingernail) bricks, fired by Calvert, rose red the color.

Watch a good mortar man on the wall and the bricks start to pile up effortlessly, as if they're all freeze frames adding up to an animated cartoon; before your eyes, the blank precast concrete support turns into the walls of a stadium whose brickwork could be in Venice.

"Brick changes color three times for you," Charlie says. "When you lay it up, it's wet. Then it dries. Then it gets washed down, it's another color still."

He notes my amusement at the perfection of his stroke.

"Like slicing lunch meat at a deli," he says. But it's not. Smith leaves no excess mortar. The line from brick to brick is perfect. It is like watching a good singles hitter, a Rod Carew, a man who makes a living from hits that don't look so much as if a baseball being violently slapped around a field, but rather like the ball is being gently, though forcefully, redirected. A good mason makes the bricks look as if they're eager to be on the wall.

It is not nearly as easy as it looks. The bullnose brick—a toenail—is heavy in your left hand; the uncooperative mortar drops and drips off the trowel. You slap it down, it's much too thick, and when you slap the next brick down mortar comes shooting out of the grout like frosting between two slabs of steel.

Several minutes later five bricks on the wall of Camden Yards have been laid not by Local One but by a bystander, and they are the five shakiest bricks you'd ever want to see.

"I seen Palmer pitch his no-hitter in '69," Smith says after we've climbed off the wall. We are walking down the stairwell, on the outside of which his men are now bricking. "I was one of the three thousand who saw Brooks beat Cleveland in the ninth in his last year. You'd have thought he'd won the Series. Gentile, Powell—I'm listening on the radio when he powdered three.

"Sometimes we'd go to the games," he recalls. "Get a six. Fill a two-liter jug. You'd buy the first cup, then keep filling it from the jug."

On our way down the stairs we run into the president of Baltimore Masonry, Victor Campitelli. Campitelli's father founded the company.

"The big one we did," Victor tells me, "is the Physics and Astronomy Building at Johns Hopkins. Where they record all the Hubble telescope stuff."

Victor calls Charlie aside, and they chat. I regard the flat concrete precast wall onto which Charlie's crew has yet to lay the brick skin. Victor is doing all the talking. I wonder if, on his way in, he'd glanced up at the wall and seen five bricks with mortar dripping from beneath them.

Charlie and I walk out of the park, to the spot where thousands of bricks are stacked.

"Here," he says, hefting two bullnose toenails. "Take these. Use 'em for bookends."

I take one in each hand. They are much heavier than the fateful five. They are extremely heavy. They weigh as much, it seems, as the earth's original ingredients. Real things could be built of these bricks.

Charlie has turned around to regard the wall. He is quiet. We look at the wall. It is hypnotic, in its scale, in its subtlety. Brick does that. Who isn't drawn, at one point or another, even to America's brick ruins? By the nobility of their stature? They have a particularly stalwart feel, even in the decomposing. In the backyards of industrial cities, the factories sit, empty windows staring blankly, unblinking; remnants of neon signs are in tatters, but the brick shells still stand, ivy curling up the walls, trying to tear them down, and not succeeding.

The sight of golden sun setting on good crimson brick is a color that is unduplicatable.

At first Smith appears to be watching his crew. In fact, he is regarding the soaring plane of red brick. The bullnoses, the detail, the arches. The wall of Camden Yards nearly matches the soaring wall of the warehouse—a tapestry of another time.

"This was designed," Charlie Smith says, with a nod at Camden Warehouse, "by an architect who knew brickwork."

"That's me," Stuart Smith says.

He means the brick face of Camden Yards, the one he designed, carefully, replete with all of the subtle ripples and ridges. He designed it after spending a few days examining, in the minutest of details, the old brick monolith of the Powerhouse building, the old power plant down on the harbor—his favorite building in the city.

But he also means, in another sense, that he and the brick are one, and that he and the park are one. After all, he spent four thousand hours with the place. That's five hundred work days, most of it in design.

Stuart Smith is no relation to Charlie Smith, although now, of course, they are bonded forever. Stuart was the project designer on Camden Yards. You wouldn't know it unless you read the in-house memos circulated by HOK, but he was. Stuart Smith designed more than the brick; the arches are his, too. The steel trusses? Stuart and Joe Spear worked on those drawings. A lot of detail belongs to Stuart Smith. But it's the brick you should know about.

When Smith arrived on the scene, off his work helping HOK to design an arena in Sheffield, England, the Camden Yards master plan had been finished. It showed a brick façade, but that's all. The eventual design—the way the bricks are used, the thirty palates that Charlie Smith so admires—is his.

"I had a piece of this pie," Stuart Smith says after thinking the sentence through carefully.

How big?

"Wouldn't we like to say all but a sliver? In my eyes, in my four thousand hours of design, I feel I brought some good ideas to the stadium."

It's not that he is looking for more credit than he deserves, although a little individual credit would be nice. While the internal memos at HOK cited Spear as Principal in Charge and Stuart Smith as Project Designer, the official history, in *Progressive Architecture,* cited him as nothing but a member of the design team. So as time passes, Stuart Smith, once a designer of stadiums, now setting his sights on buildings of more diversity of design, has found himself fading into the fog of history.

Just as troubling to Smith is that history keeps being written the Orioles' way.

In fact, Smith says, when he arrived on the scene in the middle of the steel versus concrete debate, he realized right off that the media were "not flying the HOK flag."

"We were pretty insignificant in the project, if you read the press. That's where the tensions came between HOK and Janet Marie Smith. You know, [speaking] as one of the young architects, we were trying to move HOK forward in innovative design. We wanted to market the stadium: 'Hey, this is ours!' "

Smith, for example, designed the arches. Arches were drawn on the master plan; Smith turned them into the deep arches that now stand—impressive passages, serious, weighty entrances, instead of adornments.

"We did a lot of the design work," he says. "They had input. Janet Marie had some magnificent ideas, but we were still the architects. It was a collaboration, [but] when it came to press acknowledgment, it was more toward the Orioles defining the stadium than us designing it."

In truth, Stuart Smith was not only designing the park, along with Joe Spear, who was working on other projects at the time; Smith often found himself sent alone into meetings with the Orioles. The aftertaste of that relationship, more than anything else, soured Smith on the experience of having contributed to Camden Yards.

"There were a lot of tensions," Smith says. "When you went into a good meeting, we'd present something, they liked it, you came out feeling pretty good. But fifty percent of the time, if not more, you came out saying, 'Man, I hate doing this.'

"I knew [Lucchino's] reputation. He hated HOK. He was one of the people who made it a rough deal. I was in meetings when we were doing interior design of the club level. He came in and said, 'That's an ugly color. I don't like that. Why are you doing this?' "

Even knowing Lucchino's reputation didn't prepare Stuart Smith for the extent of Lucchino's temper, which is legendary in Orioles offices. His sorest memory? Walking into a meeting in Florida and watching Lucchino, with whom he thought he was working, turn on him:

"We were doing a proposal for a spring-training facility. Janet asked Joe if I could work on that design. Nobody wanted to go. I felt kind of bad that nobody else in the office would do it except me. I go to Florida by myself. I'm supposed to have a meeting with Lucchino and Janet and USF&G [United States Fidelity & Guaranty Insurance Co.]. It was supposed to be a little presentation. I walk in and Lucchino says, 'What are you going to say?' I walk by the courtroom. There are TV cameras. A lot of people. It's a public city hearing!

"It was humbling. I got halfway through. Lucchino jumps up and says, 'No, that's not right. Sit down.' I was pretty livid at Joe for making me go down there. No one else wanted to be a support system. And here I am getting reamed by Lucchino. . . . It was like he almost enjoyed it.

"I went into these meetings a lot of times by myself. Once I came in with a graphics package, sick as a dog, walked in in the middle because my plane was late. They started hatcheting this graphics package. I took a lot of blows. I put in a lot of time. I don't want to sound ungrateful . . . but I probably do. But hey, look, I did a lot of the stadium."

Stuart Smith grew up in Lebanon, Missouri, 104 miles southwest of St. Louis. He was a Joe Torre fan. He would travel to Busch at least twice a month as a kid. His father ran halfback for Missouri; now he runs a cooperage business in Lebanon that supplies barrels for Jim Beam and Hiram Walker.

From high school Smith went to Kansas State University, Joe Spear's school, for the five-year bachelor of architecture program. He joined a small firm where he was doing design for Hallmark card stores, when he got a call from a friend at HOK. They were looking for someone with design experience. HOK took him on in 1988. He worked on a graphics package for the scoreboard in St. Petersburg, and the detail of the façade in Comiskey, and the arena in Sheffield, before coming to Camden Yards in the spring of 1989. The question of steel and concrete was not yet decided, but the stadium design—the way it would look—was set. It was up to Spear and Smith to design specific details—of the brick, of the arches, of the scoreboard.

Stuart Smith, not incidentally, never had a desire to design sports architecture. He had not been bitten by the big-bowl bug. Nor was he in it for the money. He did enjoy the perks—at least, in Chicago. Which is another thing that grates.

"After having the privilege of working on the White Sox and Baltimore . . . well, first off, the Sox' stadium will never be the Orioles' stadium, for a lot of reasons. Like the site. The Sox' stadium has bullet-proof glass on the first level, Camden Yards an iron fence, for instance.

"But the difference between the Sox and the Orioles—there were a lot more perks working with the Sox. They'd be happy to get you tickets, or baseballs, little things that said you were doing a good job. 'Even though we chewed you out in this meeting, you're doing a great job.' The Orioles never offered anything like that. The Sox gave us a suite. The Orioles? Well, we had one on Opening Day, but we didn't get it until the last minute.

"That was another sore point: They're chewing on us in meetings for virtually no reason, the attitude Lucchino had, and they're getting all the press for the stadium, and here we are—they decide, 'Let's change this,' and myself and many others were putting in seventy-hour weeks to make changes they wanted to make that we weren't even able to bill for."

Smith had no problem with Janet Marie Smith, although he agrees strongly that the credit—as in, the name of the architect—should go to Joe Spear: "He was the guy." At the same time, he insists, he enjoyed working with Janet Marie: "I was kind of put in the middle of wanting to please the Orioles, and do a good job for HOK. I had to try to be careful not to say to Joe, 'Janet suggested this, why don't we do this?' or, 'Janet, this is a lousy idea.' It's kind of tricky.

"In the long run, all of the good ideas came out, whether it took one meeting or ten meetings. It put a lot of pressures on people. Unnecessary pressures."

Stuart Smith is now out of the stadium game. He is glad of it, and not just because he was never recognized publicly as the project designer. It's because he got tired of his nickname—his second nickname. His first nickname was "youngster." It was spawned soon after he arrived at the age of twenty-six at HOK.

The second was "old-timer." "Since I worked on Comiskey, and now the Orioles, I was called old-timer. I was working on these old-time buildings. And that's not what interests me. I'm more into the new modernist architecture. I mean, once the Orioles were on board, Cleveland wants one just like it! Then Denver. The next ten will be like the Orioles."

At the age of twenty-nine, Stuart Smith didn't feel like an old-timer. He left HOK and enrolled in the master's program at Virginia Polytechnic Institute.

"I was just ready to move on. I was going to be cornered into designing stadiums."

If he was determined not to let that happen before Opening Day at Camden Yards, that day's experience clinched it. It was nothing like Opening Day at Comiskey; in Comiskey, HOK had a suite prepared for them long in advance. They still have the use of it now.

In Baltimore, on Opening Day, the HOK folks found themselves without a suite. An hour before game time, Joe Spear was sipping coffee in the press dining room. Only at the last minute was something arranged, and HOK was accommodated.

Many people in Baltimore who deal with the Orioles on a commercial basis find them arrogant. They speak of contracts broken. They speak of the Orioles' belief that, since they are the Orioles, they should automatically command respect.

They do not command Stuart Smith's.

But his brickwork rivets everyone. His and Local One's. So that now, to anyone approaching the city by car from the South, for whatever reason, whether to view baseball or not, the first glimpse is anchored by a rust-colored brick building laced with steel and arches—not as beautiful in detail, perhaps, as it is in its subtlety.

With the warehouse on its east, and the brick of Ridgely's Delight on its west, backed by the skyline, Camden Yards is at once a huddle of weight and lightness. From within the park, the warehouse is the most commanding design feature. From without, the brick compels the eye. The brick makes Camden Yards fit. The design of the brick—the details, the quoins, the arches—defines the Yards from the outside: the canvas of the brick.

I am standing amid a wash of green so beautiful and so vast that somehow, I know it should be cordoned off. It should be shaped like a baseball field. It should be rigorously framed, like a work of art, shouldn't it? Because there's nothing as immaculate and patterned, no piece of earth so lorded over, as a major-league baseball diamond. In a ballpark it is flawless—mowed into perfect whorls, into vertical and horizontal naps. A baseball field should be an exhibit.

This one is just a field, by the side of Route 13, south of Salisbury, Maryland, on the Eastern Shore. A patch of perfect green grass set amid the unruly roadside weeds, there in front of the Arby's, this square of green is the subtle but effective standard of the Oakwood Sod Farm. Take the next right, down a dirt road lined by ragweed and morning glory and lamb's-quarter, past the chicken houses, just before you get to the big farmhouse surrounded by eleven huge, elder, sleepy oaks, and there it is, on the right, sandwiched between two golden fields of soybeans.

It's nothing but a field. A four-acre field of pleasant green grass. It invites a stroll. Or a five-on-five touch football game. It invites a beautiful woman in a bathing suit reclining on a towel, accompanied by a tube of suntan lotion, a drink, and a good novel.

It's not even completely flat. It rolls. It doesn't start or stop anywhere, either. Not really. You park your car, walk beneath a few oaks, and you're on the grass.

"This is it," says Gary Wilber, with half a shrug. He is wearing a red sweatshirt, blue jeans, tan boots, and a green baseball hat embellished by a tan braid laid across the top of the visor. The legend OAKWOOD SOD FARM adorns the crown. Green and tan are the colors of the Oakwood Sod Farm. It only makes sense.

Gary is wearing sunglasses; this is to be expected, as sunlight glances off green and yellow everywhere. His expression is very calm, even nonchalant, considering that we are standing on the grass that will soon become the home of the Baltimore Orioles. Right now it belongs to no one but the buttery Eastern Shore sun—and, of course, the Wilber brothers. Technically it belongs to all of the Wilbers, including Gary and Alan's parents, but if truth be told, the sod operation on the Wilber farm belongs to the brothers. This is their mark. The family farm had always turned a profit, ever since their grandfather had come down from Connecticut to get away from the New England winters, and settled here on the Shore. The Wilbers' mother and father bought this tract in 1946. They did not choose it for its sandy soil, but it's a good thing the soil was sandy, because when the Orioles went to the University of Maryland Agricultural School in 1989 to divine which of the local sod farms had soil sandy enough to meet the specifications of the state-of-the-art drainage system they were installing, the school told them about the Wilber brothers over in Salisbury. The sandiest sod soil in the whole state, they were told, lies beneath Oakwood Sod Farm

The Wilber brothers signed the contract in August 1989, ordered the seed in September, and seeded in October. By the fall of 1991, they had grown four acres of baseball.

It wasn't that the Wilbers felt the overwhelming need to diversify; one hundred acres of corn, five hundred acres of soybeans, and twenty-eight-thousand chickens were handful enough. The family was doing quite well.

It was Gary Wilber's ambition that did it. Actually, that and the golf course association.

"Part of it," Gary says, "is we were looking to do something different. Here I was the youngest son . . . looking for a part of the farm business that I could . . . to put in a tactful way, that I was in charge of." We are walking, slowly, the length of the field. Off to each side of us, the soy acreage beckons golden. We are heading for the end of the field, which tapers off into woods and behind the woods, a stream, which is being tapped underground, and fed into the sod.

"I was an agronomy major at Maryland, and there was a scholarship available from a golf course association. You had to take a turf course. They usually give it to someone in the turf program. But at that point, there weren't that many turf people. Actually, I also ended up getting another [scholarship] from the Delmarva Corn and Soybean Association."

Gary figured he'd give a shot at being one of the turf people.

Absently, he reaches down to pull at a tuft of crabgrass. It seems as if the grass should cry out in pain when he does so. I wonder aloud if we should even be walking on it. Gary laughs.

"It has the toughness to stand up to traffic. It was top quality a couple of months ago already."

His brother Alan has joined us. Alan also wears sunglasses. For how subdued they are, though, the Wilbers emanate pleasantness in waves. They act as if they are hosting a cousin they always liked well enough and hadn't seen in a while.

"It's pretty durable stuff," Alan says. He reached down and, not without some difficulty, pulls out a plug of the grass. He holds it up, and the roots of the grass are thick and interwoven in the sandy dirt. In the clump Alan displays there seems to be more root than soil.

"Those are underground stems called rhizomes—they weave together. You couldn't pull it apart. In two weeks you won't be able to lift a piece off this ground."

"It's Kentucky Blue Grass," Gary says. "Three strains of it. Midnight, Eclipse, and Touchdown. Midnight is the dark one. The other two lighter blades are Eclipse and Touchdown. They're very aggressive strains."

On your knees, up close, you can tell the Midnight from the other two. It's darker.

"It shows up well," Alan says, "on TV."

Up close, little winged insects hop from blade to blade so quickly that one moment they're on one blade, and the next they're on another, without appearing to have flown.

Trouble? "Leafhoppers," says Gary. "They're not a problem."

The problems come with the arrival of the sod webworms and the white grubs. In addition, the summer saw an onset of a disease called summer patch, but a little patch is acceptable. At least, that's what the Orioles told the Wilbers.

We continue to walk. The Wilbers neither hurry nor dawdle. They seem to enjoy walking on their grass.

"I had a fraternity brother at Alpha Gamma Rho who had a sod farm," Gary says, continuing his tale only after some prompting. "I'd been talking about it with him. I had to do a term paper for the turf course. I did it on the feasibility of starting a sod farm. My professor said it looked profitable. I ran the numbers and it looked like you could earn more per acre than corn or soybeans. He said, 'Why not give it a try?' I went to a meeting of sod growers—The Maryland Turf Growers Association. Several of them invited me to their farms. They have monthly meetings. I learned from them."

It sounds easy. But it requires capital Gary says. Sod farming requires specialized machinery and marketing expertise.

"With corn," Gary says, "you just bring the corn to the silo. With sod you have to find a market and work with the landscaper."

"Sod has to be stronger than your typical lawn," Alan says. "And playing baseball stresses it.

"That's the real stuff—learning how to make it sod and not grass."

The fragrance is everywhere. The worst thing about artificial turf is that it doesn't smell like anything—although, in fact, that's not true; on very hot, sunny days plastic grass smells distinctly like a cheap child's toy left out all summer on the porch. And that's just the half of it. Equally unfortunate is the absence of grass smell in the artificially turfed ballpark. Without the scent of green grass in a stadium, the scents of nacho cheese sauce and beer baked into concrete become synonymous with the game.

There is no mistaking the scent of newly mown grass here.

Real grass is the stuff of baseball dreams; no one lays AstroTurf in a cornfield. A field of grass between two crops is the natural place for anyone to play a game of baseball, and our grass diamonds set among buildings are the urban echo of that rural fact. But farming, like baseball, doesn't work well when it tries to be more than it has to be. When Gaylord Perry went back to eastern Northern Carolina after his retirement to farm soy, it seemed the most perfect of matches, but his farm went belly-up. He bought all-new equipment when he didn't have to. Air-conditioned cabs on his tractors. Leased too much land. Went bankrupt. The locals sneered at him behind his back, thought he was trying to one-up them.

The Wilbers, on the other hand, seem exactly like the right farmers to supply baseball with its land.

"My dad grew up in the Depression," Gary says. "We've always had the philosophy we don't overextend ourselves. We always start small. We learn before we grow. We don't have the newest machinery. We watch how we spend our money. We make sure we pay our bills. We don't always use the newest tractor. We never got too large to the point where a lot of farmers have problems."

The Wilbers' newest tractor is an Allis-Chalmers 60–80. It's fifteen years old.

Gary and Alan Wilber have been entrusted with growing the single most sacred piece of greenery in American sport in decades. But together they are about as excitable as a glacier. There is something apt in this.

"A big order is all it was," says Gary. "We're not excitable types here."

What's odd is to see such stoicism in a young man. You would not be surprised at this demeanor in a seventy-year-old farmer; in a twenty-nine-year-old it's sort of remarkable.

Gary turns over his palms and kind of shrugs. Camden Yards, frankly, is no big deal to the Oakwood Sod brothers.

"People call us up and talk about it," Gary says, with the expression of a man who has just said something completely devoid of affect, such as, maybe, that tomorrow is expected to be the same temperature as today.

"You have people going down the road and they see the name on the truck and they honk," Alan says, leaning down to snatch at some crabgrass.

They are not surprised that they got the contract. Nor are they excited. Partly this is because they live on the Eastern Shore, which belongs to a different kind of people. The Orioles carry no weight on the Eastern Shore. It is known for two distinctly different subsets of

Maryland citizenry: the horse set, with its helicopter-to-the-District commuters; and the clam diggers and fishermen of centuries past.

Partly they're not surprised because Gary and Alan Wilber know that they're good. The sandy soil, the consistency of the summer rains, the overwhelming success they've had with every crop since their first—all of it pointed to their getting this job.

"We produce a quality sod," Alan says.

They are Maryland certified. In Maryland's certification process, they first check for noxious uncontrollable weeds, then they check your field. When you're ready to harvest, they inspect for worms.

"The second time our whole field was harvestable," Gary says. "We sold ninety percent to landscapers. Twelve cents a square foot, ten thousand feet. We made twelve hundred dollars."

"Then we did a football field at Salisbury State," Alan says.

"We're the local guys," says Gary, with a figurative shrug.

What if disaster had struck? What if some mutant strain of webworm had eaten the entire field?

Lazy smiles bloom on both faces.

"We knew it wasn't gonna die all at one time," Gary said. "We knew from experience it'd be ready if we managed it properly."

"We planted extra," Alan says. "We wanted room for error. We wanted every piece we sent them to be the highest quality."

"It'll work," Gary says, with some finality. "It's our job to grow this."

We are walking back toward the farm's office, a large sunny room attached to the north end of the farmhouse. We walk past the chicken houses. I ask Gary what kind of chickens they are.

He looks at me for a moment. Then he says, "They're just chickens."

Back in Baltimore, the stadium has garnered more publicity than anything in town since the barrage of Fort McHenry. Out here, on the Oakwood Sod Farm, nothing but calm rides the warm wind.

"It's funny," says Gary. "When we were first getting started it was a lot prettier. You become desensitized. We've noticed it a lot with houses we do. [Here,] it's part of your field. It's nothing special. But you put it next to a house and it's so beautiful."

In fact, it's very beautiful here, too. In the artificial confines of a stadium it's just another piece of the decoration. Out here, though, flanked by soy, bordered to the north by the woods and to the south by the dirt road, watched over by the eleven ancient oaks, the grass is surely as beautiful as it will ever get: grass as grass should be.

"Maybe we don't see the full picture yet," Alan says. "When we see it right now, it's a field out in the middle of two soybean fields."

A sign on the office wall in a room on the north side of the house exclaims the credo of the American Sod Producers Association: "To continually strive toward the betterment of our environment through the production of quality sod."

"We like to see clean water and air," says Alan, "and we think that sod is a good product to do that. It produces oxygen. People have gotten a good feel about trees because they know about them. I feel there's more grass with the ability to protect the environment. More so."

As I drive back toward state Route 13, back to Baltimore, the soy seems more golden than before, the grass greener. In the rear-view mirror Alan and Gary are watching my car kick its way down the road. Through the car window floats the scent, again, of newly mown grass. Perfume.

The real weave here is deeper and closer than the rhizomes the Wilbers are cultivating. The family and the farm in the very fabric of the earth, with good sand, and a lot of rain, forty-five years on this ridge—it is strong and quiet and it speaks of nothing so much as this: that the earth and the men and women who till it make a bond that is not easily broken up.

Three weeks later, the first trucks came in at dusk. Pulling a special turf-cutting device behind a Massey-Ferguson tractor, Gary and Alan Wilber peeled their turf up in ribbons sixteen inches wide, which were cut every forty-five inches and folded in half. The work was done at night so that the sun would hit the sod as little as possible; with the strips folded over, heat generates inside and bakes the blades, and cool weather is the preferred climate for shipping.

The sod envelopes were loaded onto wooden pallets, one hundred pieces of sod per pallet. Eighteen pallets were loaded onto each truck: nine thousand square feet per load.

At Camden Yards, the Prescription Athletic Turf awaited.

They laid Gary and Alan's grass on top of it, and Camden Yards became a baseball field.

WORKING MEN

◆

IN EARLY NOVEMBER, without any further fanfare or advance warning, Governor Schaefer announced on a morning radio show that he and Jacobs had agreed on a name: Oriole Park at Camden Yards.

"I sat down with him over the weekend. I went to breakfast with him, or lunch, whatever it is," the governor said. "He said to me, and I said to him, 'It's getting ridiculous.' "

Needless to say, the naming dominated the news for days. Columnists and letter writers decried its ungainliness.

No quotes from Eli Jacobs were forthcoming.

On December 3 the *Sun* reported that the sign configuration atop the park behind home plate would read "Oriole Park" in six-foot letters and "Camden Yards" beneath it in three-foot letters. Somehow, the preposition had disappeared. Schaefer exploded. He demanded equality in signage size, not to mention the immediate restoration of the preposition.

Two days later, it was announced that the letters would all be the same size, and that the word *at* would be restored.

In the *Sun,* Jim Henneman wrote, "They can call 'Oriole Park at Camden Yards' anything they want, but if Cal Ripken doesn't finish his career there, it won't matter."

No one ever proposed putting Cal's name on it, but it would have made more sense than most of the rest. Because, really, who else's stadium was it? The politicians who sold out the state to the lawyers and leveragers? The Orioles, who would stand to gross two dozen million dollars in their inaugural season, and still have the gall to insist, near the end of construction, that the state pay to install two more electrical outlets in the press box?

Who, then, but Cal? What other blue-collar town could boast a blue-collar hero whose soon-to-be-signed contract would bring him $6 million a year—a sum of which no one in the city would begrudge him a penny?

It may have been the most fortuitous occurrence in the entire birth of the ballpark when, on November 20, the Baseball Writers Association of America named Cal Ripken the most valuable player in the American League—and, for the first time, the new ballpark was allowed to celebrate the man, and vice versa.

At five-thirty P.M. on November 20, their foreman told Kevin Carlin and Tim Legg that the Orioles had decided to hold a ceremony at the field at seven o'clock to honor him.

This was a heartening thing for the Orioles. It was the perfect way to inaugurate the stadium, which was nearing completion; the turf was halfway down now, like a carpet being laid in a basement rec room. The brick skin was wrapped neatly around the stadium's shoulders. The lights had been installed.

But it was a tad inconvenient for Kevin and Tim. Not because it meant overtime; there had been plenty of overtime work during the last six months for the two men who had, by and large, handled all of the lighting. There was only one tall crane on the site, and each day the ironworkers had first shot at it, so Tim and Kevin were accustomed to waiting until late afternoon to greet the storklike arm of steel—with its headache ball, the two-ton counterweight fastened to the cable like a blot of lead on a fishing line, and painted like a huge, two-ton baseball—up on the four light racks that served as their roost for the last six months.

So it wasn't the late hours that concerned them. It was that no one had ever actually used the lights. They had never even been tested. And more important, they had never been aimed. No one had the slightest idea if they'd even hit the field.

Tim and Kevin had spent their time bolting each seventy-pound fixture to the racks while they were still on the ground, fastening them into place in general approximation of where they should point. After each rack was hoisted and fixed to its perch—above first base, above third base, above left field, and atop the warehouse (the last one a fortuitous and very important design feature of the park, because it meant that the warehouse was not just a bystander but an actual physical part of the park itself—Legg and Carlin had spent their days wiring each bulb, leading the conduit from the back of each lamp down a cable tray, into one of two panels with forty-two circuit breakers on it, through a distributor box, down the spine of a steel beam, and into the room with the "on" switch.

But they had never aimed them. They'd figured they'd have a little more time too. It wasn't like repositioning, say, a desk lamp. These fixtures could burn the skin right off your hand. These fixtures were from another league entirely. From afar they look like points of light; up close, they are on a scale that you and I have little to do with. They are the equivalent, in foot-candles, of mastering, training, and harnessing enough light to illuminate, say, your whole home town.

Legg and Carlin could not very well tell the Orioles to wait a few days. They could not very well advise Cal Ripken to find himself an empty banquet room at the Marriott.

Still, they were intrigued and excited: The first thing that their lights were going to illuminate was the man whose name had defined Baltimore baseball for all of Kevin and Tim's high school and union days.

What else had they signed on for if not to taste a little baseball?

"That's me," Kevin Carlin says. On his kitchen counter in Sykesville is a photograph of a man on a light deck 180 feet above Baltimore, holding in his hand an American flag. He looks as if he has just scaled a very large mountain, except that the landscape behind him features natural gas tanks and the Bresco incinerator smokestack instead of glaciers and Sherpa guides.

"That's him stealing that flag," says Tim Legg, his brother.

"That was done because of the war that started with Eye-raq," says Kevin. "The first lighting rack that went on had a flag on each corner.

The iron workers put those flags up. One went to the Stadium Authority. I managed to walk off with that one."

They are not brothers by blood. They are brothers by union: The International Brotherhood of Electrical Workers, Maryland Local 24, sixteen hundred strong. Not very many years ago, Baltimore was a good union town for electricians; in 1989, every union man was working. In addition, there were three hundred travelers (union electricians, in from other cities to find work) in town. Now Kevin and Tim are out of work.

Kevin Carlin is wearing a T-shirt that reads, BUILDING BETTER BASEBALL IN BALTIMORE. NEW BALLPARK CONSTRUCTION TEAM. Kevin and Tim are each drinking from cans of Coors Light.

"With a stadium, you can drive by it and see it," Kevin says. "You can show people what you've done. See, I was a welder, too. I learned how to weld when I was an apprentice. I knew they needed a welder first. I volunteered to do the light racks. I knew it was going to be sports lighting. Lighting the field. I knew that's something you're going to be able to see from all over the city—you look up, you see it.

"It's a different world. You're working upstairs and everything's visible. If you're doing work in the basement, nobody's seeing it. Up there it's like . . . recognition. Amongst your fellow brothers you want to have recognition any way you can get it. Talk gets around real quick. That builds up a person's persona, their qualities, their qualifications. Ego. And it can make a difference in getting more work."

Kevin Carlin's father is retired with a full disability from the National Security Agency. Kevin says he doesn't know what his father did before he left the NSA. Kevin's wife took the tests that the agency administers to high school students all over Maryland, and now she works there. Rather than enter the agency, Kevin decided to follow in the footsteps of his real brother, a union electrician, five years his elder, because, among other things, his brother had a nice car. Now Kevin's backyard is graced by a swimming pool, although he has no job.

He was proud of his father's service, and he speaks of it

synonymously with his love of country. "One thing it instilled in us was patriotism," he says. "He had the flag out. He was a working-type man with a briefcase in the morning."

Kevin is a handsome and hard-looking young man. You could easily find yourself getting into a discussion with him about patriotism in a Naugahyded lounge somewhere outside of Baltimore, and if you did, you would accede to Kevin Carlin's point of view quickly, and without any shame, even if you disagreed with it.

Kevin showed aptitude for electrical work in high school, but when he graduated in 1986, tuition at the technical school would have cost him six thousand dollars a year, so he joined the union as an apprentice. Five years later he was a journeyman wireman. He quit a job at a medical waste incinerator to get work on the stadium.

"I'm an American patriot, man," he says. "I go back to Frank Robinson and Boog Powell, Palmer, all of them. '69. I played Little League for the Jessup Shamrocks."

Also, he admits, and not incidentally, they were going to fire up the medical waste incinerator when he was still working there, and he didn't like that idea, because no one really knows what kind of medical waste gets incinerated in medical waste incinerators.

He signed on as the seventeenth electrician on the site at Camden Yards.

Tim Legg had joined the union out of high school in 1989. His father Jeff and his brother Ed were already in the ironworkers union, Local 16, but Tim wasn't interested.

"All their work was outside," he says. "Plus, it's not using your mind as much as your back."

Tim is softer than Kevin. His voice is a little quieter. He's more loosely wound. It is easy to understand why Tim would not want to be a connector. Connectors strut their trade; electricians practice theirs.

"They're nuts," Tim says of the high-iron people. "They're not afraid of anything."

Tim signed on as Number 198 on the ballpark site. He'd been out of work seven weeks after he was laid off at the BG&E power plant at Brandon Shores in Glen Burnie (640 megawatts, twin coal burners). When he arrived at the stadium his dad was working on the handrails and the iron gates. His brother was working on the rigging for the light rack on top of the warehouse.

Tim Legg didn't do it for the love of baseball. "It wasn't any preference for me," he says. "It was a job. As far as going there for baseball reasons, no. I played Little League for three years too. But I kept striking out."

Tim was one of several volunteers to work on the lights on the stadium. A lot of people turned it down because of the height involved. Tim didn't feel as if he was in a position to turn a job down. After all, you never know how the foreman is going to react. When they asked Tim, he took it.

"I was chosen because I was young and I had ironworker blood," says Tim.

"They didn't know he was afraid of *heights,*" Kevin interrupts, and he bursts into high-pitched, loud, very sudden laughter. Kevin Carlin's laugh is like a separate part of him; when something strikes him funny, all of a sudden he smiles and this laugh chitters out of him.

"To a point," Tim says.

"I didn't know either, 'til you told me," says Kevin. Then he laughs again.

"I can't walk a four-inch beam with nothing around me. If I can touch my finger on something, like this, I'm fine," Tim says, softly placing an index finger on the linoleum counter in Kevin's kitchen. Behind them, Kevin's wife makes spaghetti for their toddler daughter. His wife wears a tolerant expression on her face, but a skeptical one; she is happy to allow her husband his memories, but what they symbolize, at bottom, is a job that ended, that has not yet been replaced by another.

Tim opens up their scrapbook to the page that displays the picture of Kevin in the harness. The harness features five attachment points for the safety rope.

"I preferred the one on the chest," Kevin says, and Tim nods.

Only one man was allowed to climb up the racks at a time. He had to be connected at all times. The discomforts were numerous. The potential for a fall was just the start. The lights on top of the warehouse weren't as stable as the others. In order to bear the weight of the rack, the warehouse had to be fitted with a special cantilevered steel support. Tim never trusted it: "I was scared on that one. The more weight you put on the front of it, it moved more than the other ones. It shook back and forth."

For his part, Kevin was suspicious from the start about the epoxy paint on the steel they were welding. He insisted on a respirator.

Supplies came up in a bucket via a pulley system rigged up by an apprentice on the ground. In general, life on the racks was pretty spare, although it would be inaccurate to say they didn't even have a pot to piss in, because they did. Literally.

It went remarkably smoothly, except for the day the crane hoisted the rack up to the first-base side, the whole thing more than one hundred feet long with more than 250 lights in place, lifted gently, laboriously, only it was the wrong rack. But then, the ironworkers had had a dark day, too, when they tried to assemble the scoreboard frame and found out that one of the beams was an inch too long, and tried to fit it anyway, and couldn't.

Now, at five-thirty on the 20th of November, ninety minutes before Cal and Kelly and Rachel were to step onto the field for the ceremony, Tim and Kevin heard the foreman's voice squawk, "Bring up Number One," and the two of them had to run, literally, to the rack above third base. There were no moments to spare. Tim and Kevin had to turn on all four racks, and they had no specific idea of where the bulbs were going to point.

They were in such a hurry that, for the first time on the job, they didn't stop to hook the safety rope to their harnesses. There were four towers and only two safety ropes. Something had to be sacrificed. This job would not be done by the book, but by now Tim and Kevin knew their way up the ladders and around the catwalks on the racks as well as they knew their way around their own homes in the dark.

Two hundred and fifty lights were on the racks behind third and first, another 180 on the bank in left field and atop the warehouse. Each held a fifteen-hundred-watt bulb. It wouldn't be dark until seven, so it was going to be difficult to tell if their aim was true.

It was easy to tell when their aim was untrue.

Not ten minutes after turning on the first bank, the foreman radioed that there had been complaints from guests in the Holiday Inn beyond left-center and the Marriott beyond the warehouse in right. This meant that, with at least a few of the lights, they weren't even close. Frantically trying to coax each fixture to at least *hit* the field—and doing their best not to let their bare skin touch the fixtures, which would have burned them in an instant—they finished off the work behind third base, scampered down the ladder, ran out to left field, and turned on the next rack. Immediately, they were told they were blinding cars on Interstate 395, south of the park.

Legg and Carlin didn't finish their work until the ceremony had already started down on the field, amid a crowd of a couple hundred people. The Orioles, in a magnanimous gesture, had decided to open the gates of the park to anyone who happened to be strolling by. Now writers and television types and team officials were toasting Ripken.

When their foreman told Kevin and Tim that they were finished, the two hurried down in time to witness the last few minutes of the ceremony. They came down from the upper deck and walked right down to the field, over the concrete steps that did not yet hold seats.

At a podium, Cal said a few words. Roland Hemond looked around and said, "We could play right now." Everybody toasted Cal Ripken with champagne glasses full of milk—Cal's beverage of choice, as any of several hundred billboards across the state will attest.

The final aiming of the lights took place in January and February. The grid was designed by General Electric; the means of aiming was devised by Jim Wheeler of Sparks Electronics, the contractor. He had asked the union for two good electricians, and the union tabbed Kevin and Tim. They had to be good; each bulb cost $375.

Jim started out at home plate and paced off a grid of squares thirty feet by thirty feet in horizontal rows. At the corner intersections of the squares, Sparks would place a stick with a fluorescent plastic flag on it into the ground. Then he would stand at a point with a pair of binoculars. Up in the racks Legg and Carlin would aim the light by holding on to clamps on each side of the fixture. They would site the lamp according to a degree marker on the bottom of each lamp.

On the inside perimeter of each metal lamp shade was a black band painted to keep the lamps from glaring, much like the black paint players put under their eyes on sunny days. If Wheeler could see any black from down on the field, he figured the light was out of line. When he could no longer see any of the black band, he figured the lamp was aimed correctly. He didn't know for sure.

In January and February, the wind was cold enough to make them wonder if their flesh would stick to the lamps, and sometimes it was strong enough to bring the details of a 180-foot fall to mind. It was not something you could dwell on, of course. But in winter, with a razor wind, the job was less fun than it could have been.

This is what Tim Legg wore in February: A thermal shirt, a flannel shirt, a sweatjacket with a hood, a quilted flannel shirt, long johns, jeans, two pairs of socks, and a Carhardt, the quilted coveralls with all the pockets. (They're union made. Everyone wears them on a union site.)

On February 28, Carlin and Legg were up in the warehouse doing the final bulb replacements and setting the disconnect panel when their foreman came up with their checks.

"We were hoping we'd be sent to another job," Tim says, "but the whole town is drying up."

They could tell from the look on his face.

They were the last electricians laid off.

"Union is the American way," Kevin says in his kitchen. "When you think of the function of simply buying American, well, you're putting people to work. It's not that hard to understand. It's made here. It's putting someone to work. It's shipping it. It's storing it in a warehouse. It's putting people to work.

"It's like the cycle of life."

Tim waits for his brother to finish speaking. He thinks about the union. He sips at the last of his Coors. Then he says, "My father being very prounion, and my brother, as ironworkers, they take a different course in their apprenticeship. They learn about the union and unionism, showing films that go very deeply into unionism. They teach how unions started and what our forefathers went through to establish unions."

"The union fought hard for an eight-hour day," Kevin says. "So even if you're nonunion and you don't believe in unions you still have an eight-hour day because of the union. And Saturday and Sunday off."

Now 20 percent of the work in Baltimore goes to unions. The rest goes to nonunion workers who earn less money. Electricians who are not in the union earn $12 or $14 an hour. Union scale is $22.

"As far as safety," Tim says, "they're not safety first. That's why they have such a high rate of accidents. I worked seven months nonunion out of high school. I started in high school, at $3.75 an hour. If I didn't have sweat running down my forehead the foreman was yelling at me that I was dumb, I didn't know what I was doing.

"It was rip-and-tear work. I had a foreman, a mechanic, and six apprentices. The mechanic would go around and make all the splices and twist the wires around. Then he'd say, 'Now untwist the wires.' Six guys making four an hour and a guy making eight telling 'em what to do. But in the union the foreman is only making a dollar more an hour than we do. There's three mechanics for every apprentice. You're getting quality work out of everybody. That's how you're safer. And you help the apprentice. You teach."

"I feel sorry for them," Kevin says. "The contractor is charging the same as the union contractor but the nonunion contractor has the forty-thousand-dollar boat and the three-hundred-thousand-dollar house and he's taking all the money."

Kevin sips at the beer.

"It's burning me up," he says.

There's some good news. The local's new business agent says it's okay if they bungalow-hop, the trade vernacular for doing wiring on nonunion jobs that require work so unskilled they wouldn't call for union anyway. Wire a couple of houses. A grocery store.

Also now, on the side, Kevin and Tim sell firewood.

After they were laid off, Tim and Kevin went down to the hall and signed on at 318 and 319. Three hundred and seventeen men would get hired before them when jobs came up.

Five months later they were at 181 and 180.

There are no jobs on the books right now.

*   *   *

As Cal Ripken walked away from the podium on the field that night, Tim and Kevin positioned themselves to be in his path.

Tim held out his hard hat for Ripken to autograph, and Ripken stopped and said, "I never held a hard hat before." Tim couldn't believe it: Not only was he going to get an autograph, he was talking to Cal Ripken. And Cal Ripken was taking the time to be interested in Tim Legg's work. That's how Tim saw it.

He remembers people around Ripken waiting to usher him off the field.

"Do you want to trade hats?" Tim heard himself say, but before Ripken could answer, someone in a suit said to Cal, "We can get you a hard hat," and someone else in a suit said it'd be no problem, sure, and then Cal was gone, and Legg had his autographed hard hat.

"I think it was an experience for him," Tim Legg says. "It made me proud to be there."

It was the most fortuitous of meetings, but it was somehow preordained: What could make better sense than two workmen who do their job as brothers to meet the one workman in Baltimore who for so many people epitomizes the work ethic that is waning in society, and is virtually extinct in professional sports? Ripken does, now, stand alone; independent of slumps and snide comments from radio geeks, above the muck of image and greed, Cal Ripken would be a labor hero for his peers if his own peers actually had the slightest interest in their coworkers.

Who else would have understood Tim Legg and Kevin Carlin as well as Cal Ripken? Who else in baseball or sport knows the meaning of the word *labor* than a man who never fails to show up?

It wasn't Cal Ripken's 1991 season that won him the MVP; how valuable could he have been, playing for a team that finished fifth? Most baseball people figured the award would go to Cecil Fielder, the robust home-run hitter, a man whose titanic achievements attracted far more attention than Ripken's. Then again, most people aren't sportswriters, and the sportswriters who honored Cal Ripken were not only honoring his 1991 numbers. They were honoring his decade.

This includes his decade of dignity, marked by an astounding absence of whine and rant and pomp.

Mostly, of course, they were honoring Ripken's decade of numbers. They were honoring the streak, because they may not have another chance to do so, and because it may end. We will never see anything like it again. In the middle of the 1992 season, Brett Butler stood second behind Ripken in games played consecutively, but he had to sit out a few games with a bad knee. He was more than fifteen hundred games behind Cal. Cal entered 1993 at 1,735. The old Orioles record belonged to Brooks Robinson. Four hundred and sixty-three.

It was not coincidence, of course, that the Orioles chose to open their stadium by honoring their shortstop. It was fitting. It was good public relations. And it's Cal's stadium; if it belongs to any one baseball player, it belongs to Cal. Cal was so much the sire of this park that Eli Jacobs signed over a sizeable chunk of his initial profits to Cal. This was not, of course, out of pure gratitude; this was to make certain that Cal Ripken will be standing in Camden Yards in June 1995. In June of 1995—barring some unnatural disruption in the universe such as strike, lockout, or catastrophic injury—the world of baseball will be Cal Ripken's.

It will happen on the Oakwood sod of Camden Yards. The American League schedule maker will be instructed to make sure of one thing above all when he puts together the season of 1995: to ensure that Cal's record-tying and record-breaking games will take place at home.

He will tie it by being at shortstop for the first half-inning of the game. The next day, the game will be stopped at that point, because it will then be official: Cal Ripken will be baseball's iron man.

Baseball claims Cal's streak; it might as well already have stamped one of those tacky little Major League Baseball insignias on it, the ones that Ueberroth gleefully slapped all over the game like tattoos. When the day approaches, if the day does approach, the ceremony and joy will be national, but it truly only belongs to Baltimore. Cal Ripken's streak is now Baltimore's standard: more than Mencken's millions of words, more than Barry Levinson's Oscar, more than Kurt

Schmoke's address at the Democratic Convention, or Joan Jett's national anthems.

It is a blue-collar record for a town without shout. It's an X-Days-on-the-Job-without-an-Accident record. An attendance record. It represents no pinnacles, no heights scaled, just low-profile dutifulness, which is as Baltimorean as you can get. It refuses to stamp its chest.

The ground swell will be phenomenal. The season will begin with the focus on Cal, as it did on Pete Rose when the game knew that Rose was poised to break Ty Cobb's record, with this considerable difference: Cal will not be in a position of having to bunt and scratch out singles between third and short on artificial turf. Nor—and this explains the zen nature of Cal's record—will he set the record by doing anything but showing up and taking his position at short and watching his pitcher wind up and pitch the first pitch of a game. It's such a Baltimore record. It's such a nondescript way of achieving greatness.

It is not an intellectual record. It is not an emotional record, either. That's why it's Cal's record. Not that he isn't both; he just doesn't show them—his intellect and his heart.

But in the second half of 1990, when Ripken was slumping and the streak was being blamed, sometimes he'd disappear up the dark, medievally toned tunnel behind the dugout, past the dark-green warped plywood writing platform with the little lamp that no one ever saw any manager ever use—it was like a candle set into the stone wall of a turret—up to the equipment storage room. In that room someone had long ago tacked up a piece of rubber to hang down from the sloped ceiling for batters to practice their swings on between at bats. In 1990 Cal would walk up there after a bad at bat, close the door to the rest of the world, and whale that piece of rubber. But you never saw the anger out front.

You never see the joy, either. You never see any self-celebration, any hand pumps after a home run has settled into the outfield seats.

"Never really felt a big need to do that," Cal says, not modestly, not immodestly.

"The old-school mentality," he explains. "It was a code. That's easy to figure out."

If it was all Cal, this game, it would all be so easy to figure out, and so easy to root for. Which is also part of why he won the MVP. Cal Ripken is such a . . . relief.

Who's pitching for them tonight?

"I don't know," Cal says, over the telephone, from a hotel room somewhere. Cal doesn't mind talking on the telephone; it's the only place he doesn't really mind talking. Unless you count a couple of hours after a night game, after he's done his time in the weight room, and he's sitting with a carton of milk—then he's relaxed, but he's on his way out. But mostly you can't talk seriously to Cal in the locker room. On the road, though, in the afternoon, when he's trapped in some faceless Hyatt room adorned by the same pastel illustration of a Western sunset scene with awkwardly illustrated mountains hanging above the sterile headboard—the same nothingness flitting across the television screen, the only alternative a stroll through a homogeneous mall, so that even when he's in it he has no idea what city he's in, and he'll have to sign autographs anyway—Cal talks on the telephone of the things he doesn't talk about much in person. Like the streak. It's the perfect time to talk about the streak, when the monotony of the baseball life is bearing down. Because, yes, of course, the streak bears down heavily on him.

"I don't know who's pitching for them," Cal says again. "It doesn't make any difference. Everyone else gets obsessed with who pitches the next series against us—'Do we get Nolan? Do we get Clemens?'— but to me, it doesn't matter. Whoever's pitching, you're going to play. It doesn't matter who's pitching. Someone's going to pitch, you're going to play."

He says it with no emphasis either way—boast or complaint. But if it sounds as if the words should carry some weariness, of course they do. Eleven years' worth.

It began in 1980, in Charlotte, North Carolina—not technically, but in spirit: Manager Jimmy Williams awarded each of his regulars three consecutive days off at one point during the season. Ripken declined them. The next year in Rochester Cal played in every game until they called him up to Baltimore.

In 1982, Ripken missed a game on May 20, when the redoubtable

Floyd Rayford replaced him at third base in the second game of a doubleheader. Ripken was back in the lineup the next night. He played the rest of the season. Every inning.

In 1983, he played all year, too. A few people noticed his stalwart nature, but most talked about Ripken's hitting and fielding skills. In September, the Orioles clinched the pennant two weeks before the season ended. Joe Altobelli, the manager with the hounddog face, was walking through the locker room scheduling days off for his starters over the last ten days. Altobelli walked over to Ripken's locker, pointed at him, thought for a second, and passed him by. That's where it could have ended.

"The second half of that year, everything fell in," Cal recalls. "I never gave it a thought (that) I was playing every inning. If you took time to think about it, it seemed kind of remarkable, but when you go through it it doesn't seem remarkable."

He pauses. Then he utters as Ripkenesque an aphorism as you'll ever hope to hear:

"You play a game."

And he does.

"That's the way it was for the first five years," he says. "Then people started recognizing it as a streak. Then people started writing about it. It was never meant to be done, set out to do."

There is a universal appeal to Cal, Jr., that's obvious. There is no aura to him, in person or in the abstract. He has no real desire to rise above the pack, which would invite scrutiny and pressure; there's no doubt that he stayed in Baltimore for less money so that he would not, at this late stage, have to face up to new and foreign demons.

And still, he's up there, celebrated and featured, plastered on billboards and magazine covers; as the rest of the player populace grows more and more tedious and self-absorbed, as the emotional health of the rest of his peers devolves, and one by one so many of them slough off to the side, there he is, left standing, king by default.

And there is universal appeal in father and son. Baseball is a game of father and son. In Asheville, North Carolina, in 1972 and 1973, Cal, Sr., was the manager. Cal's brother, Fred, managed the visitor's clubhouse. Cal served as batboy, often shirking his duties to shag a lot of batting practice balls. Billy was the ballboy. Sister Ellie changed the score on the scoreboard.

A decade and a half later, the family saw the father managing the Orioles, and his two sons. It would have been nice if it had all worked out, if Cal's dad had been a brilliant manager, but he wasn't, and it didn't. Cal, Sr., is a coach, and coach is his appropriate and accustomed level. In his brief stint behind the manager's desk, Cal, Sr., looked as uncomfortable as a farmer asked to sit at his loan manager's desk down at the bank. Cal, Sr., was the man who herds the rookies onto the bus in spring training with a drill-sergeant's bark. Until, after Cal signed his most recent contract, the Orioles released his father.

"It should never happen again in baseball," Jon Miller says: "The son is wildly successful. The father gets the dream job, the club goes down the toilet—his failure is being reflected every night. What burden does the son bear? There's a lot of things at play."

There was one obvious burden. It was the father who broke the inning streak. The inning streak has been forgotten. But the inning streak was the most remarkable thing of all. The inning streak was 8,243, spanning 904 games. As far as anyone knows, the closest anyone in baseball ever came was in the early 1900s, when two Red Sox players named Buck Freeman and Candy La Chance each played all of 524 and 434 games, respectively.

"When I hadn't missed an inning, people became obsessed with that," Cal says. " 'How could you not miss an inning? I could see how you play the game, but not miss an inning?' It was in a period when we started to lose—you didn't think about anything else. The inning streak wasn't even a consideration."

In other words, when he and the team were doing well, Cal didn't have the time nor the inclination to think of anything else. And when he and the team were doing badly, he clamped his focus on the losing. It was when the streak came to a halt that it finally commanded his attention, in a way that his attention had never been commanded before.

"I didn't expect it," Ripken says, and the four words speak of thousands.

This is how it ended: The Blue Jays were beating the Orioles 17–3.

Cal was in the dugout, getting his bat. It was the top of the eighth inning. His father came over and said to his son, "What do you think about breaking this innings thing?"

Cal thought for a moment.

He said, "What do you think?"

His father said, "You should."

Cal Ripken did not react right away. There were so many conflicting tugs within his heart that he wanted to give them a moment to war, and let the one that deserved the most respect surface and win out.

"Okay," said Cal, finally, and that was that. It was an old-style thing. It was code. It was Dad.

Cal walked to the plate, as implacable as ever. No one at bat ever wears an expression any different from any other at bat.

He hit a single.

The next batter stranded him on first base, and his brother came out of the dugout with Cal's cap and his glove.

"I told him I didn't need it," Cal remembers. He also remembers the look on his brother's face. It did not compute. It was an expression of total befuddlement.

"See, at that moment I hadn't come out of a game ever in Billy's time in the majors," Cal says from his hotel room. "The whole time he'd been on the Orioles, when the game started I was always there and I was always there at the very end.

"I think I even wrote something in about Billy's face."

Wrote something?

"It was the only time I ever wrote anything," Cal says. "After my dad broke the inning streak. The night my dad broke my inning streak, I stayed up 'til three in the morning. I felt . . . bland."

Silence swells on the line. He is searching for a better word.

"My feelings were so scattered—good? bad? There was a sense of loss. Relief. Happiness. I felt the need to write, so I could look back. In one way I felt I had lost something, and I'll get it back."

The disembodied words seem hardly to be Cal's at all. If it weren't for the voice, it would not be he. He never talks this way. Usually, he fills his sentences with words of description; he can recount detail like a man replaying a videotape. He likes to describe processes, and he tells accurate stories about the way things happened, as if he delights in an orderly world of making sense. He can remember his time down to the second in a race he once ran, for instance. But he seldom ventures toward the core of a thought.

"Whether I blamed my dad or not . . . he wouldn't have done it without my permission," he says. "Just like the streak now—the innings thing was more of a fascination than the streak itself. And that started sending off an alarm to my dad. To alleviate pressure."

No one will suggest he take a day off from here on in. Not with just two years between him and Lou Gehrig. Because Cal Ripken at his worst is, on the average, better than most shortstops at their best. Cal Ripken will always get hits. And he will always have to play baseball.

"He has to do it," says his friend Brady Anderson. "He has the energy of a seven-year-old. He bounds in and bounds out of the locker room. He has more energy than anyone I've ever seen. You know how when you're a little kid you don't get tired? He's like that. You'll never see him taking a nap in the corner."

What did he do with what he wrote that night?

"I lost it," Cal says. "I've looked for it. I wish I could find it."

One day in 1991 it hit him: that something could happen. That the streak could end. It had not really occurred to him until then. That's what he says, and there is really no reason not to believe him when he talks about it, because he talks about it so seldom it's hard to believe that he would not tell the truth when he does talk.

"We have a kangaroo court," he says, and for a moment, it is unclear where he's going with this. First he has to get the details out of the way. "There was a seven-thirty game. I had a business meeting that afternoon. I was at the park at four-thirty. Instead of hurrying and being five minutes late, I decided to miss fifteen minutes of stretching. The way we're set out is four groups, and each has to be on the field for forty-five minutes, to spend forty-five minutes on the field no matter what, and with stretching, it's an hour. I missed stretching.

"Anyway, I got a little paranoid when I got to the ballpark late. My routine was broken. I had to make an excuse in kangaroo court. I had to get this evidence together. One of the reasons I came up with was my car was broken into after I had a flat tire and something was stolen and I had to wait for the police report. I put together my case, all of which was fabricated, so I could prove why I was late, but in the process of it I thought, 'This really could happen.'

"The reality of it is I could get into an accident. My car could break down. All sorts of things could cause me to miss a game.

"Brady said, 'The last week, I'm living with you and we're having in a bodyguard. Someone could kidnap you.' Maybe you shouldn't write that. It'll give people ideas."

He laughs uneasily.

"How crazy is that to think in those terms?"

Not crazy at all. Your car breaks down. You stick out your thumb. Someone picks you up, sees you're Cal Ripken, starts driving away from the ballpark, asks you how much it's worth to you to keep the streak alive. Or, more mundane, will some cocky utility man try to gain sudden fame by going in high to spike his knee?

Ripken laughs. He's had spiked knees. He's twisted his ankle. The worst twisted ankle preceded an off day. Also, he doesn't get sick. Which makes you wonder how come everyone else always hurts.

If it happens, it will be on the basketball court. This worries the Orioles. Cal plays hard. By now Orioles basketball is as deeply ingrained as the baseball. Baylor started it; Baylor and Blair would bring the Orioles team into the Miami streets during the spring-training off-days, taking on all comers. They used to say to Baylor, "Hey, you're going to get us killed." Baylor was tough. They'd win games in half-dozen bunches.

Now they all play at Cal's. He built a full-size court and the games span generations: Bumbry, Ripken, Ben McDonald. Cal will not give up the basketball. The basketball, he is convinced, helps ward off injuries.

The mind delights: What about the day you tie it? Do you risk going home that night, risk a car crash, or a twisted ankle in the shower, or lightning hitting? Or do you camp out in the locker room?

"Mike Schmidt has the perfect plan," Ripken says. "He said, 'You go on, you tie the record. The next day you take the day off. You make a statement that you wanted to be in the same book with Lou Gehrig, but it's a great accomplishment, and you wanted to share it.'"

Jokingly?

"Half-jokingly."

Cal's record is different because it means you have to play when you're hurt, and while in the old days you wanted to play hurt because it increased your chance to get more hits and more stats, now a sore knee may be considered a harbinger of a more serious injury that could threaten a salary that represents more than the ballplayer's grandfather, father, uncles, and brothers ever earned in all of their lifetimes. So a twinge behind the knee becomes ominous, and you rest until it goes away.

Cal's record is the only real throwback record left. It is good that it is a Baltimore record, a throwback city with a throwback hero. Pete Rose was able to achieve his record because so many of his hits bounded into the outfield off the hard plastic grass. Also, at the point when a prudent manager might have questioned the value of a weak singles hitter playing first base, Rose was his own manager, so better players sat while he pursued his ghosts. Cal's is of the old ethic. Of the top ten consecutive-game streaks, only three men—Ripken, Steve Garvey, and Billy Williams—played in the seventies. Stan Musial and Nellie Fox played in the sixties. The other five belonged to previous eras.

The other baseball records are chased, and considered quite breakable. They are a matter of lifetime achievements, but many lifetimes are yet to come. Aaron's will be broken, as was Ruth's, and Cobb's. Ruth's was a matter of time; 714 was an imposing number, yes, but enough men reached well past 500 that the rest seemed likely enough. Ty Cobb's hit total signified a remarkable achievement for Rose, but several reached 3,500 hits, and thus four and change does not represent a quantum leap.

And yet, in a sport that overflows with records, and long ago reached way beyond the stage of too much of a good thing, both of those marks stand well above the rest, for a single reason—not for the feats themselves; no one remembers many of Hank Aaron's specific home runs, and so many of Rose's last hits were so feeble and inconsequential that watching him get there was as wincingly painful as watching Yastrzemski reach 3,000; no, it was what they repre- sented: consistency. Consistency in baseball is more important than any other attribute. A pitcher who can walk out to the mound every five days and win as many as he loses, a lead-off hitter who plays at least 150 games displaying nothing more than an average batting average, an everyday shortshop you can count on—these are the mortars of a pennant-winning baseball team.

Brady Anderson does not understand the question. The question is how close he and Cal are, and what it is they have in common.

"We're friends, man," Anderson says, with a logic worthy of Cal. There is nothing complicated here after all.

Brady Anderson's ascent and his friendship with Cal Ripken coincided. Brady Anderson and Cal Ripken hang out on the road. He had been touted as the next Boston star and wasn't, and it ruined him for five years. In Baltimore, he found that he could turn to Cal Ripken. Ripken sees some of himself in Brady Anderson, which is why they played Ping-Pong for four hours in a Cleveland hotel once.

Anderson didn't win a single game.

("We were in Miami—I was seven," Cal recalls. "There was a Spanish girl next door who came over. I tricked her into moving a piece to get a six-way jump. She obviously didn't know how to play checkers well. I jumped her six men. I went back—my head hit the concrete window sill. There was blood. It wasn't as fun to trick her. Cheating wasn't as good. Playing hard to win honestly was better.")

"One day he asked me, 'What does it mean?' " recalls Brady Anderson. "I said, 'What does it mean? *What does it mean?* It means you're going to go down in history as one of the greatest players of all time. You're doing what no one else is doing.' "

Anderson shakes his head as if in wonder, but actually in admiration. To not know what it means—how much freer can you be? But Brady Anderson knows, firsthand, something most of us don't; he has seen some of the vulnerability in Cal Ripken.

"I've seen it in his face, that he wasn't happy. I walk up to him one time: 'What's the deal? You got the greatest life I can think of.' But you know, parts of the game, your total life, can wear you down. I think what wears you down and makes you tired is the mental exhaustion.

"Emotionally," says Brady Anderson, "he has so much happening."

"It'd be real nice," Cal says, "if you weren't swinging well and Clemens was the first day of a series and you could take a day off, I could see the value, mentally and physically. But I can't."

He can, of course. He just won't. He talks to Brady Anderson about it, but he can't really talk to anyone about it. Lou Gehrig isn't around.

"I'm in a position that no one else has played in the games I've played in—no one else can give me advice because they haven't experienced it," Cal says, and his voice is neither up nor down.

He has resorted to looking for any variation he can find in a world in which he's allowed no variation. He might shag with the pitchers. Join into the catcher's routine. Into the outfielder's routine.

"It turns the clock back to Little League days when you'd play every position," he says. "It makes my concentration refocused. I used to think if I missed BP I wouldn't be ready. If I didn't take ground balls, I'd make an error. Now it's better to break the routine, take little mental vacations. Like when I come out of a blowout game, getting into the shower, and [being] dressed when the club comes in. It's a break.

"I'm a pioneer of sorts. Where an off-day might be a mental break, miss Roger Clemens, take two days off, get an off-day, I can't. I started thinking how can I get a mental vacation.

"Because every single day it's the same."

Silence crowds the telephone line.

"Talk about a routine," Cal says, and then a moment later, "You do the same exact thing every day."

What if it were ended prematurely?

"In some weird way it'd be nice," he says. "The worst thing that could happen is that you become obsessed with the streak and you lose sight of your normal goals and your focus. I keep trying the best I can; I know it's impossible, but the longer you play the more you want to maintain the approach you had in the first year—I want to be enthusiastic, I want to be in there every day. Sometimes when comments come out—the streak this, the streak that—I try to take myself back, to winter ball, your desire to play, when nothing else mattered, it's just you playing. The reason this all happened, in my mind, is because of how I approached it my first year.

"Maybe when it's over it'll take on a certain level of importance to me the same as everybody else. Maybe I'll look back with a certain sense of pride and feeling."

Until then, it's all in a day's work.

COUNTDOWN

◆

IN LATE NOVEMBER 1991, with Opening Day just over four months away, Janet Marie noticed that the dugouts were so high that the view to the on-deck circle was blocked in certain seats. She also noticed that the dugouts were longer than they'd ever have to be—a full twenty feet longer than Memorial's. At a cost of $100,000, paid for by the Orioles, a crew came back in and chopped and channelled the dugouts. The Orioles gained more than 100 seats in the process; the annual added revenue would be $90,000.

Then, on a very cold January afternoon, with all the seats at last in place, the Orioles held an open house for season-ticket holders to look at their new locations. Although the Orioles served hot chocolate, many of their fans were not pleased. Many were outraged. That night, the sports talk shows spoke of nothing else.

"What they've done is take the real fans for granted," one man told the *Sun*. Another, who had had seats behind home plate in Memorial since its inaugural season, found himself out beyond third base. Several complained about being bumped farther out. And it was obvious that the sight lines down the left-field line could have been better. Preserving the old-style shape of the park meant that the seats had been designed to face the outfield; in several thousand seats, the fans would have to turn their heads to see home plate. Still unnoticed was that several seats out in the bleachers in right-center had no view of first base; they were blocked by the tall wall scoreboard.

"There will always be those concerns," Larry Lucchino said of the seat-location controversy, "in any sports facility where there is a limited number of tickets. There are certain seats that are held by the club. There are seats that go to other officials. It is not a perfect formula."

But a more perfect formula had been promised. A man who has long been closely involved with the dispensing of season tickets for the Orioles, a lifelong Baltimorean and a passionate baseball man, addressed the issue of how so many longtime fans had been assigned bad seats.

"The Orioles flat out three years ago set up a procedure, a priority list to assist with the relocation, and then ignored it. They found themselves in a bind, and they had to get it done.

"[But] they said in 1989, to existing customers, 'If you buy more seats now you'll be able to consolidate your seats when we move. Even if they're bad, it'll get you good seats in the new park.' It made a lot of money. A lot of people bought lousy seats—upper, lower, grandstand—with the expectation they'd be able to consolidate when they moved. Then when the [computer] model assigned [new] seats, it did not give them any consideration. The people who got seats were season-ticket holders they sent questionnaires to. People who had four and said they wanted eight got their six or eight—without buying those lousy seats for three years. So the people who did what the O's wanted them to do got shafted.

"Those who waited until this year got the cream, and those extra seats compounded in pushing everyone further out. They had three years to plan this relocation [but] didn't get going until the end. . . . They had so many other things to do that that became something they couldn't worry [about]. They just screwed people. . . .

"[But] you can't really say, well, ownership doesn't have a right to certain prime seats. No one else stepped up with the dollars to [buy the team]. . . . Ownership held up the relocation process until they could ascertain the number of seats they needed. Lucchino's friends got taken care of. His friends outnumbered Jacobs in a big way. . . . The state of Maryland got plenty . . . they went whole hog in what the Stadium Authority was able to get [for] their friends."

For his part, Eli Jacobs screwed his face into a frown when it was suggested that it was a common belief among citizens and journalists alike that he had reserved the first three rows from dugout to dugout for himself.

"That's bullshit," he said. "The reality is that on any given day few of my friends are there. And if I chose friends to have there, that's my prerogative."

The final days before Opening Day should have been Janet Marie Smith's time for glory. Instead, they were a time for breaking into tears at a key staff meeting and fleeing the room.

It wasn't the niggling details that led her to distress, although that would have been an understandable reaction from a design manager for whom the smallest detail could mean worlds. And, six days before Opening Day, it was true that the last-minute bugs were eating at her. Recreating the past was turning out to be harder than everyone had thought.

First off, the foul screen they'd erected, a white mesh net, had turned out to be anything but transparent, although it wasn't so much the material that was faulty as the way it was designed to be installed—like a tent with a flat roof, stretching from right behind home plate back to the base of the press box, which lay low to the field. If the mesh had been stretched up and over the press box, the view from the home plate box seats would have been fine.

But the Orioles did not want to give the press a view through a net. The Orioles knew that the success of the product they were selling was going to rely heavily on its front men, the baseball press, whose power had rocketed exponentially in the modern big-revenue era. The press could hardly be expected, after all, to have to gaze through a net; the producers of a Broadway show would not be foolish enough, after all, to seat the critic behind a pole, in an obstructed seat, would they?

And by now, the line between theater and sport was becoming increasingly blurred. Camden Yards was threatening to become nothing so much as sheer entertainment—a theme park of baseball nostalgia, a carnival tent promising a quick glance at a world of simple, old-time values—built at huge public expense, yes, by the modern profiteers, but profiteers who were nonetheless operating in the name of all that made this great game great. After all, they'd put in nostalgic telephone booths, hadn't they?

The admission price would be steep, yes, but who could expect to pay on the cheap for a chance to get a hands-on look at the game in its simpler days? A hundred-dollar day at the park, certainly, was not too much to ask in return for a glimpse of steel and brick and asymmetry.

And if the asymmetry of Camden Yards was entirely artificial; if some of the bleacher seats furnished no view at all of a base because the old-time scoreboard got in the way; and if thousands of seats faced center field and not home plate only because Janet Marie Smith had decided the left-field wall had to adhere to the street grid—even if the street it adhered to was one that, unlike the predecessors she was copying, had no foot traffic on it at all, and no commerce, just speeding cars; and if the grand, towering, arched, awninged central entrance to the park behind home plate, reminiscent of Ebbets Field and Baker Bowl with their lovely street-corner entrances, was in fact an entrance foyer primarily for the press and the people with luxury-suite tickets who needed access to the mahogany elevators, and this elegant approach had been placed in a spot virtually 180 degrees removed from where the city could actually enter the park—well, fields full of dreams don't come easy.

This was a show about to open. The Opening Day reviews would be papered and broadcast to every corner of the country, if not the world.

So the Orioles decided to give the press a clean view, and stretched the foul screen taut, eight feet above the seats—and the mesh, at such an acute angle, became impossible to see through, obscuring much of the view in the most expensive seats in the house.

It would have to be replaced by Opening Day.

The tiny lettering on some of the outfield advertising presented another last-minute concern. Janet Marie was furious at that, after all the time she's spent on recreating the old-style look of the signage. In addition, the lights mounted in the underside of the sunscreen for the upper deck were too dim for Janet Marie's taste.

Beyond that, most appallingly, in full view of all—whether walking out on Russell Street or patrolling the wide concourses inside—lacing amid the beautiful steelwork on the underside of the upper deck were the cylindrical, snaking, huge plastic sewage-disposal pipes of gleaming white PCV—an aesthetic gaffe for which, John Pastier suggested, unable to control himself, "Janet Marie should be shot."

"It's frustrating when you know something could be better and it isn't," Janet Marie says in her office, her voice nearly quaking, her eyes like dull iron. Smith's office is in the fourth floor of the warehouse. Down the hall is an exhibit case filled with old pictures of the ballparks that influenced Camden Yards—although there are no pictures of Baker Bowl or Huntington Avenue Grounds, with their warehouses.

"You only get a chance to make a first impression once, and the photos are going in the scrapbook."

One set of plans, however, was working out to perfection. The Orioles would be hosting the Babe Ruth Museum's annual Base Ball on Saturday night, two days before Opening Day, on the luxury level at Camden Yards. Thousands of Baltimore's moneyed best, at $125 a pop, were going to be the first to experience the luxurious feel of velveted old-time excess. For days in advance there were whispers, there was talk: A big surprise would be the focal point of the evening. A real surprise. Something huge.

Remember the marketing of Memorial's closing? You thought that was spectacular? Wait until Saturday night. Black tie, of course.

If you can't wait, though, or if you suspect that from here on in the pomp will begin to blot out the purpose—if, in other words, you want a last chance to see a new ballpark be born, to engage in a ceremony actually related to the building's purpose, unencumbered by frills and frippery—you can leave Janet Marie's office that evening and sidle down into the center-field seats where a man sits alone in the dark.

Jim Wheeler of Sparks Electronics is awaiting the final test of the lights. The dim lamps under the sunscreen in the upper deck are on, the lighting around the park furnishes a little illumination, and the windows of the warehouse are lit. But the stadium seems a sleeping hulk; it is an eerie gloam, smelling of newly mown grass gathering dew for a cool spring evening.

"Those two kids," Jim Wheeler says, "were incredible. Do you know, when the American League came in to inspect the lighting, they didn't have to change the aim of a single bulb? Tim and Kevin got every one right the first time around."

All of a very-subtle sudden, it is slightly lighter. Then lighter still. Now it feels a little like dawn. Then, more quickly, the place begins to glow, and the lights take on a life of their own. There is no way to trace the shine of each bulb; there are no visible beams. It's as if the bowl is becoming illuminated from an invisible filament in the middle of the park, perhaps suspended above the infield.

Jim Wheeler glances around, with a dutiful and professionally honed eye; his aim was true; he could spot a dark spot a mile away; there are none. The park is lit, brilliantly, perfectly, and the warehouse light rack seems to lean in over the field, as if we're sitting at the base of a large luxury liner and looking up at the brilliance of a party up on the first-class deck. The warehouse itself, because of the lights burning on top of it, seems much, much closer, and the brick on the warehouse looks very much like the brick wall of a tobacco-town minor-league park from a fictitious baseball past.

It is like day.

"Wait," says Jim Wheeler. And it grows brighter still.

Within a minute or two, Camden Yards is literally brighter than day. Every nook, every cranny, every blade of grass is etched aloud. The steel glows sharply dark green. It is a wonderful, resonant, permanent color.

The Oakwood sod is of a green that comes entirely from nature, but more so—surreal, in a way that Irish meadow grass can seem real and unreal at the same time.

It is as if the park, two years in the making, has been sleeping, and has now, finally, awakened. The park is somehow, oddly and excitingly, alive. Even more so for its emptiness. For one final moment, before it gives itself over to the game, Camden Yards can be itself, for itself.

It wasn't the design flaws that got to her. It wasn't the pressure leading up to the exhibition game on Friday, or the Base Ball on Saturday. It was the question of taking too much credit, the trait that caused her design consultant, Pastier, in a moment of uncensored pique, to confide, "I've seen her get full credit for everything. And frankly, she knows very little."

It was an article about the ballpark in *The New York Times* that started it—an article that appeared in the nation's great gray chronicle of record, one month before the first game. The piece was accompanied by a photograph of Janet Marie Smith. It described Smith as the "architect" of the stadium in its fourth paragraph.

It wasn't just that Smith was the center of attention once again; a smart, savvy, aggressive, hard-edged woman in the business of building stadiums is naturally going to attract attention in 1992. A female vice president of a baseball team is going to be noticed—that's a given. And no one was going to begrudge her a rightful share of the marquee.

It was what wasn't in the *Times* that attracted attention around the stadium site: the name of Joe Spear, for instance. Never mentioned. The architect of three modern and celebrated baseball stadiums. Absent without reason.

Hellmuth Obata Kassabaum was given one mention, two-thirds of the way into the story; HOK was described as "a Kansas City firm." The author didn't specify what kind of firm. It could have been a meat-packing firm—or, of course, a construction company.

Nowhere, in fact, was there the slightest hint, amid the lyrical quotes from George Will and Roger Angell, amid the eloquent waxing rhapsodic about the "green jewel," that Joe Spear and HOK had anything to do with the design of the stadium.

Furthermore, the *Times* informed us, the park was being built by "the Orioles and the Maryland Stadium Authority," when the Orioles were, in fact, paying for very little of it.

It also said that the most important design feature of the park was "the Orioles' initial decision to retain and restore the warehouse."

Spear and HOK were furious. The Stadium Authority was no less exasperated. And when Herb Belgrad relayed everyone's fury and indignation, at the beginning of a regularly scheduled meeting the following week, Smith broke down and left the room.

Aside from being more than a tad irked, Belgrad had a personal reason to be dismayed. As the project reached fruition, he'd planned a large dinner party for all of the principals. Now Spear and his HOK team had told him in no uncertain terms they would not attend.

On Friday April 3 the Orioles hosted the Mets in an exhibition game. It was meant to be a dry run. The team sold only two-thirds of the seats; they wanted to be able to test the park's efficiency without stretching it if something was wrong that they hadn't anticipated. The decision to christen the building with a meaningless exhibition in a half-empty park in the middle of a workday was roundly vilified on the talk-show dials.

And the day was surprisingly empty of feeling. It was only a baseball game; unable to market it or pump up its importance, the Orioles seemed to be trying to pretend it wasn't happening. Played in a cool wind beneath scudding gray skies, Camden Yards' dry run felt dry. As workmen frantically jury-rigged a foul screen out of chicken wire two hours before the first pitch, Rex Barney's first announcement ever in Camden Yards, crisply at twelve-thirty, warned people to move their cars from out in front of the park or they'd be towed.

Down on the apron, Rick Dempsey, who'd been signed to rejoin the team as a coach and emergency catcher three months earlier, cast a glance around the park.

"It feels like baseball," he said.

Reporters swamped Janet Marie: "What did you do from the feminine part of things?" asked one. She smiled as graciously as she could, resisting the understandable temptation to ram the man's microphone down his throat.

Tom Rogers watched the game from the box seats beneath the open press box holding a walkie-talkie, and fielded reports from his crews: The bathroom with no sign in the picnic area beyond center field was confusing women and men alike. In another bathroom, squawked a frantic voice from the box, the toilets wouldn't stop flushing. A leak had sprung in the concession kitchens in the warehouse.

At one point, the huge Sony JumboTron screen went black. A circuit breaker had been tripped. It was back up in fifteen minutes. And, with four times the clarity of the old Diamond Vision board in

Memorial, it continued its mission: showing replays of Orioles games played in Memorial Stadium.

Cal just missed a home run, and hit an RBI single. Eddie Murray, now with the visiting Mets, hit a double off the Ryder truck sign and refused to acknowledge the crowd's pleading applause. Sam Horn struck out trying to hit a ball into the warehouse.

It was so cold that in the sixth inning Rogers retreated upstairs to the Stadium Authority's suite.

Afterward, Johnny Oates smiled widely. Asked what he thought of the park, he paused for a moment, then said he wished his dugout were on the third-base side instead of the first so that he could talk to his third-base coach. But the Orioles had wanted the dugout and the manager close to the Orioles offices up in the warehouse.

Oates was asked if he'd seen Frank Robinson's spacious office in the warehouse, with the best view of the field.

"How'd he get that office?" Johnny Oates asked.

It's something to look forward to, one writer offered, when you get fired.

Johnny Oates laughed long and loudly.

On Saturday night Janet Marie Smith was in a far better mood. Standing amid the Honduran mahogany trim, surrounded by a few thousand lubricated revelers in black tie on the club level, she was nearly laughing. Nearly.

This was the Babe Ruth Museum's annual Base Ball. Over in the museum's concession counter, two blocks away, $10.95 would get you a vial of Memorial Stadium dirt: A restricted number of authentic limited-edition certificates signed by Brooks Robinson and Jim Palmer, attesting to the authenticity of the dirt, were available for a higher price.

On the luxury level on this cool evening, if you could afford $125 for a ticket, you could enjoy the company of a few thousand Baltimoreans feasting on the old-time atmosphere and the catered hors d'oeuvres.

The theme for the evening, naturally, was old-time baseball. The programs featured photographs of the century-old Orioles. People dressed in Gay Nineties attire herded the attendees into the park and straight up the escalator to the club level. Those whose curiosity prevailed and who managed to avoid the ushers, splintered off and strolled through the new magnificence, noting not only the fine attention to detail seldom seen in a stadium—the gray and green tile on the walls of the concessionnaires, the strong but spidery-graceful steel trusses with their hexagonal gusset plates—but the several direct nods to the past: the cast-iron seat standards from the 1890s, for instance.

To Baltimore's moneyed, given this exclusive glimpse of Camden Yards, the pride was a thing as thick as the puffery.

At nine-fifteen, the celebrants were led out of the carpeted concourse into the club seats to enjoy the evening's entertainment. They filled a few thousand of the exclusive club-level seats and, for all their sartorial finery, looked quite insignificant in the huge expanse of emptiness.

The nature of the entertainment had not been announced. To many, further entertainment was unnecessary; the view was drama enough. Beyond center field, downtown Baltimore's office buildings were alight, and beckoned like a Broadway stage set. The lit cityscape presented the perfect portrait of a nighttime city: alight, vibrant, diverse.

"It's the perfect urban setting," said one woman. "It's what we think it should be, to create what we think urban perfection can be. What's beautiful about cities is man conquering nature. It's open to the danger of urban life. But isn't actually threatened by it. It's a fantasy of a city."

It was true. The real city out there was not a city any of the tuxedoed gentry in attendance that night would want to explore. The night city peeking into Camden Yards was not the gentle city that had beckoned from beyond the walls of Crosley and Griffith and Sportsmen's Park.

Likewise—a meditation driven home as the huddled thousand sat awaiting the mysterious main act—the past that Camden Yards was meant to evoke was, in many ways, equally an illusion. Most of the time it was as sordid and exploitative as it is today.

We know this is true of the world at large; it is every bit as true in the baseball world. World Series games were fixed in glorious old Comiskey Park and Crosley Field. Ball players battled booze in the good old days, with results as devastating as any seen with the drugs of today. Players may have loved the game then—as they do today—but that doesn't mean they weren't playing for money, as much money as they could wrest from their owners, who were in turn charging the public as much as they dared.

The marketers of Camden Yards, whether they truly set out to exploit an illusion or, instead, merely found they'd stumbled upon a gold mine, had also hit upon a truth that applies most emphatically in our troubled age: The past is comfortable. You can go there and be safe. Nothing unknown is going to happen in the past. But blind obeisance to the past is surely as useless as blundering into the future, and the marketing of that past as something that can be recreated in the present—when the values underscoring that present bear no relation to the values of the past—is deception at its worst.

The players know to distrust the past. The players will not come to history's defense. In baseball, the most damning epithet a man can utter of a foe is, "He's history." To a baseball player, always aware of how brief his career on the diamond can be, the past is often an enemy, because its comforts cannot stop the erosion of skills or the slowing of reflexes. The baseball player learns, from Little League on, to distrust the talents that got him here; every coach along the way will tell him that to rely on his talent is to ultimately fail. Living on past accomplishments is to shortchange today's efforts. "History is wonderful if you can learn from it, but other than that, it can't do you a lot of good," Jack Morris told me a few years ago, when he was a Tiger. "It's not something you can thrive on."

Unless you're selling tickets to it.

At nine-thirty, the fantasy took full flight, in the guise of a piece of theater acted out by a man who has come to be synonymous with the game as fiction.

A spotlight lit the pitcher's mound, and James Earl Jones, our favorite huckster, walked up to a microphone and began to talk, in his remarkably resonant voice—the voice that daily sells us everything

251

our manufacturers can conjure for the marketplace, the man whose lilting syllables can convince us of the beneficience of the telephone cartels, of the moral purity of CNN, of the legitimacy of Rush Limbaugh, the man whose gently rocking cadences have come to underscore the national tone as surely as the music of Sousa once did—James Earl Jones, hired for a reported ten thousand dollars, began to declaim about baseball and Maryland, in the unmistakably self-important tones of baseball fiction:

"The sport as played here seems to have epitomized what is good about our national pastime," he said, biting off the words and flicking them into the night. "It represents a community forged from railroads and sailcloth."

Jones was an almost perfect symbolic choice to speak on a night dedicated to the triumph of illusion. In addition to his *Field of Dreams* role, he gained great critical acclaim a few years ago when he starred in the brilliant Broadway play *Fences,* in which he portrayed an aging former Negro Leaguer.

When Jones finished his monologue on the mound, Frank Robinson stepped to the plate, illuminated by a spotlight. Jones pretended to throw a baseball. Robinson pretended to hit one. As he swung, a rocket—a Roman candle—shot off its stand next to the plate and soared off in the direction of the scoreboard. The scoreboard exploded with one burst of fireworks.

Everyone hurried back into the club level for the end of the party.

"I was so relieved," Janet Marie said, standing near the shrimp, "that someone didn't charge off the mound and say, 'You can't play baseball in this stadium!' "

She was complimented on the green color scheme.

"Green," she said, "was just like telling the truth."

On April 5, the day before the park opened, the *Chicago Tribune* ran a story about Janet Marie. It was entitled, "Baseball Fan Coaches New Stadium into Its Rookie Season." It spoke of her philosophies of design, and how she helped implement them in the park. It quoted her complimenting the Orioles at length. It made no mention of HOK and Joe Spear, who had given their city Comiskey Park. There was no mention of the Maryland Stadium Authority.

*   *   *

One day, talking to Bruce Hoffman, I observe that, in person, Smith had always mentioned several contributors' names to me; she even seems eager, I say, to spread the credit around.

"I don't know if she does," Bruce Hoffman says. "She says she does. . . . Deep down, she must need credit. I don't. My job is to get it done and not worry about credit."

The view from Bruce Hoffman's office in Baltimore's World Trade Center is astonishing; from the conference room of the Maryland Stadium Authority the city lies below like an architect's model, and the most prominent feature on the whole plane is the warehouse.

"I used to sit up here at seven in the morning," Hoffman was saying one day, "and if the cranes weren't working, I'd want to know why."

They usually were, and for this the state of Maryland and the Baltimore Orioles have Bruce Hoffman to thank. That's what the governor says, anyway.

Hoffman is an engineer. His experience is in water and sewage and land development. He comes from a world where strutting your stuff makes no sense. Which is why Janet Marie has angered him.

"Sometimes she'd take credit for things she didn't deserve. They've designed stadiums before she got here and they'll design them after. She was one of a million people at Battery Park. She was a coordinator. And did Pershing Square ever get built?

"Yes, she poked at the [design] team and made them be more creative—I'll give her a ton of credit. She's smart. She did her homework. She got a bunch of old pictures and made some trips to other stadiums.

"But you've got to be careful. Unless you want to take all these people we spent six or seven millions dollars on and push 'em aside, you gotta be careful. [Her] not even mentioning HOK? That's beyond belief. That's unfair. You can't do that to people who work for a living.

"Ask her," Bruce Hoffman says, "how many stadiums she's designed."

On Sunday, the day before Opening Day, the Baltimore Orioles paraded down Pratt Street, past the stadium. Then they held a public workout in their new home. They charged five dollars to park and three dollars for admission.

As they held practice, in a cool sun, the scoreboard said, "The Orioles and McDonald's welcome you to a workout in the park."

"I remember how I found out the old stadium had burned down," said Bob Maisel, the retired *Sun* sportswriter, a quiet and ruly man, and an advocate for a new park since the late sixties. Bob Maisel's dad led the American League in steals in 1914. From 1919 to 1925 Fritz Maisel played for the Orioles of the International League, and managed them for the last four years.

Bob was patrolling the grass on the first-base side. Behind us, fans hollered and screamed and squawked for autographs.

"I was in Italy during the war. You couldn't call home whenever you wanted. There were only a couple of places you could call from. That night my time was four A.M. My dad said, 'It's funny you should call now,' he told me. 'Oriole Park just burned to the ground.' "

Maisel had epitomized Baltimore sportswriting for three decades. But he had retired the year before. I asked him why.

"Near the end, you were like the enemy," he said.

It was an odd phrase, considering we'd just been talking about the war, and the sour look that crossed Maisel's pleasant face struck an odd note; more than anyone else, Maisel had asked for a new stadium here over the years, ever since 1972, when he repeatedly told his readers that the black hole of downtown Baltimore could only be revived by a ballpark. Now, twenty years after those first columns, he was standing in the palace that he had helped to spawn.

He was speaking slowly, and somberly, about the game and the day.

"I didn't like that feeling. In the old days you could rip 'em and if they deserved it they'd still be your friends. Now—every word, like every pitch, is lost revenue.

"What I thought was a game," Bob Maisel said, "is now a business."

Over near the visitor's dugout, Larry Lucchino defended his decision to charge admission to, in effect, a total charade: a baseball team walking through a listless workout with all the animation of men checking out groceries at a supermarket. For the past several months, the Orioles had given fans free tours of the park. Today they made them pay.

"We were concerned we couldn't control it," Lucchino said. "We didn't know how many would be coming from the parade. People were fried. It was a way to control them."

As the Orioles began to duck into their spacious dugout and leave the field, a kid yelled at me, leaning over the railing with a baseball. He was wearing the kind of jacket you get at sporting goods stores, one that has Day-Glo greens and pinks, set against black. He had a hard face, even for a twelve-year-old. He looked as if he would be very wealthy someday and not know at what cost.

"I'll give you ten bucks to get this signed by Glenn Davis," he said.

The next morning, as Opening Day dawned, the camera lights flicked on in center field, where, on three benches in a row, sat Joe Garagiola and Janet Marie Smith and Larry Lucchino.

"I'm sitting here," Garagiola told the nation, "with the architect of the stadium."

She didn't blink. And she didn't correct him.

OPENING DAY

◆

IT IS A SINGULAR MOTION, Rick Sutcliffe's windup, a thing of self-evident simplicity. Nothing is out of place, and it's open for everyone to see. His mechanics are plain and sound, everything's balanced, and everything makes physical sense. It has no tricks, no high-tucked legs, no eye-glance-to-the-sky, no twist of the torso. It is a straight baseball windup, culminating in his characteristic bent-wrist low point, and it's followed by a straight baseball unwindup, the long and rubbery limbs all unfolding in perfect balance.

At three-twenty, beneath a gentle, cloudless sky, the air a cool 63 degrees, Sutcliffe brought the ball up and over the top, and into the vacuum of the hush of the crowd he let the ball go.

In the batter's box stood a highly regarded rookie named Kenny Lofton, himself as nervous as a twig in a gale, trying his best to stand tall against a veteran of two decades, and, on the first pitch anyway, succeeding—Sutcliffe's pitch sailed in high for a ball. With the thwack of the ball in Chris Hoiles's glove, the crowd noise started up again; the bubble of sweet anticipation burst, and the regular baseball noises spilled out of the upper deck of Camden Yards.

Rick Sutcliffe didn't hear them. A ball high is the worst place for a ball to be, on Opening Day, in a new stadium, coming off a dreary season. Facing oblivion. When your manager should have started any of three other pitchers, but gave the ball to you, for reasons you still couldn't fathom, and didn't care to.

In that split second of follow-through, as Sutcliffe watched his pitch sail high, you could see the anger in his eyes if you looked hard enough; he likes to think he hides all his expressions behind his woolly red beard, but Rick Sutcliffe's eyes always give him away. At times, he's as gentle to look at as the man behind the counter in the general store on the back highway somewhere out west. But sometimes his eyes are those of some mountain man driven by a deep old rage, and when his first pitch sailed high, you could see it in their glare.

Hoiles snapped the ball back to Sutcliffe immediately. As Sutcliffe caught the ball, Lofton stepped out of the box, to exhale, to calm himself down.

In that infant moment, tens of thousands of Baltimoreans leaned back to savor, at last, the overwhelming rightness of their new palace: the crook of the stands down the right-field line, as if the upper deck were cradling the outfield; the warehouse, long and thick and chthonic, the oldest wall of any major-league stadium dominating the newest playing field; the open wedge of downtown office buildings representing ninety years of urban architecture peeking in; the left-center-field seats slicing across the outfield, those fans seeming right atop the field. Nothing shouted for attention—not the warehouse, not the steel, not the comfortable slant of the grandstand. It fit. The outfield had been mowed neatly, so that the nap looked like a new haircut. The infield grass had been mowed in concentric rings. It looked like crop circles viewed from an airplane. Nothing was amiss.

Did it satisfy the purists? Not even close: too much stylistic confusion for John Pastier's taste. A futile attempt at recreating the architecture of the past with the materials of the present—"Mimicking . . . funny . . . phony," was Dale Swearingen's take. No, it was not a thing of seamless beauty. Even Eli Jacobs conceded that: "Is this great architecture? Probably not. It's not intended to be a great work of architecture. This is not intended to be a great public edifice."

And, no, it didn't take an architect's eye to see some of the oddities caused by two years of rival architectural camps butting heads: how clumsily the outsized video screen chopped off the entire north end of the warehouse; how the ballpark's huge open archways contrasted sharply with the warehouse's aesthetic of tiny windows and nondescript appeal. But on this day the ballpark was quite above reproach. On this day it was both a magnificent and an intimate place. On this day, it felt as if the game had come home.

Rick Sutcliffe may have been glancing at the park around him, but his eyes were not seeing. Sutcliffe's gaze was directed inward, at the curious set of circumstances that had put him at center stage. As Kenny Lofton stepped out of the box, Sutcliffe had one last moment to pause over his own anxiety—very little of it having to do with the shimmer of adrenaline that was washing over the beautiful brick-steel ballpark.

"You realize what a chance he took? I was a thirty-five-year-old guy that more than half the teams in baseball gave up on," Rick Sutcliffe said later. "Then he names me for Opening Day? When he has Mussina? And Ben McDonald? What does he have to gain? He has everything to lose. What do you think Jacobs and Lucchino and Hemond are thinking? What if on Opening Day in front of millions of people I give up five runs in five innings? They're gonna be putting a microscope on Johnny's every breath from then on in."

"I read people saying that the only reason he's here is because he's my friend," Johnny Oates said. "That had nothing to do with wanting him on the ball club. It was that I knew about him. I knew him. So many times you go for guys you know nothing about. But I'd caught him. I'd coached him.

"I knew he'd be fine. I saw what he did in spring training."

In spring training, while most of his teammates paced their game and metered their emotions, slowly cranking up for the marathon of a season ahead, Rick Sutcliffe pitched as hard as he's ever pitched. In spring training men who have won Cy Young awards and have signed huge contracts and have seen themselves on *Lifestyles of the Rich and Famous* generally arrive with a smile and a yawn. In 1992 Rick Sutcliffe arrived with his eyes set fierce and, from the first pitch on the first day, tried to get everyone out.

In his own words, Rick Sutcliffe had reached a fork in a path. One path led to three or more years in the game, the other led to going home within months, or weeks, or days.

Something else was pushing Rick Sutcliffe, too: the desire to prove to the skeptics that he wasn't standing out here because of his friendship with his manager.

"He was no fun to catch," Johnny Oates said one day. "You had a tough time thinking with him. And then he didn't have the control, either. He was a thrower. He had the worst mechanics I'd ever seen. He'd throw a fastball onto the screen, or over a right-hander's head. I'd be afraid to call a curve on the second pitch."

They'd had two years as pitcher and catcher on the Dodgers, two years of Rick Sutcliffe veering away from Johnny Oates's game plan time and again, until Oates, a simple man not familiar with spontaneity and anarchy, wanted to scream.

"He'd shake me off," Johnny Oates remembered, "then a lot of times he'd come back to the same pitch, the same location. That's stubbornness. That's the height of stubbornness."

Johnny Oates never knew when Rick Sutcliffe was going to stop paying attention to their game plan. All he knew for certain was that Sutcliffe would. He'd never met a man that stubborn in his life. The catcher in him hated it.

The baseball man in him loved it.

In 1984, Oates was a bullpen coach for the Chicago Cubs when Rick Sutcliffe came over from the Indians. Sutcliffe made a conscious decision not to get close to any of the Cubs, because he was about to be a free agent and he desperately wanted to be playing in Kansas City, where he'd grown up. So he befriended the bullpen coach, Johnny Oates.

"You know what I have now? I have videotapes and tendencies and statistics on everyone I pitch to," Rick Sutcliffe said. "You know what I had the year I went sixteen one and won the Cy Young? Johnny Oates. Every game me and Jody Davis would talk to Johnny, and he'd tell us how to pitch guys. That was it. I went sixteen one and won a Cy Young in a half season. We just listened to Johnny. That's all we did."

"Rick used to call me from the dugout when I was out in the bullpen and ask for advice on how to pitch to guys," Oates recalled. "I'd be out in the bullpen and he'd call and ask me how to pitch to someone. Then he'd go out and do what I suggested."

Some of the time.

"I remember one game in September in Montreal in '84," Sutcliffe said. "We hadn't clinched it yet—we didn't clinch until four days from the end. Johnny says, 'Don't throw Dan Driessen a slider.' Well, at that time, my slider was the best slider in baseball. I had a better slider than anyone in the game. So Driessen comes up in the first inning and Jody calls fastball outside. I shake him off. Curve. I shake him off. Change, fastball in. I shake him off. He calls a slider. I nod. Driessen hits a fucking home run.

"I'm down one to nothing. We take the lead two one. Now it's the fourth, there's two on, two out, a man on second. Driessen's up. We do it again. I shake off everything he calls. But he won't call the slider. Driessen steps out. Jody looks at me and says, 'What?' And I just go into my windup. I threw a slider. He hits this one farther than the first one. But it's five feet foul. Then I get him out on a fastball.

"I get back to the dugout and I call up Oates in the bullpen. And I say to him, 'I told you I could throw the slider to Driessen for a strike.' "

Johnny Oates did not laugh at the retelling of the story, eight years later.

"He still does stuff like that," Johnny Oates said.

One day in Oates's last year on the Cubs, he was leaving the locker room when Rick Sutcliffe motioned for him to come over.

Sutcliffe handed Oates a check.

"Not a small check, either," Johnny Oates said. "See, he knew I'd never make any money. Chicago was expensive. I wasn't making any money as a coach. People don't realize, for a lot of people in this game, moving around all the time, our cost of living in some of these cities, it can be rough.

"He probably doesn't even know how handy it came in. I'm jumping up the steps to get to the phone to call my wife. I tell her, 'You won't believe what's happened.'

"That's the type of guy he is. Of course, he probably needed a tax write-off anyway."

By 1990 Johnny Oates was coaching for the Orioles. Rick Sutcliffe was not pitching for the Chicago Cubs. In the middle of the 1990 season, Rick Sutcliffe was entertaining his friend Bill Murray in the Cubs' weight room under the third-base seats in Wrigley Field—the room in which Rick Sutcliffe would spend half the season, the other half in the trainer's room. In 1990, Rick Sutcliffe did not throw a pitch in a game.

He was wearing a pack of ice the size of a small bowling ball taped to his right shoulder with an Ace bandage as he and his friend traded stories. They remembered the time Murray had leaned over the lip of the Cubs dugout at Shea to offer Sutcliffe a Heineken and some cajun fries after Sutcliffe had been knocked out in the third, as Don Zimmer glared in disbelief from his pitcher to the comedian, back to his pitcher, the veins in his neck throbbing, the metal plate in his head glowing red. They remember how the two of them had walked around Shea a dozen times that night, at one A.M., looking for a cab, Sutcliffe jumping like a cat at each sound in the dark, Murray cradling his son, asleep, over his shoulder.

They remembered the night that Murray had spelled Harry Caray for one game, and teamed with Steve Stone to call a Cubs game that Sutcliffe was pitching. And how Sutcliffe, to give his friend something to talk about, decided to steal a base, although he'd never stolen a base in the major leagues—and stole it, head first—and when Sutcliffe slid head first, safe, and looked up, instead of seeing Doug Harvey signalling "safe," Doug Harvey was down on one knee, staring Sutcliffe in the face, saying, "What the fuck are you doing?" They remembered the time Sutcliffe stole home the next year—a pick-off went awry and Sutcliffe was given credit for the first steal of home by a Cubs pitcher since Jim "Hippo" Vaughn. His friend Mark Harmon was in town filming *Stealing Home* with Jodie Foster. Two days later a jacket arrived at Sutcliffe's locker, a leather jacket with the words STEALING HOME on the back, and on the front, on the breast, instead of Rick Sutcliffe's name, it read "Jim 'Hippo' Vaughn."

They reminisced like that for a while. Murray went off to talk to Zim. Sutcliffe played with Murray's kids. Then Murray came back and collected his kids and Sutcliffe asked him if the tickets he'd left for Murray were good, and Murray said, "No, we're up with the weird and the damned," and they both laughed.

Then Murray asked his friend how his shoulder was.

"I'll be back," Rick Sutcliffe said, with a nod. Murray nodded back.

Outside of the trainer's room, Murray said, "He will, too."

He missed all of 1990. He missed two-thirds of 1991. Then he started to pitch again. In the final six weeks of 1991, he was the Cubs' best pitcher.

But when the season ended, the Cubs told him they were no longer interested in his particular talents. Sutcliffe's playing career now seemed as frayed as the tissues in his shoulder.

Meanwhile, his pal Johnny Oates's managerial career was finally beginning its ascent. And when Roland Hemond was getting ready to go to the winter meetings in December of 1991 and he asked his manager what he thought they needed for the Orioles, Oates told him about his friend, and Roland Hemond told Larry Lucchino.

Instead of first going through Sutcliffe's agent, Larry Lucchino asked Johnny Oates to make the call to his friend.

"Johnny called me," Rick Sutcliffe recalls, "and said, 'Are you healthy?' I said, 'John, I wouldn't lie to you. I feel better than last year.' He said, 'That's all I need to know. What do you have to have to sign?' "

So Sutcliffe flew into Baltimore a week after the meetings in December 1991, after Johnny Oates had called him up. Hemond met him at the airport. Then they took him to Camden Yards. It was near freezing, and splotches of snow covered some of the mud inside the ballpark. There was no turf on the ground, but when they led Sutcliffe to the mound and he looked down the lines, he smiled.

"I looked down the first-base line and saw through the rafters," Sutcliffe said, "you could see the supports, just like Wrigley. You look down the third-base side and it looks like the old Comiskey. It's like a whole bunch of old friends, packed into the same place."

Rick Sutcliffe had then said to his agent and friend, Barry Axelrod, "Let's see if we can work something out today."

When Ewing Kaufmann had courted him in Kansas City, nearly a decade earlier, the Kansas City owner had taken him to an elegant restaurant and ordered a $250 bottle of wine. On this day, after the

Orioles had shown him the mound of the new park, they bought him a turkey sandwich at the construction site lunch wagon called The Oasis, then took him to the only heated room in the stadium, a storage locker beneath the first-base side box seats. And Oates and Lucchino and Hemond and Sutcliffe's agent sat down and signed a contract for $1.2 million, on folding chairs.

Oates and Hemond drove Sutcliffe and his agent back to the airport. "Hemond turned to Johnny, and said, 'There's your Christmas present,' " Sutcliffe recalled. "I said, 'What?' And Roland said to me, 'Johnny said to me that if he got you, he didn't have to get a Christmas present.' I was his Christmas present."

On the second pitch, in on the fists, Kenny Lofton inside-outed a foul pop fly down the third-base side that hit the rubber warning track and bounded high, unnaturally high, into the stands. Now they were even, Sutcliffe and Lofton, and this time Sutcliffe took the ball back with a more settled swipe.

On the third pitch, Kenny Lofton flied out to left field. Lazily. So did Glenallen Hill, the designated hitter, and Carlos Baerga, the second baseman—all of them looping, powerless pop flies, etched against a sky so blue you could follow the baseballs forever.

With the third fly ball, Sutcliffe stepped off the mound, his head resting on his chest, and walked in to the dugout accompanied by the ripples of applause, the fans shifting colorfully and comfortably the way they do after a good half-inning for the home team in a new stadium. Now, for the first time, the Camden Yards crowd could pause and take the day in, and let the park settle in around them.

In the bottom of the first, the first Orioles batter, Brady Anderson, hit a ground ball down the first-base line. Paul Sorrento, the Indians first baseman, ran in to snare the ball several feet up the line toward home plate, and as he stepped on the chalk, the ball was ruled foul. Sorrento trotted back out to his spot wide of the bag, leaving small white ghostly footprints in the dirt.

In the second inning, after one out, Mike Devereaux misplayed a line drive by Sorrento, and Joe Orsulak overran it too, and Sorrento had the stadium's first hit. He was on second base. Then Sutcliffe threw a pitch to Sandy Alomar, and when Alomar swung, the ball left his bat so quickly that Sutcliffe didn't even snap his head around to watch its flight.

In center field, Devereaux froze. The ball had seemed invisible to him in the split second after it had left the bat, because of the green tarp that covered the walkway the umpires used to get to the field. When his eye caught up with the ball, Devereaux realized it had been hit farther than he thought. He turned his back to home plate, put his head down, and began to sprint.

Sutcliffe was watching now, but reluctantly. When an outfielder turns his back to home plate and puts his head down to sprint, the chances are slim that anything good will happen in the next few moments.

But Devereaux looked up, saw the wall, turned his head, held up his glove, watched the ball settle into the web, and just managed to get his arm out to cushion the shock as he hit the padded wall with enough force to make the entire park wince in pain—before it exploded with applause. Devereaux threw the ball in, then turned to look at the replay. But what he noticed were the hundreds of people standing out on the terraces on the 24th floor of 250 West Pratt Street, the glass office building a quarter-mile beyond center field. The terraces were full. Devereaux found himself wondering how they could see from that far away.

One out later, when Devereaux reached the top step of the home dugout after his long jog in, Rick Sutcliffe was there to slap gloves with him. In Wrigley, it would have been an easy home run. Sutcliffe turned to walk down the steps.

He did not look over at Oates. If he had, he would have seen that Oates was not looking at him. Neither of them heard the buzz of the crowd that said that a grand ballpark had just been christened as surely as if it had been smacked with champagne.

In the bottom of the second, Glenn Davis hit a solid single to center field for the first Orioles hit, but he got no farther. Up in the broadcast booth, George Bush joined Jon Miller to call Rick Sutcliffe's next half-inning. Sutcliffe was unaware of the frippery. After the inning, in the booth, Miller said, "All the networks are calling." Bush said, "What do they pay?"

Sutcliffe came back strong: He struck out Brook Jacoby swinging. Mark Lewis popped to Glenn Davis at first. Lofton flied out weakly to Devereaux. In the fourth, Hill popped to Hoiles, Baerga grounded out, and after Albert Belle walked, Sorrento took a called third strike. The second inning was erased. Sutcliffe was back on track.

In the concourse, amid the concession stands, there were no smells baked into the walls yet. There would be no cooking oil; the cooking was being done over in the concessionaire's kitchen in the warehouse. No cigar smoke, of course.

In the main concourse behind home plate, someone had left thirty-two bricks stacked against a wall, waiting to go somewhere. They looked lost.

In the bottom of the fifth, Sam Horn drew a walk, and Camden Yards stirred with a few pockets of applause as the big man rumbled his way down the base path. You could feel his footsteps on the dirt, it seemed, even from the top row in the upper deck in left-center field, where the game below played out in miniature. To the south, beyond the park, industrial South Baltimore beckoned, the view that the architects had turned the stadium's back on: The huge Resco smokestack, the Baltimore Gas & Electric oil tanks, the weave of the interstate, the glint of the river.

From the upper deck, the baseball game seemed an adornment. The view to the rear, over your shoulder, out of the park, was just as enticing: the tarred roofs of Ridgely's Delight; the Metropolitan Life Insurance Building, squat brick and masonry; the Grinding Company of America.

But when Leo Gomez singled, the game muscled its way up to the top. The crack of the bat reached the top row a full half-second later, and then the cheer of the crowd washed up to the stadium's brim.

Charles Nagy's next pitch floated in, a speck from these heights, and rocketed off Chris Hoiles's bat much more quickly than it had come in. The sound from down in the park grew louder and louder, and as it became clear that the ball would not be caught, the top rows were suddenly on their feet, spurred by the dramatic—even five hundred feet away—sight of Sam Horn running full tilt, like a scared bull.

Horn scored, Gomez stopped at third, and Hoiles chumpfed into second. Now the game seemed at our fingertips. The landscape was unseen. The setting was finally just a setting; the play was the thing. On the next pitch, Bill Ripken dropped a suicide squeeze down the third-base line, and the Orioles led 2–0.

In the dugout, Sutcliffe allowed himself a quiet nod. He'd pitched five shutout innings. Everything else now was gravy. This is the way some pitchers think. But this is not the way Rick Sutcliffe ever thinks. He wanted a complete game.

"You put my name down to start the motherfucker, I'll finish the motherfucker," Rick Sutcliffe said after a game once. "I work too fuckin' hard to be taken out. The middle relievers, the lefties and the righties, don't even try that shit. Because I'm gonna be waiting in your office after the game."

In the sixth inning, Sutcliffe was about to glance over to the Indians' dugout, because he likes to gauge the readiness or weakness of an opposing team by reading the faces in the dugout. Then a strange thing happened. He found he didn't want to do it. He was rolling through the Indians' lineup now, with no effort at all, and the Indians' manager, Mike Hargrove, was one of his best friends. They'd played together with Cleveland. Sutcliffe couldn't look over, because he was afraid Hargrove would misinterpret the glance as a gloat. He had retired the Indians in order.

By the top of the seventh, Camden Yards had settled into a gentle, joyous hum, graced by billows of Boog Powell's barbecue smoke in right and center, and the scent of Italian sausage redolent on the Eutaw Street promenade—a bustling marketplace, the park a shifting, ephemeral sea of color, laced through by steel, framing the game on all sides. In center field, hundreds of fans crowded the railing above the stacked bullpens, and the whole place seemed to be leaning in closer to the game.

The Orioles had stopped hitting the ball, but no one cared, and when Sutcliffe took the mound for the top of the ninth, pitching a five-hitter, the crowd's applause had a fullness to it.

Carlos Baerga hit a hard ground ball up the middle. Sutcliffe ducked and the ball hit him on the left shoulder. The crowd gasped, Sutcliffe contorted, and Billy Ripken picked up the carom and threw

Baerga out. It had been a glancing blow, and when it bounded straight to one of his fielders, Sutcliffe and everyone else in the park knew that the outcome of this game was a given.

Albert Belle popped to Ripken at second for the second out.

Paul Sorrento stepped into the batter's box. Sutcliffe worked the count to 1–2.

The crowd rose to its feet and began to applaud, loudly.

Rick Sutcliffe went into his windup, all lazy and elastic, the beard peering out from beneath the brim of his cap, and as the ball left his hand, it happened again—the sound diminished, the volume dropped, everyone caught their breath. It was like air being sucked into vacuum.

The ball clipped the outside corner.

Paul Sorrento's bat never left his shoulder.

Umpire Larry Barnett pumped a right hand into the air, but if he uttered the word *strike,* it was buried in the avalanche of sound. Sutcliffe gave a glance to the sky, sighed, and stepped off the mound to accept Hoiles's handshake. His team engulfed him. Slowly the pack made its way to the dugout, where Johnny Oates stuck out his hand to shake his pitcher's hand.

Rick Sutcliffe looked him in the eye, and put the baseball in Johnny Oates's outstretched hand, and Oates had only the smallest slice of a second to be surprised before Rick Sutcliffe hugged him.

In the Orioles locker room, dozens of reporters and radio men and television men and people with credentials from cities and newspapers no one has ever heard of rushed straight for the locker of Rick Sutcliffe.

"I knew what he'd done in spring training," Johnny Oates said in his office. A small smile graced Oates's face as two dozen writers scribbled and the TV lights bathed him, but his eyes were clear. When he was asked about Sutcliffe giving him the ball, Johnny Oates said, "It was kind of sentimental for both of us," but no more than that; he was not going to share the emotions with a random pack. He was going to keep that feeling inside, to draw upon at his leisure, on his own.

At the food table, Mike Devereaux put some ribs on a plate. "After

I saw I'd misjudged it, I thought, 'Oh, shit,' " he said. "Don't write that, though. I knew I had to take off. I was thinking it was carrying a lot. I said, 'Oh, fuck.' Don't write that, though."

Devereaux's fork had stopped in midair, and he'd forgotten the plate; the fork poised above the salad, waiting for him.

"I was running as hard as I could. I looked at the wall. I thought, 'Okay, let's see where the ball is.' I knew if I hit the wall full speed, I'd still be out there. That wall is concrete behind four inches of padding.

"But if the elements are correct, you can run to a spot where you think it's going to be, and sometimes it's there."

But no one, it was observed, had ever done so in this park, in this geometry, in these conditions.

"That's true," Mike Devereaux said, with a small smile. "With the situation we had . . . we'd had a good spring . . . we had everyone in the city pumped up, a brand-new ballpark, it's Opening Day . . . in the past we've been behind early in the game . . . there's a runner at second, there are two out, you look at all that, it was . . . one of my greatest catches."

And it was the first great moment in the new park. It had stamped Camden Yards with its first piece of baseball.

Mike Devereaux measured his response.

"That's what makes that my number one catch," he said, nodding. "Tops."

Now, for the first time, the new locker room, which had earlier seemed cavernous—much too big—was now full, and comfortable. Players drifted happily, aimlessly, savoring. It was a room now.

Rick Sutcliffe emerged from the trainer's room with a pack of ice wrapped around his right shoulder held in place by an Ace bandage as, red-faced and aglow, he headed for his locker. Silently, the pack parted, and Sutcliffe walked in and turned.

He praised Mike Devereaux—"I don't know if I've ever seen a better play." He talked about how in Wrigley it would have been gone. He talked about the baseball game, about how he hadn't had to shake off Hoiles at all, and how he had to use the deep part of the park if he was going to be successful.

Someone handed him a cup of Gatorade over the bowed heads,

hand to hand, like a water brigade at a fire, and Sutcliffe took it with a nod. That's a baseball thing.

Then someone asked him about Johnny Oates.

"I wouldn't be here without Johnny Oates," Rick Sutcliffe said, softly. "We have a great friendship off the field. But I'd be real disappointed if I found out that I got Opening Day because of our friendship. I'd be hurt if it were."

Much later, with no one else around, Sutcliffe was asked why he gave Oates the ball.

"What else could I do for him to show him how grateful I was? I mean, he wouldn't take money."

Then Charles Barkley showed up at Rick Sutcliffe's locker, and they shook hands and started laughing, and out of nowhere a television camera appeared, its light blinking on like a huge white eye, and another moment began.

In the hallway outside of the Orioles' locker room, wives and children and friends and relatives waited. Johnny Oates appeared, to applause, and went straight to Gloria Oates, the poet, and they hugged.

Rick Sutcliffe went straight to his wife.

Roland Hemond smiled at it all.

"One thing about our sport," Roland Hemond said. "It captivates for a lifetime. I don't think any other sport accomplishes that."

Hemond started to walk a few feet behind Sutcliffe and his entourage, down toward the loading dock and the ramp and the players' cars.

"I told Rick's wife," Hemond said, "that he became an instant hero in our town today."

We were passing the storage locker.

"This is where we signed him," Roland Hemond said. "Rick," he said. "Remember that day?"

And Sutcliffe peeled away from his pack, and he and Hemond ducked into a large storage room, and headed for one of the stainless-steel doors. They weaved their way between startled young men packing up hot dog rolls. Hemond opened the door, and the men walked in. Floor to ceiling, kegs of beer were stacked like ordnance.

"On that day," Hemond said, "it was the only heated room."

269

"They bought me a turkey sandwich," Sutcliffe said.

Then they walked out. Hemond ducked into the underground tunnel to go over to the warehouse. Sutcliffe climbed into his car, and drove it up the loading ramp, out into the parking lot, into the night.

It was dark inside Camden Yards now, again. Long ago the last rays of sun had crawled up the side of the warehouse, painting it rust, then disappearing over the roof, and the whole field had been set in green shadow.

The lights of the warehouse were all illuminated. The Orioles' offices were alive, the second and third floors lit up like those lights on the passenger cars in a model railroad set. Up in the Camden Club, men in suits lingered over the last beers.

From behind home plate, the lit cityscape out beyond center field looked like a perfect stage set for a Broadway show.

There was a resonance now in Camden Yards. Of lives, of moments, of reality.

And down on the darkened field, there was the distinct echo, at last, of baseball.

INDEX

◆

Irma the Rose, 45
Irsay, Robert, 46, 49, 60, 64, 65,
    93, 95, 97

Jackson, Andrew, 83
Jackson, Joe, 113
Jackson, Pam, 98, 99–100
Jackson, Reggie, 76
Jacobs, Eli, 15, 20, 64, 148–55,
    157, 162, 167, 171, 172, 176,
    194, 218, 229, 242–43, 257,
    258
Jacoby, Brook, 265
Japan, Orioles post-season tour of,
    66, 69
Javits, Jacob, 150
Jett, Joan, 230
Joe Robbie Stadium, 104, 107
Johns Hopkins University, 87, 90,
    204
Johnson, Dave, 41
Johnson, Philip, 140, 152
Jones, James Earl, 40, 251–52

Kansas City Royals, 146, 259, 262
Kansas State University, 207
Kaufmann, Ewing, 262
Keeler, Wee Willie, 32, 136
Kelly, Pat, 41
Kennedy, Ethel, 148
Kennedy, Robert F., 149, 152
Kentucky Blue Grass, 212
Kindred, Dave, 62
Kohn Pederson Fox, 116, 159
Kornheiser, Tony, 75
Kovens, Irvin, 47
Kraft, James, 50
Kram, Mark, Jr., 57
Kuhler, Otto, 85
Kuhn, Bowie, 56–57, 60, 70

La Chance, Candy, 233
Lacy, Lee, 73

Lapides, Jack, 91, 95–96, 97,
    98–99
LaRussa, Tony, 74
Law, Vern, 116
League Park, 170
Legg, Tim, 219–28, 246
Levinson, Barry, 229
Lewis, Mark, 265
Lifestyles of the Rich and Famous,
    258
Limbaugh, Rush, 252
Lincoln, Abraham, 84
Lindsay, John, 150
Lofton, Kenny, 20, 256, 257, 258,
    263, 265
Los Angeles Dodgers, 259
Los Angeles Kings, 55
Los Angeles Lakers, 55
Los Angeles Times, 105, 168
Louie's Bookstore and Café, 47
Lowenstein, John, 27–28, 75
Lowry, Philip, 107
Lucchino, Larry, 14–15, 54–55,
    58, 63, 67, 91, 93, 96, 102,
    114–21, 126, 148, 158–60,
    162, 171, 184, 241–42, 255,
    258
  background of, 116–17
  cancer of, 117–19
  design competition and, 140–41,
    158–59
  HOK disliked by, 114–15, 121,
    141, 158–59, 207, 208
  and old-style design of Camden
    Yards, 128, 130, 153, 158,
    160, 167
  physical appearance of, 14
  press and, 15, 120, 184
  and signing of Sutcliffe, 262,
    263
  temper of, 120, 141, 145, 207
  warehouse opposed by, 128,
    130–31, 138, 155

277

HOK rendering of Camden Yards, March 21, 1990